WILLIE MAYS: *My Life In and Out of Baseball*

# WILLIE MAYS:
# My Life
# In and Out
# of Baseball

*As told to* **CHARLES EINSTEIN**

New York　　E. P. Dutton & Co., Inc.　　1966

Published simultaneously in Canada by Clarke, Irwin & Company
Limited, Toronto and Vancouver

Library of Congress Catalog Card Number: 66–11554

FIRST EDITION

GRATEFUL ACKNOWLEDGMENT IS MADE FOR PERMISSION TO QUOTE
THE FOLLOWING:

Excerpts from article by Milton Gross which originally appeared
in the New York *Post,* as reprinted in the San Francisco *Chronicle* of September 13, 1965.

Excerpts from "The Fearless Spectator" column by Charles
McCabe as it appeared in the San Francisco *Chronicle* of May
25, 1964.

"I'm an Old Cowhand," words and music by Johnny Mercer.
Copyright 1936 by Leo Feist, Inc. Copyright renewed 1963 by
John H. Mercer.

Willie Mays's home runs record compiled exclusively by the
Elias Sports Bureau, publisher of *Little Red Book of Baseball.*

From pages 106-109 of *Baseball Has Done It* by Jackie Robinson, edited by Charles Dexter. Copyright © 1964 by Jack R.
Robinson and Charles Dexter. Published by J. B. Lippincott
Company.

*This book is for my son Michael*

*List of Illustrations*

WILLIE MAYS: *My Life In and Out of Baseball*

# 1

*I remember what I think nobody else remembers, from that one day: the way the clouds were against the sky. It was a good day, but it was October and it was getting late, and they were no longer white but ribbed with gray too, and you had the feeling that if you could reach high enough you could get the gray out of there.*

They tell me there was a hippopotamus being delivered to the zoo in Central Park that day, and the keepers who were changing him over from the crate to the hippopotamus pit had a radio going and were paying more attention to the radio than they were to the hippo. They say it was like when Roosevelt died, when forever after that, people kept remembering where they were when it happened.

Me, I remember the clouds.

*The New York Times* had it on page one next day, with headlines equal to only one other story: the Russians had successfully tested an atom bomb.

But I remember the clouds.

I saw them, looking up automatically the way you always did when you came up out of the dugout at the Polo Grounds, carrying two or even three bats, to go out in the on-deck circle and await your turn to hit.

The date: October 3, 1951.

The most famous single date, I suppose, in baseball history.

It started—that last half of the ninth—with the player I admired

11

'most. We—and when I say "we" in this book, anytime I use that
word, it means only one thing: the Giants—I say, we'd come a long
way. In a short time. We'd won 38 of our last 46 games, 13 of our
last 15. A long way in a short time, and all for nothing. Or so it
seemed. Because it was the end of the final play-off game against
the Dodgers for the National League pennant, and they were ahead
on the scoreboard, 4-1. And that was that.

Or was it? The player I admired most—his name: Alvin Dark—
was at bat first for us in the bottom of the ninth, with Don Newcombe pitching for the Dodgers.

Leo Durocher, still jaunty as ever, had made a little speech in
the dugout, before he went out to coach at third. "All right," he'd
said, in what for him was a normal tone of voice, meaning loud,
"we've come this ——— ——— far already and we've still got a
——— ——— chance to hit." And then he went striding out to coach
at third, with that number 2 sitting on his back like he didn't have
a worry in the world.

And Dark came to bat and slapped a hard grounder to the right
side. Gil Hodges, at first for the Dodgers, and Jackie Robinson,
playing second, crossed each other's paths like the blades of a
scissors coming together—but the ball was through and into right
field for a single.

Now Don Mueller, and he hit the same kind of ball; a little more
to the right of Dark's, maybe, but the way they were defending him
it came out the same.

And again the two gray blades of that scissors flashed—and missed,
and the ball was through, Dark stopping at second, taking no
chances.

Monte Irvin, our big hitter, at bat now. Out in the Dodger
bullpen, a sleeper jump away at the left-field turn in the stands,
everybody and his mother was throwing like crazy for the Brooklyns.

But Irvin fouls out to the right side, so sick about it he actually
breaks his bat when he slams it down, and the hitter is Whitey
Lockman.

And suddenly it's a new ball game, because for the third time that day, Lockman doubles to left. I stand up in the dugout, saying to myself "Go, Lock—Go, Man!" which has a meaning all its own because like most ballplayers Lockman writes his name on the inside of the tongues of his shoes, so you can tell whose shoes are whose, but he does it by writing "Lock" on the left shoe and "Man" on his right, so if he can't spell his name when he looks down he knows somebody else has got one of his shoes.

The double scores Dark. Mueller slides so hard coming into third he sprains his ankle—so bad a sprain they have to carry him off on a stretcher, that long, long walk to the clubhouse in center field. Next morning, Red Smith will say in his column that here was the perfect final touch for the Giants: stretcher-bearers.

Hartung goes in to run for Mueller. Time out too while the Dodgers change pitchers. It's a rare scene at the pitcher's mound. Ralph Branca comes in. Newcombe waits for him, then solemnly—emotionally—shakes his hand before he leaves.

Bobby Thomson at bat now. He had a home run off Branca at Ebbets Field two days before, in the first game of the play-off. First base open—Mays up next, then Westrum. Charley Dressen, the Brooklyn manager, has to decide—walk this man intentionally to set up the force and get to the weak end of the batting order? —or pitch to him?

On the one hand, the walk must appeal to Dressen. He knows, among other things, that the Dodgers still have a two-run lead. That's important when you're thinking of deliberately loading the bases, because when you load them, then another walk or a hit batsman or a tipped bat, and you force a run in. Here though he has the luxury of taking that risk and still being ahead even if something goes wrong.

On the other hand, the oldest "book" in baseball says you never put the winning run on base. Once in a while, they go against the book. When was the last time? Wasn't it Bucky Harris, in the '47 World Series, and didn't Lavagetto kill him with the two-run double that broke up Bevens' no-hitter and gave the Dodgers a 2-1 win?

Dressen knows one other thing. No matter what he does now, if Brooklyn wins he was right. If Brooklyn loses he was wrong. It's that simple.

He's got that two-run lead. He goes with the book, decides to pitch to Thomson.

I never told him this before, so if he reads this now, so many, many years afterward, he will be hearing it from me for the first time. But when he decided to pitch to Thomson instead of walking him, Willie Mays, in the on-deck circle, nearly wept with gratitude.

The first pitch to Thomson: "Strike one!" says Lou Jorda, umpiring back of the plate. A fast ball, down the middle, but Bobby might be guessing and deciding to take the first pitch. After all, they may not walk him intentionally, but they don't have to give him setup strikes all the time. An *un*intentional walk will be better than giving him something too fat. So he's watching the first one.

And Branca cuts the plate with it. Rube Walker, the catcher, has talked things over with him. They're thinking with Thomson and one step out the other side of him. Pitchers can do that. They know where the pitch is supposed to go. The hitter doesn't. The first guess has to be the hitter's.

Now what will happen? Another fast ball, but maybe not so fast as the first?

That would make sense.

And that's what Branca throws.

He wins the guessing game.

But we win the baseball game.

Because Thomson swings and connects and the thing goes tracking out toward the left-field stands, and in the on-deck circle I drop the bats and stand up, watching Pafko in left for them, and he's got his butt up against the wall, but his arms at his sides.

It seemed like forever.

Since then I've seen the movies, and Thomson was only halfway to first when he stopped running and started jumping instead, and went around the rest of the way like a kangaroo, and that's how Hartung and Lockman were running too, and Fitzsimmons, coaching at first, bellowing one thing as Thomson passed him—"Touch the —————— —————— —————— —————— bases!"—and Durocher going crazy at third, to the point where Eddie Stanky came out of nowhere, from the dugout, the fastest I ever saw Stanky run, and threw his arms around Leo out there at third and wrestled him to the dirt. And afterward everybody said, wasn't that a sight, Leo and Stanky, who weren't supposed to be the best of friends, rolling on the ground and hugging each other, except some other people said Stanky, who's always thinking, wanted to pin Leo so he couldn't interfere with the runners as they went around third.

And that was it—the home run heard 'round the world—victory for the Giants, 5-4, climaxing the greatest miracle finish in the history of baseball, where a team that was 13½ games behind on August 11 came on to win the pennant from another team which itself had played better-than-.500 baseball in the same span of time. We'd won 39 of our last 47, 14 of our last 16.

The roaring sound of those Giant fans—more so because they'd had nothing to roar about till that one moment—was something that will stay in my ears as long as I live. And the way they came cascading out of the stands like the death of a waterfall. And Jorda, the plate umpire, trying to protect himself in that mob scene at home plate, to make sure Thomson touched home.

He touched it. That last kangaroo leap, and he came down on the one open spot, seemed like, in the whole ball park. And then we fought for him, clawed at him, lifted him up. You've seen pictures of guys being carried in triumph by their teammates, but was one guy every carried by so many? I'll swear 30 men had a piece of him. And the guys in our bullpen, 'way out in right field—they didn't know what to do. I saw two of them, out in the outfield there, along with a fan and a cop, and the four of them had joined hands and were going around in a circle like an Israeli dance act.

Afterward, long, long afterward, Leo Durocher said: "The spark was Mays. When it looked like we couldn't win, he carried us on his back. He carried the whole damn team on his back." Come to think of it, he didn't say "team." That's how it appeared in print. Baseball men never say "team." They say "club" or "ball club."

He was talking about the season, of course, not that game of October 3, and in a way he was being kind, because if you believed him then you must have believed *he* believed that if they'd walked Thomson, or something else had happened so I came to bat that day in the ninth inning, then I would have won the big game.

I don't think I would have.

I was so scared, out there in the on-deck circle when Thomson went up to hit, scared I'd have to go up there with the game depending on me, that I was shaking, near sick to my stomach.

I was a 20-year-old kid from Birmingham—and frightened kids from anywhere will know how I felt.

# 2

SOMEWHERE ON ONE of the downtown streets of Cincinnati—don't ask me what street it is, but it's only three blocks or so from the Terrace Hilton, where the Giants stay—is a furniture store. It sells new furniture and old furniture and reconditioned furniture, but the accent is on the older stuff and the low prices, and they don't have any new appliances. That is, all the radios and TV's are old and second hand, and they don't have refrigerators or washing machines, or things like that, at all. You know the kind of a store I mean. One of those blocks right downtown but still low-rent.

And this one afternoon—it was about three or four years ago—I passed by there, and looked in the window, and I went inside, and the man inside was funny, because he recognized me right away, and he must have wondered what is Willie Mays doing in here, where about the only thing you can buy new is filing cabinets or desk lamps? I mean, what does Willie Mays want with a second-hand couch in Cincinnati?

He says to me, the guy, "You're Mr. Mays."

"Yes," I said.

"I'm a fan of yours," he said. "My boy Arthur is twelve and he sleeps with your picture under his pillow."

"Does he play ball?"

"Captain of his Little League team."

You get to meet all kinds of kids, and they level with you when you talk with them, but according to their fathers there's got to be more captains than there are teams.

"I wanted to see that radio," I said, and pointed to one I'd seen through the window.

He said, "Mr. Mays, I don't . . ."

"Just to look," I said.

"Well, of course," he said, and he didn't know if I was putting him on or not—maybe now, he'd already recognized me but he was beginning to wonder was I really Willie Mays, is there another guy who looks just like him? And he yelled in the back, "Hey, Lionel!" And after a while Lionel, who must have been his partner, came out of the back and they both stood around looking at me and whispering, and I heard Lionel say, "Sure it's him!"

Me, meantime, I was looking at this radio. It had to be 25 years old. It was a square box, a console, with that cloth in front, so worn you could see the circular mouth of the speaker, where the sound came out, back of the cloth. And it had a lid that you raised, like today's stereo-radio phonograph sets, only there was no phonograph set at the top under the lid, only the controls for the radio.

Finally the first guy came up to me and said, sort of halting-like, "You want to hear it? I'll turn it on."

"I don't want to hear it," I said.

"Of course he don't want to hear it," Lionel, the partner, said.

So the two of them stood there and watched me, and finally I turned away from the radio and said to the first guy, "What'd you say your son's name was? Arthur?"

"Arthur," he said.

"You got a card?" I said.

He brought out one of his business cards. I took it and turned it over and wrote "To Arthur, best wishes, Willie Mays, S.F. Giants." I gave him back the card and said, "Thank you, both of you. Thank you very much." Then I went out of there and back to the hotel with the two guys, the first guy and Lionel, staring after me as I went out.

Maybe they didn't understand, but you meet a lot of people who don't understand. Take the record book. It doesn't even have my name right. My name is Willie Mays. It's not Willie Howard Mays, or Willie H. Mays, or any of those three names with a "Jr." after it. My real name is Willie Mays.

My father's father was Walter Mays, a pitcher in Negro ball in Tuscaloosa around the turn of the century. My father is William Howard Mays, because William Howard Taft was President when he was born.

One Southern sports writer actually said to me one time, "Willie, you must be descended from slaves."

"For your sake," I said to him, "I hope you're right."

I don't think he got it—him with his professional worship of "Southern womanhood"—but you can't draw any lines just for any one or two categories of things. Say there's a man on first and the next guy singles to center sending him to third, and you pick up the ball in center field and throw it to third anyway, hoping against hope something'll go wrong—he'll fall down or miss the base or overslide. And on the throw the hitter, who had a single, moves on into second. And now you walk the next man intentionally, and next day it comes out in the paper, "The Giants lost the game when So-and-So moved into scoring position on Mays's foolish throw to third base."

What the writer doesn't know is that, in that situation, it didn't make any difference, because if the hitter got on we were going to walk the next man anyway—whether first base was open or not.

The point isn't that I never made a wrong throw. I've made my share—maybe, when I was new, more than my share. The point is that in the situation I just described, I'm being paid to think about the next hitter and the writer isn't. I think it's as simple as that. I've seen ballplayers and managers thinking five hitters ahead. I once saw Herman Franks thinking six.

One time I saw Ashburn take off from first on a high pop-up

down the left-field line—the kind where it might be foul, or the third baseman or shortstop or left fielder, any one of them, might catch it—and there was only one out, and they finally caught it, and he was to third base by that time, so he was the easiest double play in history when they threw it back to first. And next day one of the writers said, "Ashburn ran because he made a mistake and thought the ball was going to fall in," and another said, "Ashburn ran because he made a mistake and thought there were two out, whereas actually there was only one out."

I think *whereas actually* must be the baseball writers' favorite all-time line.

What they didn't think was that Ashburn's team was tied 0-0 in the first inning and the next hitter up didn't do good against that pitcher. So Ashburn took the risk—either score if the ball fell in or be back at first with two out and a weak hitter coming up. Which actually is no risk at all. If you've got a choice between the good chance and the bad chance, try for the good one.

In the 1965 season, I tripled down the right-field line with McCovey on first, only he stopped at third and I was around second before I realized it, so they had me in a rundown. So at this point McCovey broke off of third, and, while they were running him down, I reached third. Then he came back into third, and they tagged both of us, and of course he was out, because he was the one who occupied the base last before the tag.

Some people might think having two runners hung up when you only need one is stupid base-running. Big-league baseball thinks what we did is the way to wind up with the faster man on third. If you've got the choice between the good chance and the bad one, try for the good one.

They ran Milt Stock out of baseball—the writers did—for the way he coached at third in the last of the ninth of the final game of 1950. Stock was coaching for the Dodgers. He had men on first and second, none out, tie game against the Phillies. Snider was up. He singled to center, and Stock waved Abrams, the man from second, around toward the plate. Ashburn threw him out, and Roberts pitched out of the inning, and next inning Sisler hit a three-run homer so the Phillies won the pennant.

So they descended on Stock for "taking a chance with none out" by waving Abrams into a "suicide" out at the plate.

It can be argued whether it was a "suicide" out or not. Abrams was a fast man. Ashburn had a notoriously weak arm. Stock figured he had a chance to win the game right there. At worst, he'd wind up with men on second and third and one out—which is exactly the result a perfect sacrifice bunt would have produced, if Snider had been bunting in what was a classic bunt situation.

Reason he didn't bunt was that he was a left-handed hitter and, at that early point in his career, not a good bunter. And the Dodgers were the home team and didn't want to lift this big man for a man who could bunt better. And Snider was fast, with a real good chance of staying out of the double play.

So they went against the book and let him swing away, and he delivered. If you've got the choice between the good chance and the bad one, try for the good one. Stock, coaching at third, had an easier choice than that. His choice was between two good chances. He had nothing to lose, so he went for the better one.

And like I say, they ran him out of baseball for it.

I could make a book out of this. I'm not going to. There are writers who understand. We have some in San Francisco.

As for the ones who don't, there's no difference between them and the furniture man in Cincinnati and Lionel his partner. Of course you didn't expect him and Lionel to understand. I don't expect all the writers always to understand either. It works both ways. You do something right and they don't know it. Okay. You do something wrong and they don't know it either. Things have a way of coming out even.

Late in 1954, I set what was then the all-time record for extra-base hits in one season by a Giant, breaking Mel Ott's old record. I did it with a double. It was in a game held up by rain, and the double was a fly ball to center, the easiest fly ball in history, but by now it got caught up in the setting sun and false twilight, and the center fielder lost it, and put his hand over his head to protect himself, and it dropped behind him for the hit.

Afterward, they asked me, "Did you want to set the record on a hit like that?"

I said, "How about the real hits they took away from me?"

It evens up. A lot of things in life even up, I think. The best you can do is the best you can do.

But the older you get, the harder it is. I remember DiMaggio, when he announced his retirement, saying he thought night baseball had taken three years off his playing lifetime. For a long time, I couldn't understand that. I mean, I could understand it, but it didn't apply to me. After all, Joe D. had been brought up on day ball, so he was used to it, and I could see where he wouldn't want the changeover to more and more night games. But I was playing night baseball when I was 15, and I've always been used to it, and I always said I liked it better, that there was no sun to bother you, that it seemed like you could see the ball better a lot of times when you were hitting at night.

Now, though, I don't know anymore. The nights—especially in San Francisco—may not be any colder than they were four, five, half a dozen years ago. But they seem colder, or maybe the warm clothing isn't as warm as it was. Maybe the water in the hot-water bottle we keep on the bench at Candlestick Park isn't as hot as it used to be. Maybe it just seems like a summer cold hangs on for two weeks instead of two days. Maybe I just think that my hands shake when we play a day game right after a night game.

Maybe Willie Mays isn't as young as he was. Baseball has its "old men." Satchel Paige—still pitching when I last heard, and he must be in his sixties. Warren Spahn. Appling. Musial. It happens. Guys get to their forties and still play in the majors, especially pitchers. But the nonpitchers—look at the list of them, and you see an interesting thing. Either they don't play every day, or, in their final couple of seasons, you don't find them on contending ball clubs. An "old" ballplayer can take the aches and pains, and he can take the pressure and the mental strain, which the fans never see, but he can't take them both together. And the worst part, I think, is the pressure, because it results in your being sick and getting hurt. Baseball is a young man's game. If you play it when you're old, it's because a lot depends on you—a lot of things and a lot of people, looking up to you, expecting leadership and the big play. Musial gave it to the Cardinals, but he was down to .255 his last season, and as a fielder, which is a better guide to how many games he appeared in than the hitting chart, he was in less than 100 games. Yet he still helped them, sometimes by just sitting there on the bench and having the other team know he was there so they'd have to let the tired left-hander go on pitching rather than bring the fresh right-hander in and take the chance The Man would get up there and kill them with one swipe.

Yet in that final season of his—1963—the Cardinals were just one game out in mid-September—I can see him, this truly great hitter, wishing somehow he could make the years roll back.

In my own case, there are no rules to go by except my own experience. I've been the "dean" of the Giants since before I was 30. Pressure? The last time there wasn't pressure was the last year we played in New York. We finished sixth that year.

Then we moved to San Francisco and suddenly, out of nowhere, we were driving for a pennant. The mayor of San Francisco said to Horace Stoneham, the Giants' owner, "You know what you were doing back there in New York last year? You were hatching the biggest explosion since they developed the atom bomb!"

"It was the best-kept secret since then too," Stoneham answered. "Why do you think we moved?"

But from 1958—our first San Francisco year—through 1965, as this book is written, we were up there in the pennant fight every season, year in, year out. Our worst finish—fifth place in '60—we were the preseason favorites, led the league for more than a month, had a shot at it for more than half the season.

On me, the pressure told. What happens to "old" ballplayers happened to me long before I was supposed to be old. I collapsed —just from plain nervous exhaustion and fatigue—in September of 1962; again in September of 1963. Yet what also happens to "old" ballplayers—they start becoming part-timers—didn't happen to me. I'd wind up playing in my 150 games a year, season in, season out.

I have said some things about baseball that were untruths, I know that now, but they seemed true when I said them. I said I preferred night baseball, and it was true when I said it. Maybe it's not true anymore. I said I never wanted to be the kind of player who wound up his career sitting on the bench, just getting in there once in a while. It was true when I said it. I want to think it's still true.

I told somebody once it always seemed like I started slow when the season began, but I said this the year after my worst start, and I shouldn't use the word "always" the way I do, because in my whole career—looking back and checking the book, I see it now— I've had only two real bad couple of opening months—'60 and '63— and all the rest have been either pretty good starts or tremendous ones, like in '55, '64, and '65.

If this book is what I think, and what has happened, then it is what I want it to be. At places it will sound like me when I talk and at places it won't, but there is nothing phony about that, because I don't ever talk book-length to begin with. Main thing, I want to be understood. Maybe you'll settle for that too.

I'm the highest-salaried player in baseball history, and the first Negro player to be named captain of a team—and that was the idea of a white Southerner who was manager at the time and who called me the greatest player he'd ever laid eyes on. My being a

Negro is a part of this story—more than you might suspect, but probably, also, less than a lot of people would like. I can say this: the sun doesn't rise or set on whether I hit a home run. For me, it rises and sets in a little guy whose name is Michael Mays: my son. He will know his father not as the first Negro player in the major leagues, because I wasn't, but as maybe—all things considered—the first you could point to and say, "Look what he did," instead of saying, "Look, he's colored."

I think just about all the Negro players who came up to the majors before I did—barely more than four seasons, from Robinson in '47 to me in '51—had the same scouting report. First they said the player was Negro and then they said he was great. With me they said great, then they said Negro. No question about what Jackie Robinson started. But maybe I started something too.

Before I came to the majors, no Negro player had the right to take one drink too many and break training. That was for white players only. Since I came up, we've had a couple of Negros in trouble too. Not me—I don't drink. And I don't mean to say, either, that my coming to the majors was a signal for the other Negro players to all shout, "Now we can sin along with the white boys!" No. What I mean is much simpler than that, and I think whoever reads this will know what I'm saying. I mean that with the timing, and the breaks, and what talent I had, there was put together, my first year in the majors, a kind of new set of values, where the Negro man stopped being equal just when he did good, but began being equal, period.

It may have been innocence on my part. I don't know. The "riding" I get from an opposing bench comes from Negroes and whites alike, and isn't racial talk. The only fight I ever had on the field was with a dark-skinned Latin player. I came close to tangling with a white boy once—a catcher for Pittsburgh who didn't last much more than a month or so of one season—and it wasn't so much what he said as what he did. He went out of his way to hurt me in

a play at the plate—this was 10 years ago, at the Polo Grounds—
and I came up with my eyes smarting and my hand was in a fist, but
then my mind said, *What for do you want to hit a busher?*

As captain of the Giants, I've had other players come up to me
with the most intimate problems you can imagine—things they
wouldn't even tell the manager, which is what captains are for—
either for advice, or to relay word to the manager, or just for somebody to listen to. I could say, and truthfully, that these players have
included white Southerners, except it never was that. It was two
people talking.

I don't picket in the streets of Birmingham. I'm not mad at the
people who do. Maybe they shouldn't be mad at the people who
don't.

# 3

I ALMOST EVEN became a Dodger.

I say "almost"—actually, it never got that close. Artie Wilson, who played with us around Birmingham and served as sort of a Dodger scout too, told me he'd recommended me to them and wanted to take me to spring training with him. This was a good two years before the Giants signed me. I couldn't have been more than 16, maybe 17.

Funny thing, it turned out they'd had reports on me already, from other scouts, and the word on me was no.

"He can't hit the curve ball," the reports said.

They were right. I couldn't hit the curve ball. Most 16-year-old kids can't, and I wasn't that much different from most 16-years-olds.

So I didn't become a Dodger.

But I heard they were after me again, just before the Giants did sign me. There have been all kinds of stories about the way I was signed. I guess the best and most accurate is contained in a letter Eddie Montague, one of the Giant scouts, sent to Tim Cohane, former sports editor of *Look* magazine, more than ten years ago. Charles Einstein, who is collaborating in the writing of this book, got a copy of the letter from Montague a couple of years ago, and probably the best thing is to print it here and now. It contains some things even I didn't know.

Here is the letter:

November 20, 1954

Mr. Tim Cohane
Sports Editor
Look Magazine
New York City

Dear Tim:

I have your letter of November 11, and I will try to give you a blow-by-blow account of the signing of Willie Mays.

In regards to Bill Maughn stating that he gave me my first tip on Willie Mays, I believe that he should correct his statement and say that he spoke about a young Negro ballplayer around Birmingham with a great arm, but I do not recall that Maughn ever mentioned the name of Willie Mays. However, that is beside the point, as I know it is a fact that Bill Maughn probably knew about Willie Mays before any other scout and I understand that he tried to get his organization to purchase the boy from the Birmingham Black Barons. I did not go in to see Willie Mays because Bill Maughn talked about him. The reason that I went into Birmingham was that, while at my home in Jacksonville, Fla., I received a call from our farm secretary, Jack Schwarz, to scout a player with the Birmingham Black Barons, named Alonzo Perry—a first baseman. This fellow had had a pretty good day in the Polo Grounds on the preceding Sunday and some of our scouts saw him and recommended him. I was told to scout Perry and see if he could help one of our Class A clubs. (Willie Mays may have played in the Polo Grounds also but no report was made on him.) The Barons toured through the Carolinas on their way back to Birmingham. One of our scouts picked up the club there and followed them into Birmingham. Still no report on Mays, who I know was with the club on this tour. When I arrived in Birmingham for the Sunday doubleheader I had no inkling of

Willie Mays, but during batting and fielding practice my eyes almost popped out of my head when I saw a young colored boy swing the bat with great speed and power, and with hands that had the quickness of a young Joe Louis throwing punches. I also saw his great arm during fielding practice, and during the games his speed and fielding ability showed up. This was the greatest young ballplayer I had ever seen in my life or my scouting career.

During the ball games I moved around watching the action from different angles and saw most of the games from on top of the roof. It was here that I met Mr. Hayes, owner of the Barons. I asked him about the young center fielder and how much he was asking for the boy. He told me $15,000 was the price, half now and half when the boy reported, and also that he wanted to use Mays on his club for the balance of the season. After the game I went down to the locker room to meet Willie Mays. He had just gotten out of the shower and I saw a well-built young fellow. I talked with Willie for a few minutes and I was impressed by his likeable attitude. I told him I would see him play the following night at Tuscaloosa, Ala.

I then went to my hotel and called Jack Schwarz at his home and told him my report on Alonzo Perry, who I said was not a major league prospect but o.k. for Class A. But then I gave him my report on Willie Mays and asked him if he had any reports on the boy. He said no, never heard of him. I told Jack I would see Mays the following night and if I still liked him I would try to purchase his contract from Mr. Hayes.

I was at the ball park, in Tuscaloosa, very early the following night. In fact, if it weren't for the groundskeeper I would have been lonesome. When the Barons came in to the ball park I immediately cornered Willie and asked him if he would like to play professional baseball, and he said, "Yes, sir," so I told Willie that I would speak with Mr. Hayes about his con-

tract. Willie said, "What contract? Mr. Hayes don't own me," so
I told Willie if that were the case that I would deal directly with
him. I got his address and phone number at Fairfield, Ala., and
told him I would call him the following morning. The next
morning I called and Willie told me that I would have to
speak with his Aunt Sarah, so I asked her how much they
wanted to sign a contract, and the answer was $5,000. I told
her I would contact my office and be at their house that afternoon. (Incidentally, I felt that I had to work fast, as I had seen
Ray Blades, Brooklyn scout, in the stands at Tuscaloosa, and
I was sure that he was there to see Mays. Willie had a great
night, hitting line drives to all fields and making a great catch
and throw.)

I told my farm secretary that I could get Willie Mays for
$5,000 and that he was not under contract with the Birmingham
Black Barons. I told Schwarz that Mays would be playing center
field in the Polo Grounds in two years, and Jack said, "If he's
that good, go and get him." He also told me that I had better
put a clause in the contract that Willie Mays was not orally
or writtenly obligated to any other baseball club and then have
it signed and notarized. Schwarz also asked me what classifica-
tion Mays could start playing, and I suggested Class B so
that he could get the feel of pro ball and gain confidence.

That afternoon I was at Willie's house in Fairfield. Willie's
aunt and young sister were at the house, and about 4 P.M.
Willie's father came home from the steel mill where he was em-
ployed. Mays senior was a former semi-pro ballplayer and he
was a proud man that day when Willie signed his first contract.
After talking about the Giant organization and professional
ball and what I thought of Willie's chances of getting to the
majors, I drew up the contract, and then Willie, his father, his
aunt and young sister proceeded to a notary to have the
contract signed and notarized. After I left the Mays' house I
went directly to the post office and mailed the contract in,

air mail special delivery. I then went to a drug store and called Jack Schwarz and told him that I had just signed a great young kid and that the contract was in the mail. At that time Jack Schwarz told me that we might have to pay Mr. Hayes something for Mays after all, as the Giant officials felt it was the right thing to do, so Mr. Hayes was sent a check for $10,000 which made everyone happy and also proves again and again what a grand organization the Giants are.

I understand that other clubs were interested in Mays at the time I saw him, but they were dealing with Mr. Hayes. We signed Mays and dealt with Mr. Hayes later, which in my opinion is the reason Willie Mays is playing for the Giants today.

These are all true facts in the scouting and signing of Willie Mays.

Sincerely yours,
s/ Eddie Montague

The year is 1950—the one Montague is writing about in that letter—and my recollection is that one of the reasons that kept me from joining the Giant organization the day after I signed was not just that the Birmingham Barons wanted me to play out their season with them, but also that I had to finish high school that June before I could play organized ball.

Where he recommended in the letter that I start in Class B "so that he could get the feel of pro ball and gain confidence," I guess it didn't hurt me any. In fact, I'm sure it didn't. But nobody, including Montague in the talk we had at the house that day, was fooled into calling Class B a step up from the Negro National League. In my judgment, the Birmingham Barons played Triple-A baseball. The main difference was—then as now—that the major leagues have 25 men to use, whereas the Triple-A minors only have 21. That's four more moves a game, and that, I think, is the real day-in, day-out difference between the majors and Triple-A. Sure, you get a steadier brand of ball in the majors, but you can go weeks on end and your Triple-A players will make every play the major leaguers can make, hit a ball just as far (maybe, because the pitching's shorthanded, even farther).

And it was the same with the Barons, where Piper Davis was the manager and played first base and was one of the great ones. Sometimes we had 21 men in uniform, sometimes less than that, but no league that included Satchel Paige and Josh Gibson was a Class B league.

(I got to hit against Paige one game. I was 1 for 2.)

I think maybe one of the nicest and truest compliments I ever got came from a guy named Jack Hardy, who played shortstop against us for some other team. "Buck?" he said. "He don't drink. He don't smoke. The only thing he ever done wrong was take a bath on Saturday night."

"Buck"—that's me. The ballplayers have always called me that, though they also say "Willie" and "Will" and "Mays" and "24." That last, of course, is the number on my back. In the middle of the 1965 season, we signed Warren Spahn to see if he could pitch for us, and somebody said to me, "Hey, Spahnie's number is twenty-four and he wants to keep it. After all, he was pitching when you were in second grade."

"Then you better call up Giles and tell him we got two twenty-fours on the Giants," I said.

"Can't do that," the man said. "Can't have two of the same number on the same team."

"Why not?"

"Confuse the fans, that's why. How could they tell you and Spahn apart?"

"Easy," I said. "I'm the one who bats right-handed."

Actually, Spahn's number has always been 21, but when they spring something on you in a hurry like that, sometimes you don't remember right, and for minute, there, even though I remembered him wearing 21, I thought maybe I was wrong and his number *was* 24.

(Way it worked out, Gabrielson was wearing 21 so they took it off him and give it to Spahn and gave Gabrielson 7, and Gabe regarded it as a promotion, because the last Giant who'd worn 21 was Ernie Bowman, but the last one who'd worn 7 was Harvey Kuenn.)

Players get that way about numbers. The Giants told me long ago that no one will wear 24 after I'm gone. They've retired one other number—Mel Ott's 4.

I heard a story about how Babe Ruth got to be 3 and Lou Gehrig got to be 4 with the Yankees (two more numbers that have been retired for all time). When they started out, there weren't any numbers at all. Then they came into being, and in recent years some clubs have gone farther and started putting the numbers on the front too, and on the back they now put the player's name, some of the clubs. I don't ever want to be married to the seamstress who has to sew Santoniowiscoatovich on the back of some guy's uniform. He'll look like a soup advertisement or something. And if he only lasts in the majors for a cup of coffee, they'd better farm the uniform out with him when he leaves. It'll have too many holes in it to be useful to anybody else.

Anyway, Ruth and Gehrig—Ruth got to be 3 because he batted third in the order. Gehrig was 4 because he batted fourth.

The word "cleanup" for the number-four hitter is, incidentally, a wrong word. It implies he's your greatest hitter. He isn't. Your greatest hitter bats third, for obvious reasons—you guarantee him two innings (the first and the second) when he doesn't have to lead off, and over a season you get him up to bat that many times more.*

But that means he has to have a big man batting fourth too.

* Once in a very great while, the number-three hitter will lead off the second inning. But if he does, it means you got 11 men to bat in the first inning, and by then you're happy past caring.

A Ruth had his Gehrig. A Ted Williams had a succession of big men up behind him, from Joe Cronin to Vern Stephens. This is known in baseball as "protection." The reason's simple. Without a big man coming up behind you, they don't have to throw you strikes you can hit.

It works the other way too. Although most of my career has been as a number-three hitter, we were without Orlando Cepeda as we went into the 1965 season, so for about half the season Manager Herman Franks fell into the pattern of batting Willie McCovey third and me fourth. It had its drawbacks, chiefly that I could do less running if I got on with McCovey ahead of me. This isn't because McCovey's that slow. More, it's because his main way of getting on base—outside of the home run—is singles and walks, so with him I had a bigger potential than with a lot of other guys to come up with a runner only 90 feet in front of me.

But it had its good side too, mainly that the pitchers didn't want to put an extra man on with me coming up. Having a man on first may have denied me the chance to stretch a hit or steal a base, but it also denied them a place to put me when I came up. And so they were less likely to tempt McCovey with bad pitches, for fear he'd let 'em go by and the umpire would call them balls.

When I talk about ballplayers, I use their last names, mostly, and so do all other players when they're talking about you, not to you. There have been a few exceptions. Williams was usually just "Ted." Paige was his full name: "Satchel Paige." But Musial was "Musial," Spahn is "Spahn." Durocher was "Leo." Dark is "Dark." Sometimes it's nicknames, or what they call diminutives. Bill Rigney is "Rig," when other people are talking about him. Fred Hutchinson was always "Hutch." Danny Murtaugh, though, was "Murtaugh." Red Schoendienst is "Schoendienst," because too many other guys are called "Red," and nobody knows what his real first name is anyway. But Casey Stengel was "Casey." Tom Sheehan has always been "Clancy," for some reason I don't know. For some other reason, the former commissioner of baseball, Ford Frick, was "Frick," the president of the American League, Joe Cronin, is "Cronin," but the president of the National League, Warren Giles, is usually "Mr. Giles," almost as though "Mr." was his first name.

The only flat rule I know where names are concerned is for umpires. Umpires are known by their last names only. The one exception to this rule was Jocko Conlan. Him, we referred to as Jocko. Once again, I don't know what his real first name is.

I've never been thrown out of a game by an umpire. Maybe the closest I came was in the second game of the 1962 play-off against the Dodgers, when Jocko signaled safe, then out, when I was safe at third and he knew it. I didn't call him names, but I said everything else. The funny thing was, I could have called him names—even the one thing you can call an umpire that means automatic ejection and a $50 fine—and I still wouldn't have got thrown out. My reputation, over the years, for not arguing, would have been in my favor. More than that, no umpire is going to have it on his record that he threw Willie Mays out of a play-off game. Actually, when you look at it that way, I am a privileged person in this respect. I do believe, though, that I earned the privilege over the years—and, having earned it, do not abuse it.

The first game of that '62 play-off was played at Candlestick, and I'll never forget Jocko on the field before the game, shouting at Manager Dark because the grounds keepers had watered the dirt around first base to keep Maury Wills from stealing.

By then, Dark had gained the nickname of "the swamp fox," and during our last series at Los Angeles all the fans had those little duck whistles and blew them at him. And it was quite a show, the way he'd have the men with the hoses water the dirt around the turn at first and along the base line toward second, when we were playing at home and were in control of the field.

We were taking batting practice that day, the opening day of the '62 play-off, and Jocko, still not dressed as an umpire but wearing his street clothes, went out to first base and looked and said to Dark, "Alvin, that's too wet."

"I don't know what you're talking about," Dark said to him.

"Call your grounds keeper," Jocko said to him.

"Call him yourself," Dark said.

"I don't have to listen to this," Jocko said.

"You don't have to listen to anything," Dark said.

They were shouting at each other, and the rest of us started gathering around, having fun. "Give it to him, Jocko!" we yelled. "You tell him, Jocko!"

This isn't to say we were rooting for Jocko. Of course we weren't. Maybe that mud at first was going to mire their base runners, but it was going to mire ours too—worse than theirs, because we had nobody as good as Wills, and whereas it might slow him up, at least he could stay upright in it. Our guys would turn first base and go flat on their backsides in the stuff.

The whole thing, instead, was part of a bigger thing, and I don't believe this particular part of the story—the main part, really—has ever been told before.

The day before had been the last day of the regular season, and the Giants have a last-day promotion called Fan Appreciation Day, and they give away something like four automobiles to four lucky fans.

And the ceremony takes place after the game, and they drive the cars in from the outfield just inside the third-base line to home plate.

Only on this day, Matty Schwab, our grounds keeper, went to Joe Orengo, who was in charge of the festivities, and said, "Joe, whatever you do, keep those cars off the infield on the third-base side."

"Why?" Orengo said.

"Because they'll sink in up to the hubcaps, that's why," Schwab said.

For practically all the season, unknown to anybody, Dark had been systematically watering down the grass on the left side of the infield, which is where our slower fielders were. Between our fielding, our pitching (including our main stopper that year, Billy Pierce), and the fact that other clubs hit more ground balls to the left side than we did, Dark wanted the infield as slow as possible on the left side.

That's where the water was going. The stuff at first base was for show and for distracting attention. And now, the day the play-off opened, the more Jocko screamed about first base, the more everybody started screaming—whether for or against him, it made no difference.

Jocko had been smart and was there at 11 in the morning and saw them watering first base. If he'd been smarter he would have been there at nine in the morning to watch them watering third. When those L.A. fans started calling Dark the swamp fox, they never knew where the real swamp was.

Jocko did the one thing he could do. He went and got the grounds keeper and made him put sand around first base. With two left-handers going that day, Koufax for them and Pierce for us, nobody was going to hit the ball there anyway, but Jocko was supposed to see mud and that's what he saw. The phrase "Here's mud in your eye" should have been invented that day.

Meanwhile, the grass on the third-base side was slow as soup. And nobody watered the dirt around third. Just the grass, where you couldn't see it. If they'd watered the dirt, somebody might have put two and two together and looked at the grass too.

Though what they could have done about it, I don't know.

Swamp fox is right—though "swamp fox" is a made-up nickname, and nothing that lasts. The very opposite, I guess, from "Buck," which is what they call me. I can't even trace where I got the nickname. I think Charley Willis hung it on me. He was my closest boyhood friend, back in Fairfield, Alabama. He called me "Buck-duck," and so did other people, and I don't know why, but it got shortened to "Buck" and that's what it is today.

"When Buck pounds that pood," Ed Bailey once said, "I know

we're all right." Something like that needs translating. What he was saying was, when Mays taps his glove, it means he knows he can catch the ball. Which by itself is usually true.

Charley Willis may have hung that nickname "Buckduck" on me, but he called me something else too.

We were just kids then, throwing a ball in a vacant lot.

He used to call me "DiMag." I know why he called me that. It's because I asked him to.

# 4

AT FIRST, I didn't want to be DiMaggio.

I wanted to be a cowboy.

My oldest memory is singing the words of a cowboy song. Not really a cowboy song. More, a popular song that was a takeoff on a cowboy song. You remember it:

> I'm an old cowhand
> From the Rio Grande
> And I learned to ride
> Just to beat the band
> I'm a cowboy who never saw a cow. . . .
> Never roped a calf 'cause I don't know how. . . .

And on and on it went, and wound up:

> Yippee-I-oh-ky-ay*

They tell me I was four years old at the time, and I memorized the words from the way they came over the radio, which was the great piece of furniture in my Aunt Sarah's house in Fairfield. I will never forget that radio. A quarter of a century later, I saw it, the

* "I'm an Old Cowhand," words and music by Johnny Mercer. Copyright 1936 by Leo Feist, Inc. Copyright renewed 1963 by John H. Mercer.

same model, looking through the plate-glass window of that second-hand furniture store in Cincinnati that time I've already told about, which is why I went in to stare at it.

"You going to be a singer when you grow up?" Aunt Sarah said to me.

"No," I'd say. "A cowboy."

"A singing cowboy," she said. "We'll call you Bing."

"He's not going to be a singer," my father would say, "and he's not going to be a cowboy either."

"What's he going to do?" Aunt Sarah would ask him. "Work in the mill like you?"

"Not work in the mill either," my father said. "He's going to go to college."

"How's he going to get into college?"

"Play football," my father said. "He'll go to Pittsburgh."

"They don't take 'em up there."

"Sure they do. What's the matter? You don't read the papers?"

"They take 'em," Aunt Sarah said, "from around Pittsburgh. Ain't nobody in Pittsburgh ever heard of Alabama."

"You crazy?" my father said. "Pittsburgh *plays* Alabama."

"Yes?" Aunt Sarah said to him. "Well, you just let me tell you: he's got a better chance being a singing cowboy." She reached and rumpled at my head. "You tell him, Bing."

"Yippee-I-oh-ky-ay," I said.

I lived with my Aunt Sarah and her family. I was born, May 6, 1931, not in Fairfield but in a nearby place with almost the same name—Westfield—but the marriage of my father and my mother didn't last much more than a year after that, and then I went to live at Aunt Sarah's house in Fairfield.

They were kids themselves, my mother and father—no more than 18, either one of them, when I was born. But he was a baseball player, and my mother was a wonderful athlete herself—a star runner who held a couple of women's track records in that part of the country (which, if you look at the makeup of our Olympic teams, produces the best women sprinters). I say this here because I remember, more than 30 years after I was born, I was in Mt. Zion Hospital in San Francisco for a complete medical checkup, and this famous heart man there, Dr. Uhley, went to hook me up to what they call a vectorcardiograph, which is like an electrocardiogram except it measures you in all three dimensions instead of just two. And he had to fasten kind of a rubber suction cup to my back, and he tried and he tried, first putting it one place on my back, then another, but each time the suction didn't work and the thing would pop off.

Finally, he said to me, "Don't tell me baseball did this for you."

"Did what for me?"

"Your father," he said. "He was an athlete?"

"My mother too."

"Well, I guess that explains that," he said.

"Explains what?" I said.

"According to the textbooks," he said, "every human being has kind of a layer of fat on his back. That's why they design these cups this way. It gives them something to glom onto.

"So?"

"*So?*" he said.

"I mean," I said, "what's the problem?"

"The problem," he said, "is you don't have any fat."

"I thought you said everybody does."

"I didn't say everybody does. The book says everybody does. Up till now, the book's been right."

"Well, if I don't have the fat," I said, "what do I have?"

"Willie," he said to me, "all you've got for a back is one continuous muscle."

I grinned. "That's nice to know. I wish I could bottle it and sell it."

"You already do," he said. "Bottle it and sell it, I mean. You know, I saw you in a game against the Mets last season and you hit two home runs, and the first one tied the game and the second one won it. I'll never forget that."

"I remember it too," I said. "The first one went a lot farther than the second one. I didn't hit that second one real good."

"That's right," he said. "That's the way I remember it too. Except it seemed to me that you hit that second one with only one hand on the bat. And the next morning it said in the paper Casey Stengel had said the same thing—that he didn't mind the first one but he didn't like to get beat one-handed."

"I'm not sure I remember that part of it," I said.

"I remember it," he said.

"Maybe I was ducking away."

"All I know is the ball went out of the park. Now that I've seen your back, I begin to see it's possible."

"I don't know," I said. "Seems to me like people are built pretty much the same."

"If they had your father and your mother they would be," the doctor said.

Actually, I am "big brother" to 10 half brothers and sisters, the result of my mother's remarriage after she and my dad were divorced. They didn't live at Aunt Sarah's, but we were always close, like relatives are, over the years.

Even despite what happened with that doctor and his machine, I don't know if there's anything you could really call "baseball muscles." Most athletes are good at a lot of sports. A whole raft of great baseball players—Jackie Robinson, for one—were football stars first. Al Dark was a football star who went to college on a *basketball* scholarship.

Where baseball's different, I think, is in two ways—first, baseball alone has a place for the little man who isn't sized to be good at other sports. And second, baseball has always attracted more than its share of stars from California and the South—because you can only play it when the weather's good, and that's where the weather is good the longest time each year. You think it's just a mistake that both Arizona and Arizona State come up with top college baseball teams year in and year out?

The only thing that will stop warm weather from producing base-ball talent is a lack of competition. That's been Hawaii's problem so far. Ten years from now, look for that state to be producing more top players per capita than any other. Ball clubs will fly over there in less than two hours, and for less than $10,000 for the whole team for a whole week including round-trip transportation, and they'll make the expenses back plus some more in six games over there, and for months after that you won't get a kid near a surfboard. He'll be out with a ball and a glove, throwing and catching, throwing and catching. . . .

Throwing and catching. Throwing and catching.

My oldest memory is of a radio and a silly cowboy song, but even before that, from the time I was less than two, my father started me with a ball. He was Kitty-Kat—that was his nickname, that's what the other players called him on the pickup semipro teams around Birmingham. And they called him that for a reason. He was the most graceful fielder, they said, that anybody ever saw.

"Buck," Piper Davis said to me, last time I saw him, a couple of years back, "you get the greatest instinctive jump on a ball I ever saw, except for maybe Joe D. or his brother Vince. But you've got more range than either of them, and you field ground balls better, and your arm is maybe the most dangerous since Ruth himself and more accurate than anybody except maybe Henrich's. And you don't know how to look bad under a fly ball."

"Sounds like I'm pretty good," I said.

"Only one better," he said. "Your old man. Kitty-Kat. Lot of things you can do, he couldn't do. But *graceful?* Man, he was a poem. He was Shakespeare and that other cat Dante rolled into one. Know the difference, Buck? You don't *pounce.* You're a grabber. The old man, though—that's why we called him Kitty-Kat—now, *he* knew how to *pounce!*" He grinned. "I've seen you on the bases. Passed ball, no more than three foot away, and you *explode.* Explode, that's the word for it. Better than Jackie, better than anybody. But, Buck, you don't *pounce.* You just never learned how."

And that was the game. When I was two years old. My dad would roll the ball at me, easy, and I'd stop it and then take it in my right hand and throw it back. And that was it—no matter how bad I threw it, he'd catch it. Like Piper said, Kitty-Kat would *pounce*. Till I wanted to pounce too, so instead of rolling it, he'd loft it a little ways in the air, and I learned to catch it.

The older I got, the more complicated the game got, but it was still the same game. When I was 10 years old, it was Kitty-Kat throwing the ball at me so it would bounce just in front of me and I'd have to "scoop" it—make the "pickup." For many big-leaguers, this is the most difficult fielding play of all. For me, simply on the basis of all that training over all those years, it actually became easier than some catches.

Here's a story in the San Francisco *Examiner*, about a spring training game in 1961. . . .

Did he or didn't he? Maybe only the ball-park hairdresser—er, groundskeeper—knows for sure, and then only if he knows how to read a divot.

But one of the liveliest discussions ever to center around a play in an exhibition game continued far into the night and the next day as to Willie Mays' unbelievable nab of a sure two-run base hit in Saturday's Giants-Indians game.

Mays said he caught the ball, and most of the Giants—and a couple of Indians—agreed.

Most of the Indians—and a couple of Giants—said he trapped it at grass-top level and conned the umpire into calling the out.

"It was straight magic," a prominent Clevelander said. "You've got to give him that. One minute he's trapping the ball and seconds later he's holding it out and showing it in his glove, and the ball's so far out of the glove you say he couldn't have trapped it. He'd have had to catch it."

Muttered Indian manager Jimmy Dykes: "He didn't catch it.

Why didn't I say anything about it? Because I knew that umpire, that's why. What was the use?"

"He's still Willie Mays," said Cleveland coach Mel Harder. "He had his reputation going for him."

"I thought he caught it," Giant manager Alvin Dark said. He grinned. "What's the fuss about, anyway? It's routine for Willie." Then, thoughtfully, Dark pointed out: "If he doesn't catch it, then he comes up throwing the ball."

There might be a point there, for not only were three runners in motion, but the situation—with two out in the bottom of the sixth and the Giants ahead 2-1—was nothing if not critical.

Though the Giants went on to win, 4-1, there was no doubt that, as coach Salty Parker put it, "Mays saved us the ball game."

He also saved manager Dark from the first concerted second guess he would have had to defend against. For with two out and a man on second, Dark had ordered an intentional walk to Willie Kirkland—going against the book by putting the lead run on base in a late inning.*

Runners moved up on a passed ball, and Jack Kubiszyn's sinking liner well to Mays' left was ticketed as a sure bet to score them both. Till Willie did what Willie did.

"The percentage didn't mean anything to me," Dark said later. "What's the difference if you go out to tell the pitcher don't give him anything good, or just go ahead and walk him?† If you tell him go ahead and pitch, you might hear the sound of that base hit leaving the bat before you get back to the bench."

Further, said Dark, "In a case like that, I want the responsibility. My pitcher has enough worries of his own."

* Shades of Charley Dressen! (See pp. 13–14.)
† Dark had another story next day. "Thinking about it," he said, "if I'd known how Kubiszyn could hit I would have thought twice before walking the man ahead of him."

But Mays' catch—old-timers who have seen him in New York as well as San Francisco called it one of his all-time best—got everybody off the hook.

As to whether he actually caught it, two things can be said. First off, those who think he didn't may be possessed of logical minds that tell them the ball simply could not have been caught, regardless of what their eyes tell them. Unbelievable is surely a correct word for it.

And secondly, Giant pitcher Sherman Jones summed it all up in one short sentence:

"If he traps it, it's still a hell of a play."

P.S.—Mays made an excitingly similar catch during today's 15-9 loss to Cleveland to end the fourth inning when it looked as though nothing would end it. But so disorganized was the situation, and so meaningless to the final result was the catch, that it almost escaped notice.

In case anybody's interested, I didn't catch the ball—I trapped it. As for that "P.S." at the end of the article, referring to another play the next day, I didn't catch that one either. Both times the umpires ruled I'd caught it, not trapped it, whereas I'd trapped them both. I don't mean to say I make a career out of this one play, or that umpires never call anything right, but it is possible to trap a ball so effectively you might as well have caught it. Possible, that is, if you have a father named Kitty-Kat making you do it day in, day out, from the time you're seven till the time you're 14.

It does no good for a father to work with a son who doesn't want to play. It does no good for a father to work with a son who does want to play if the father doesn't know what's coming off. But in between you get people like my father, and Bob Feller's father, who painted a circle on the barn door out there somewhere in Iowa, and had the kid throw to that circle. I don't believe Feller ever had an inning of minor-league baseball behind him when he came up to the Indians. Walter Mails tells me Walter Johnson was faster. I think probably Johnson was faster over a longer period of time. But I have had baseball men tell me that for those first two or three years that Bob Feller was in the big league, starting when he was something like 18 years old, he threw a ball faster than anybody in all history.

Bobby Doerr, the famous Red Sox second baseman, told me how he became one of the very few who were able to hit Feller. "Cronin gave me the tip," he said. "The idea was that, to begin with, you couldn't hit him. So you conceded him half the strike zone to start with. You decided not only to set for the fast ball, but only in one-half of the strike zone. No matter what came, you were concentrating just on that one-half of the strike zone. Figuring called balls and foul balls, there had to be some pitch—at least one—that would be where you were swinging. So you had a chance."

I have seen great pitchers, and by great pitchers I mean not just day in, day out, but a man who could get one hitter out when you had to get one hitter out. Rate them? I'll try to, right here:

I will have to do one thing—eliminate my own teammates. That knocks out some fair hands—Marichal, Maglie, even (as of late last season) Warren Spahn. Many people think I've taken care of Spahnie over the years. He's taken care of me too. And when I say "take care," I don't mean "protect." I mean, I hit him, or he strikes me out. The ledger's been a long one, and a pretty even one, between us.

So the names that are left: Koufax, Drysdale, Roberts, New-combe.

Those are the big four in my book—of the pitchers I've had to hit against.

They have one thing in common, and what they have in common is not common. Get a no-balls-two-strikes count on a hitter you *have* to get out. Now you're ahead of him 0-and-2. You can afford to waste one now, to tempt your hitter. You've got him on the hip.

Ever wonder why it is the great pitchers seem to be the ones who give up home runs on the 0-and-2 count? It's because that's when people notice it. They don't notice it when the 0-and-2 count busts the edge of the plate for strike three. They don't notice the other pitchers who'd never risk a strike 0-and-2.

But a Koufax, a Drysdale, a Roberts, a Newcombe—they'd challenge you 0-and-2, and for every one of those pitches your bat even connected with, there'd be, seemed like, two times you'd trudge back to the dugout, with that umpire saying "Strike three" in your ear and you knowing he was right.

That's the pitch that separates them: the 0-and-2 pitch.

I hear tell, from the ballplayers who were around before I was, that Dean had that pitch. And Hubbell. And Mathewson.

Old-timer after old-timer has told me how Johnson could throw. They're supposed to have timed his pitch at 117 miles per hour. I heard Feller threw 112 mph. Allie Reynolds, the Indian, is supposed to have been clocked at 108.

I'm not fixing to hit any pitch traveling at that speed.

But they tell me something else. It may be a myth. By now, nobody rightly remembers. But the story is that, back in the mid-thirties, there were two postseason barnstorming teams, one headed up by Lefty Grove and the other headed up by Satchel Paige, and they met up for a game in Honolulu. And Satchel and Lefty got together before the game and made a $1,000 side bet between them, as to who'd win.

The story that comes down, through the mists of time, is that with that side stake working, the two of them took the mound, and they went 16 innings, till darkness ended the game, and NOBODY hit the ball.

I believe it.

I should say here that I can't say what I suppose you may expect me to say—what pitchers do I like, what pitchers don't I like. There is no pitcher who's ever gotten me out consistently. On the other hand, there is only one pitcher I've ever hit consistently, and I'm not even sure about him, because it got to the point where when I came up, he went out. And he was a pretty good pitcher. His name: Harvey Haddix. I think he had a case on me.

There have been some pitchers I hit pretty good but never saw again, so they don't count. But Labine would get me out. Then I'd hit him. Brewer would get me out. Then I'd hit him. I'd hit Ellsworth. Then he'd get me out. I'd hit Cardwell. Then he'd get me out. I have batting weaknesses, but they're my own doing. The "book" on me is: (1) move the ball around, and (2) don't change up. Yet I look my worst being fooled by a pitch which repeats the pitch before—or swinging and missing out in front of the change.

Some pitchers figure I should be pitched inside, then outside, because if I go down from a pitch, I'll be "bailing out" from then on. That's probably true. What's also true is some of my best hits have come while I was bailing out. Maybe it's the muscular back that doctor was talking about.

Jackie Robinson said on TV during the 1965 season that the Dodgers used to throw at me, but they found out it made me mean so they stopped it. With all respect to Jackie, that's the greatest single piece of fiction I ever heard.

In the first place, the Dodgers still throw at me. They never stopped. Drysdale, who's a good friend of mine, like to kill me a couple of times and he knows it.

In the second place, anybody who tries to promote the myth that a guy's a better hitter after he's eaten a mouthful of dirt is throwing a kind of junior-birdman dust around that's nothing more than a bad joke. The idea is that if you make some hitters mad they're tougher to pitch to—you didn't leave sleeping dogs lie, you stirred the juices.

Let sleeping dogs lie, they say.

You ever see a sleeping dog who was as good as one who was awake to begin with?

It's the worst piece of 1,000-percent nonsense I ever heard.

No man who's just had a baseball thrown at his head at better than 90 miles per hour is going to be as good a hitter on the next pitch, and the sooner people get sensible about this the sooner we may be able to get this pitch out of the game. As of now, the way to stop the man who throws at your head 90 miles per hour is to wait till he comes up and then throw at his head 90 miles per hour.

It isn't just one pitch, either. Some pitchers throw at you again the next time. Maybe even the time after that.

Out of all the ace statisticians who've made names for themselves keeping baseball records, you'd think one would have come along who clocked duster pitches. How many of them come with no balls and two strikes? How many of them with nobody on base? How many of them with lopsided scores, so putting a man on won't matter?

One game I hit two consecutive home runs off Dick Farrell of Houston. Next time up he hit me in the left arm with a fast ball. They'd already blown the ball game by then. Was this just a pitch that got away?

Even this has its funny side. When Harvey Kuenn came over to the Giants from the American League, in 1961, he hadn't seen much of me and I hadn't seen much of him. But I knew his reputation and he knew mine, and we both admired each other from afar.

Anyway, we got in this game at Palm Springs, and Harvey was on first and I was up, and Dark wanted to try the hit-and-run, and they threw at my head. So I went down, but I had the bat stuck up in the air, and the ball hit it and went to the left-field wall on two bounces and Harvey scored all the way from first, and afterward in the dugout he said, "That's enough! I'm a believer! I'm a believer! The guy gets a hit-and-run triple while he's lying on his back! I didn't know whether to run or laugh or go blind!"

But let me tell you about Harvey Haddix, which is what started all this.

I'm not going to measure the longest home run I ever hit. I've hit some shots I remember—some off pitchers I *don't* remember, because they didn't last long—but one of the longest came in 1954, at the Polo Grounds. I hit it into the last rows of seats upstairs where the stands came around to meet the bleachers, just to the left of deepest center field, which has to be more than 500 feet to that point, and the thing was still going up when the stands stopped it.

Yet Haddix, who'd thrown it, had given me a low outside change-up. Now, it's conceivable you can pull a low outside pitch if your bat comes around in time, and that's possible if the pitch is a change-up. But to hit it that far is something else, because a baseball, essentially, is a rubber ball. That's what the center of it is. And if you've ever played tennis, or bounced a rubber ball against a wall, you know the harder it hits the racket or the wall, the farther it bounces back. Just lay your bat in the way of a fast ball, and it goes a long way. But on a change-up, *you've* got to supply the power. Ken Raffensberger, the Cincinnati left-hander, made a career out of this principle. He'd just lob the ball in there and make the hitter supply the power. Same with Stu Miller.

Yet here's a ball that had been hit more than 500 feet and was still going up, off a low outside change-up, and it made Haddix stop and think.

We faced each other time and again, after that, over the next five years, and he never once threw that pitch to me again.

In a way, he might have been building a strength, because after five years of not throwing it, he could well have figured in his mind that I'd never expect to see it again.

But now it was a summer afternoon in Forbes Field in Pittsburgh, and it was the top of the eighth, and we were behind one run with a man on, and the year was 1959, and Haddix decided he'd try it one more time.

It was still going up when it left the park, over the scoreboard in left.

It might have been an accident. I don't know. Two pitches, five years apart, and the same result on each.

But apparently it was enough for Haddix, because the next time he faced us, in San Francisco a couple of weeks later, we had a tie score in the eighth inning and I was up. And there were two out and nobody on. And Haddix signaled his manager Murtaugh, to come out from the bench, and said: "I want to walk him."

Murtaugh was a little surprised. He said: "You got bases empty and two out and you want to *walk* him?"

"That's right."

"What if he steals?"

"I'm left-handed. I can hold him on."

Murtaugh shrugged and went back to the bench. And then and there I got the closest thing to an intentional base on balls with nobody on that I guess anybody ever gave up. There wasn't any of those pitches anywheres near the plate.

Now McCovey was up for us next, and he was new to the club then, and Rig, the manager, called him back and said, "Take the first couple. Give him a chance to get to second."

On the second pitch I stole second. Then McCovey singled to score me and we won the game.

A couple of years after that, Haddix was beating us 7-4 and we had a man on first with none out in the top of the seventh and I came up. My previous three times up that game, I'd had a double, a triple, and a walk. Murtaugh came out of the dugout and Haddix just tossed him the ball and left. No waiting.

I might add, they brought Labine in to pitch and I promptly hit into a double play. Maybe the Haddix thing was as mental with me as it was with him.

I think I'm something like .700 lifetime against another real good little left-handed pitcher—Whitey Ford—except I never really came up against him that much. Just in a few All-Star games and the '62 World Series. But it got to the point where, when I was playing in the '63 All-Star game and he wasn't, I got a telegram from him: DEAR WILLIE—SORRY—WHITEY.

When I say that there's no pitcher who ever got me out consistently, I mean of course in terms of what passes for "consistent" in baseball. If a pitcher can get you out seven times out of every 10 official at bats you have against him, some people might say he was getting you out consistently. But you also happen to be batting .300 against him—3-for-10!

Instead of gabbing on and on about who I hit good and who I don't, I think I can offer proof here that I don't own any pitchers, anymore than there are any pitchers who own me. Art Santo Domingo, the Giants' statistician, showed me a table last season, giving a breakdown of my average number of base hits per season for the previous three years, ever since the league expanded to 10 teams.

My average number of hits per season *vs.* each of the other nine clubs were:

St. Louis—22
Philadelphia—19
Cincinnati—20
Milwaukee—19
Pittsburgh—20
Los Angeles—20
Chicago—21
Houston—21
New York—22

By comparison, Orlando Cepeda, who had 12 fewer hits than me over the same three-year period but outhit me .307 to .305 for that span of time, averaged as few as 16 hits per season against one club—the Cardinals—but as many as 27, against the Phils!

Yet Cepeda has been accused, over the years, of far less "streaky" performance than me. Later on, I will have more to say about this—not about Cepeda, who's one of the strongest and best hitters I've ever seen, but about the business of Mays being "inconsistent."

Maybe you can tell—maybe you can't—the secret thing that amused me about that table printed just above. It was in 1965 that I was shown those figures, and the previous year—the latest year of the three counted in that table—the Cards finished first and the Mets finished last. So I wound up doing my top hitting against (1) the best, and (2) the worst teams in the league!

I think I've been more consistent than a lot of people believe. But I also think something else: I think maybe my upbringing had something to do with it.

Not just my dad—that's the good part. But also the fact that—if you want to put it this way—I was "underprivileged." So was just about every other kid in the country, at the same time I was growing up, whether he was born in Birmingham or Newport, Rhode Island.

Us poor kids of my generation—we never had any Little League.

Don't mistake me. I believe in Little League. But I believe in it because at today's prices, for everything from tape to wind a ball, to a vacant lot to play in, a lot of places it's Little League or nothing.

But in my day we didn't have to worry about that. We found a roll of friction tape and we found a vacant lot, so what we did was play ball. I don't say there's a choice today, but I do say we had it better. We didn't have uniforms or screaming mothers or concession stands or crazy men who didn't know a thing about baseball but wound up managing because (1), their son was playing, and (2), because nobody else wanted the job. We didn't fill out insurance forms so in case somebody got hurt somebody else paid. Maybe that was a bad part. I'm all for insurance. Matter of fact, I sell it, for Pennsylvania Life. The point is, if a kid didn't get hurt playing baseball, he'd get hurt doing something else. Today so many more of them spend so much time playing baseball it's a good thing there's insurance, and it's a good thing they've got good equipment and adults around.

Main thing, what's going on today isn't like what was going on when I was a kid. More kids, higher prices, less land.

Today has its good side, and it's necessary. But my day had its good side too. Chances were, adults would either leave you alone or, if they took an interest in you, they knew what they were talking about.

In the Bay area of San Francisco, there's a rich man I've been told about who has a back yard so big it's a Little League field all by itself. And because he wanted his own kid to play he installed a pitching machine back there and managed a team and makes all the kids on the team report to his house for practice against the pitching machine. He also drives two Cadillacs.

He doesn't know very much about baseball, either.

The only wrong thing with that is, it's not the kid's fault. In my day he would have found something else to do. Today, it's play Little League or nothing. Who did this? You supply your own villain. All I know is, the kid didn't do it.

It's not just Little League. It's Babe Ruth League and Bronco League and Colt League and Senior Little League and anything else you can think of.

Do the men know what they're doing? Or not? I guess a few of them do. Most of them, I'd guess, no.

It's a fact that some young players can be overcoached, one way or another, and that it can hurt them. The classic case I know of is that of a boy whose first name is Lewis, son of a good friend of mine, who was in the Pony League (for 13- and 14-year-olds) after a real good Little League career.

Now in the Little League, and even in the Pony League, a good player can play almost any position, but by the time you get to high-school varsity play, you should be stationed where you play best. If you're not, it's not the end of the world, but if you go on in baseball from there, somebody's going to have to come along and make you over.

Sometimes this "making over" doesn't even take place till the player actually reaches the big leagues. You all can think of players who came up at one position—Mickey Mantle was one—only to be shifted to another. Some men in the big leagues play more than one position routinely. I can even think real fast of two men—Bucky Walters and Bob Lemon—who made their mark as *pitchers* in the big leagues even though they came up to the majors at other posi-

tions. Walters, in fact, spent several years as a third baseman before
he became a pitcher instead.

So that part of it isn't too bad, and in the case of my young
friend Lewis, he was good enough to play varsity ball his freshman
year in high school. He was going to be a pretty good outfielder,
but they used him instead as a catcher on the high-school team, for
an obvious reason, but one that sometimes people don't think of—
they didn't have another catcher.

In the Pony League, when he was 13, he pitched and played some
shortstop. Now in high school, at 14, he was catching. The rule was
that you couldn't get into Pony League play till the high-school
schedule had been played out. So at 14, Lewis didn't join his Pony
League team till it had played a couple of games. Incidentally,
this Pony League team wasn't very good. It was one of the two
worst teams in its league, as things turned out. Also, and again
incidentally, Pony League dimensions—the playing field—are halfway between Little League and high school (regulation). Little
League bases are 60 feet apart; Pony, 75 feet; high-school (and
regulation), 90 feet. And pitching distances are staggered to con-
form.

Anyway, Lewis didn't get a hit in his first three Pony League
games, so his coach decided he must be doing something wrong at
bat and changed his whole stance. And for the rest of the Pony
season Lewis didn't hit good, and his team finished last.

Remembering that Lewis had been playing on a regulation-size
diamond, and now had to adjust to smaller distances, especially
pitching distance, I wouldn't have done a thing with his stance if
he didn't hit for three games. An added thing was that his Pony
League team wasn't going anywhere. Let's say it took the league
three games to find that out. After that, since in the Pony League
you play two seven-inning games a week but no pitcher can pitch
in more than something like 10 innings a week, obviously they were
going to be seeing easier pitching, because the other teams would
save their best pitching for the pennant contenders.

So—just at the point where Lewis was about to start hitting normally—not only that, but even start to see relatively easy pitching . . . his coach goes and changes him around. Now he's being artificial and he never gets a hit.

And the local high-school coach sees some of the Pony League games. He knows Lewis didn't hit real good as a high-school freshman, but that's understandable. For a freshman playing varsity ball, that first year is a learning year, especially when you've got him working a new position in the field. Now, though, all the high-school coach knows is that Lewis isn't hitting *easy* Pony League pitching either. The high-school coach doesn't know that the Pony coach made Lewis change. Or, if he does know it, it doesn't occur to him that this was the one thing *not* to do. Sure, maybe the Pony coach says to the high-school coach, "Yes, I know I changed his stance, but he wasn't hitting the other way," and they leave it at that. Since Lewis hadn't hit too good the old way his freshman year in high school, the high-school coach puts two and two together and gets a big fat five and says to himself, "Well, Lewis could do it in Little League, but, like a lot of kids, he's got no real future in baseball."

And this is what happend to Lewis. On account of two men who were both good baseball men, and who meant nothing but the best for Lewis himself, he was literally coached out of what should have been a good and easy and confidence-building Pony League season as a 14-year-old. He knew now that his high-school coach had real doubts as to how he might perform as a sophomore. And what might have been a baseball career for a boy just went down the drain.

This, as I say, was a classic: a product of overcoaching. The point is not that this is an isolated case. The point's a different one, and far more interesting, I think.

Here it is:

I think youngsters who have a future in baseball can survive undercoaching—things they're not taught because their Little League manager just doesn't know them to begin with—far better than they can weather overcoaching!

Knowing *how* to play a Little Leaguer is one thing. Knowing *when* to play him is a far greater gift, I think. If you've got a new 10-year-old who obviously isn't a match for the real good pitching in the league, don't go changing him around because he isn't hitting. And don't go letting him play every game—although I know there are some parents who think the only object of Little League is for every boy to get into every game. For the boy's sake, whether he's a real good player or not, spot him against the "off" pitching.

I've found that the parents sometimes think the boy's happy if he gets up to bat. I think the truth is he's really happy not by getting to bat with no chance, but by getting to bat with a real chance. What doesn't occur to the parents is that he doesn't want to go up to bat for the sake of going up to bat. He wants to go up to bat for the sake of getting on base.

The same parents who think it's a crime if a boy doesn't get into the game would think it was cruel of the manager who not only put him in the game but made him pitch to the big hitters on the other team. Sometimes I think we should all remember that all of us—and that includes 10-year-old boys—don't just want to *do*. What we want is the chance to *do good*.

It isn't a crime to want to win at the Little League level, either. Not because winning is so important at that level. But because if you criticize a boy after a defeat, it sounds like blame. When you spell out his mistakes after the team has won, he *learns*. The difference between criticism and blame is not what you did but how the team did.

If I talk about boys with talent and coaches without it, nobody should think I believe baseball is only for winners. Baseball is for any boy who wants to play it. And losing isn't the worst thing in the world (but winning isn't either). What I don't like to see is boys who are *made* to play because "everybody else does it." Beyond that, I think today's programs, for Little Leaguers and others, are considerably more on the plus side than the minus. Like I say, 25 years ago I would have said no—but 25 years ago is a different world.

In San Francisco last year, Joe DiMaggio was the guest of honor at the opening ceremonies for one of the Little Leagues, and all the kids cheered him and rushed him for his autograph. Those kids all had one thing in common—when Joe D. hung up his spikes, none of them had even been born yet. It's been a long time, and times do change.

That radio in my Aunt Sarah's house, the summer I was 10 years old, was still playing cowboy songs. But it had news too—the news of Joe DiMaggio's record-setting 56-game hitting streak. That's when I stopped wanting to be a cowboy.

Instead, I said to Charley Willis, "Call me DiMag."

"You crazy?" Charley said.

"I mean it," I said. "That's my new name."

"That means you got to play center field," he said.

"I don't care about center field," I said. "Just so long as I hit like him."

I'd seen a newsreel of the Yankees in spring training, and they had a picture of DiMaggio, closeup, then taking his stance in the batter's box, then swinging and hitting the ball over the fence.

Years later, I found out how they do that. The way they do it, it looks like one continuous shot. What actually happens is, they take your picture closeup first, before the game, just your face. Then you get in the batter's box and they take some pictures of you swinging. Then during the game you hit a fly ball to left, say. They take a picture of that, and of you dropping the bat and running toward first, but they cut away the part where the guy catches the ball. If you or somebody else hits a home run in that general direction, they take a picture of the ball leaving the park. Then, if you *do* hit a home run, maybe the camera won't be on you when you actually hit the ball, but it'll pick you up as you round the bases. They call this "intercuts." When it comes out after, it looks like one continuous sequence, from the close-up of your face to the swing to hitting the ball to the ball leaving the park to you coming home and getting congratulated.

One of the sad things in growing older is learning what isn't glamour about what you used to think was glamorous. One time, outside of a flower store, I saw an emblem of this guy with wings that said you could send flowers by wire. And when the wind blew on the overhead utility lines and made the wires sing, I'd always think to myself that must be flowers going through the wires, somebody sending them to somebody else.

And five or six times—maybe more than that—when I was a kid, I'd get to sneak into games of the Birmingham club of the Southern Association, and the thing that thrilled me most was that they were the only team in the league that was allowed to wear white uniforms. Everybody else had to wear gray.

My daddy even pulled the old joke on me one time, when I couldn't have been much more than five, six years old, taking me to a ball game and then announcing he was a magician, and when he said, "Stand up," everybody in the place would stand up, and when he said, "Sit down," everybody would sit down. I didn't learn about the seventh inning stretch till long after that.

My dad could do the card trick with the four bank robbers too. You take out the four jacks, and they're the robbers, and you take out a king, and he's the policeman, and the rest of the deck is the house. And the four robbers go into the house, one on the bottom floor and one on the next floor and one on the next floor and the last one stays out on top to be a lookout. And he'd put them into the deck at various places, then turn the top card over, and sure enough, there was one of the jacks—the lookout. Then the lookout spotted the policeman coming, so he yells to the rest of the robbers down on the lower floors. "We've got to make a getaway by the roof!" And now my daddy would turn over the next three top cards, and lo and behold, they were the other three jacks! Somehow, he made them come up through the deck.

He lived for the sandlot and semipro and Negro leagues that he

got to play in, as a change from his work at the steel mill. We weren't
rich, but we didn't go without. Long as I can remember, my father
had work. In fact, as far back as I can remember, FDR was President in his second term. I was born at the height of the Depression,
but I don't remember those times. I remember people saying times
were getting better and thank God for Roosevelt. It's an interesting
thing—up till Roosevelt's time, the Negro people in the South
were all Republicans. Which is why my father was named "William
Howard," for Taft. But FDR changed that. Now everybody was a
Democrat because FDR was for the little people.

I don't have a deep political philosophy. To me, the difference
between the two major parties has always been that the Republicans
believe in expanding manufacturing, creating more jobs, increasing
the number of paychecks, so giving the people money to spend.
The Democrats, on the other hand, believe more in cutting taxes, and
relief, and that kind of thing, which also has the same result—
giving the people money to spend. The difference is that the Republican way, it takes maybe six months for that money to trickle
down to the little guy, whereas with the Democrats he's got it to
begin with. May wind up it's the same amount of money. But I've
seen what can happen to people during that six months. For that
reason I'm a Democrat.

The president of Chrysler, or one of those, said, back in the
thirties, that if the union came in, the grass would grow in the
streets of Detroit. My daddy always said he'd like to have bought
500 shares of Chrysler the day the union moved in, and held onto it
till now.

The business about government spending doesn't really bother the
little guy too much. They tell me Barry Goldwater, who's as opposed
to government spending probably more than anybody, was the first
U.S. Senator to line up for Federal drought relief, back ten years
or so ago, when his state, Arizona, was being hard hit. "Big
government" is supposed to be a Democratic sin, but it's based on
the idea of the holding corporation and interlocking directorate,

which were Republican inventions. Same goes for all these union tax dodges. There isn't a stunt the unions have got, except they learned it from big business.

If these sound like strong reasons, they're strong reasons why I don't feel strongly about politics. I think most of them are kidding a little bit anyway. Where the unions and the politicians and the steel mills were concerned, my father had one piece of advice for me: "Don't go into the mill." Not that he was mad at the unions or the politicians or the steel mills. He just didn't want to see me doing it.

There's a story about me that the only job I ever had as a kid was washing dishes at a lunch counter, and that the job just lasted one day, and I took a look at the pile of dishes and said, "Tell the boss I said good-bye, and don't worry about one day's pay either."

The story happens to be absolutely true.

It implies, though, that I never earned any money—and that part *isn't* true. From the time I was 13, 14 years old, my old man would take me along as an extra man whenever there was a ball game to be played. And if the score was lopsided or we didn't have enough players or something, I'd get to play. And they'd pass the hat or maybe charge a small admission or something, and afterward they'd split up the money, and even though I was just a kid and an extra hand, they always made sure I got a full share just like everybody else. Some days it didn't come to more than $10 or $12, but it was money, and you'd get maybe 20 paydays a summer.

What I remember most, though, is the way the other older guys insisted that I get paid right along with everybody else. In 1951, when the Giants won the pennant, there were two or three guys on the team, including a couple I admired the most, who didn't want to vote a decent share to Al Corwin, a pitcher who'd joined us late but who'd helped us real good in the stretch drive. And they didn't want to vote any money at all to Frank Shellenback, the scout who'd discovered Corwin. I remember the Giant front office felt so badly about it that they stepped in and ordered a fair slice for Corwin and Shellenback.

Anyway, when we had these semipro and pickup games back home, if I got in at all, it was as an outfielder. I was a big kid, and I played all sports and all positions. You'd have to say basketball was my best sport. Jim McWilliams, the football coach at Fairfield Industrial High School, made me a passer because I could throw for long distance, but some of those big linemen racked me up good a couple of times, and Charley Willis, who player on the same team, got smeared so bad one game he was out for the rest of the season. So I started going more for basketball. The year I was a sophomore I was high scorer in the county.

I've never minded physical contact in the sense of being afraid of it—except maybe with a catcher named Foiles, who used to play for Pittsburgh, and man, don't go sliding into *him*—he was built like a brick wall. But I'm not one of those people who get some special kick out of it either. In fact, I wish once in a while some *small* pitcher would throw at my head. Seems like all I get is the big ones.

I did, though, have one thing, and it came out mostly in basketball. It's kind of a disease, if you want to call it that. They call it "peripheral vision." Otto Graham had it. I'd be coming down the basketball court with the ball and suddenly I'd throw a perfect pass to somebody else without even looking at him. The fact is, I *was* looking, but my eyes could see a lot farther to either side than most people's.

It's for this same reason that I've had so few collisions with other fielders going after fly balls. And so few accidents from running into the fences. Seems like I can see the ball and somebody or something else all at the same time.

This of course is a real help playing the outfield, but even though DiMaggio was my idol, I kind of accidentally fell into playing that position. My ambition was to be a pitcher, like my grandfather. My father'd gone for the outfield for himself because, he said, "Pitchers don't work every day."

In my case, though, what happened was this: One day I was pitching for a sandlot team, and I went nine innings and then hit a home run inside the park, and after I finished crossing home plate I suddenly went all dizzy. My eyes were open, but I couldn't see anything. When I came to, my father was bending over me. "You were bearing down too hard out there," he said. "This is what happens."

Fifteen years later, a team of doctors would look at me solemnly and say those same words: "You were bearing down too hard out there. This is what happens."

Anyway, with one thing and another, I stopped pitching and became an outfielder.

It had been only a passing dizzy spell, anyhow. I only had one injury that meant anything while I was growing up. I guess you could call it an athletic injury. I shinnied up a tree to watch a football game, fell out, and broke my leg.

# 5

IT GOT SO I saw some high times.

Eddie Montague said in his letter he didn't think I'd played at the Polo Grounds, but I played there. I remember it because our uniforms got lost and we had to suit up wearing the other team's clothes. And we played at League Park in Cleveland, back in 1949. I guess I wasn't paying too much attention to my surroundings, because the next time I was back in Cleveland it was at the major-league All-Star game there in '54, in Municipal Stadium, and somebody said to me, "What do you think of this ball park, Buck?" and I said, "It sure has gotten bigger since last time."

The first major-league game I ever saw was in St. Louis. I was with the Birmingham Barons then and we had a day off and I went out to watch the Browns play the Red Sox. I got there early, and it had to be the 10 or 15 most wonderful moments of my life, watching Ted Williams in batting practice. This has got to be the most perfect batting swing in all baseball history. I just sat there with my mouth open. The wrist action was all the more amazing because, like most great hitters, you couldn't even see his wrists. His arms, the forearms, seemed like they just came down in two straight columns of muscle to his hands.

Years later, I heard Birdie Tebbetts tell how, when he was catching for Detroit, he found out the only way to pitch to Williams. "I'd ask him what pitch he wanted, then I'd signal for it," Birdie explained. "So everything that came up there was exactly what he'd ordered, just like I'd told him it would be. The thing was, he never quite believed me, so he'd always be looking for us to cross him up, and he'd let the pitch he wanted go right by."

I saw Williams, and I saw a lot of the greats, and the Negro boys who were in the majors by then used to come through on barnstorming trips and let me play with them, so I got to know Irvin and Robinson and Campanella. Campy took me to New Orleans once and said, "They tell me you field outfield like a shortstop."

"I *am* a shortstop," I said.

"Let's see," he said, and started me there for that day's game. After the first two balls that came my way, he stopped the game and put me in center field. "You get the chair for murder in this state," he explained.

Alvin Dark, who played short, said years later that I would make one of the great shortstops in the game. "You pick up the ground ball," he said to me, "and you've got the reflexes and the jump and the speed and the arm. As for going back on a short fly to the outfield, you'd be the greatest in history."

"And if you play me there," I said, "Horace will kill you."

"I believe you're right," he said.

Officially, Dark's reason for not wanting me in the infield was that he would be giving up the top defensive center fielder in the game, which was flattering. But the real reason, of course, is that there's more contact play around second base, and nobody—not Dark, not Horace Stoneham, not me, for that matter—wanted to be the one who said "put Mays at short" the day Mays got himself killed at the new position.

Actually, in recent seasons I have played a few innings at first, short, and third, and in left field and right field too. It was either that I had a bad leg and couldn't do the job in center, or that we'd be at a late stage in a wild ball game where we'd used so many infielders there was nobody left.

One time in Los Angeles, in 1964, I made McCovey look real

bad. It was unintentional on my part, but all the fans knew was what they saw. McCovey had made an error the inning before, and then when we came to bat I pulled a leg muscle running to first. So we talked on the bench, and next inning Manager Dark put me on first, where I wouldn't have to run, and put McCovey out in left field, so it looked to the fans like McCovey was being punished for making a mistake.

Actually, with a couple of exceptions—Rogers Hornsby was one, and (it's surprising, but they tell me it's true) Connie Mack was another—most managers not only won't make a change to punish a mistake but actually, if the mistake's bad enough and the kid's a newcomer, will stick him back at the same position next day. The fastest way to destroy a kid's confidence is to bench him in front of thousands of people.

Veteran players don't mind it so much, and all the time you see defensive changes made in late innings. Even there, though, it pays to be diplomatic. I remember in 1959, when Bill Rigney was managing the Giants, if we were ahead late in the game he'd bench McCovey off first and move Cepeda to first from left field. Rig always told the newspapermen this was to get more defense at first base. Actually, as everybody realized—and by "everybody," I include Cepeda and McCovey—it was to get more defense in left field. Cepeda and McCovey were equally good at first base in those days, but Orlando, by his own admission, was a "butcher" in left.

Also, the ideal time to make that move was when McCovey had just hit and Cepeda was still left to come up to bat next inning. That way you didn't lose any power out of your lineup.

(One of the real skillful touches in drawing up a batting order, if you can get away with it—and one the average fan never even heard of—is to spot your big hitters so the ones who're likely to come out for defensive reasons, if you've got a lead late in the game, bat before the ones who'll stay in. That way you can take them out without costing them a time at bat.)

Outside of getting hurt or pulling up lame, I've never come out

of a game for defensive reasons. But I have been pinch-hit for, and
they have walked hitters in front of me intentionally, to get to me.
It hasn't happened often, and it's only been when what they call
"extenuating circumstances" were at work, but it's happened. They
say they've never seen me drop a fly ball for an error. It's happened twice. They say I don't get picked off base. I've been picked
off. I've even forgotten how many outs there were.

No excuse for any of that—or maybe there is an excuse. The
excuse is that I've played in 2,000 major-league games; closer to
2,500, if you count All-Star, World Series, and exhibition games.

The greatest play I ever made came on a long shot to right-center
with a man on first. I caught the ball with my back to the plate; the
runner on first had already turned second, and had to hustle back,
and a good throw from me to first might have nailed him there.
Instead, I threw to second, and after I threw I started pointing toward the ground. So the shortstop, who took my throw, followed
my instruction and stepped on second, and sure enough, the runner
was called out for failing to touch second on his way back to first.

Did I see the man miss second on his way back to first? No. My
back was turned at the time. Did I throw to second because I knew I
had no play at first? No. I did have a play at first. Was it simply a
case of a lucky mistake? No. I knew exactly what I was doing. I even
signaled the shortstop what to do with the ball when he got it.

I can't explain it. My best guess is that something in that
runner's action, as he was going back to first when I turned after
the catch, told me instinctively that he had missed second. I know
as sure as I'm sitting here now that he had missed the bag, and that
I was making the sure play for the out. Yet I actually hadn't seen
him miss it.

"Certain things in baseball," Joe DiMaggio said, "are instinct.
They can't be taught. They're just there."

I believe that.

The plays you *don't* make in the outfield—or the ones nobody sees you make—can be as important as the ones you do. Bill Corum, who saw them all, said I had the finest outfield arm he'd ever seen. Yet I don't believe I've ever led the National League in outfield assists. I'd just as soon have it that way. The man with eight or 10 assists for a season is doing a job. The one with 30 is a man they must be running on. Also, the one with 30 isn't playing for a pennant winner. Anybody's hitting that many balls to the outfield, something must be wrong with the pitching. You can even tell it from the number of put-outs. The center fielder on the pennant winner never leads the league. Or, if he does, it's the accident of his having played considerably more innings out there than anywhere else. Pitching is what wins pennants, and the better the pitching, the less work the fielders have to do.

I understand things like this now. Again, this is the result of 2,500 ball games. The one thing that never stops amazing me is the number of things I still have left to learn about baseball.

At the beginning, my daddy went to Piper Davis and said, "Give him a contract. He can play."

"He thinks he's DiMaggio," Davis said.

"What's wrong with that?"

"He's a smaller man, that's what wrong. More he copies himself after Joe D., more he's got to unlearn."

"Then unlearn him," my father said. "But he can play for you, and you know it."

"Ain't much money," Davis said.

"How much ain't much?"

"Seventy a month?"

"You're right. That ain't."

"I'll up it five every month he's over .300," Davis said.

"With you changing him around," my father said, "he'd never collect."

"Why don't you talk to him?" Davis said.

So my dad talked to me.

"I can get you down in the mill," he said. "Only trouble is, once you get in you never get out. I think maybe you can make better money doing something else."

"Baseball?"

"Doesn't have to be baseball. You got a trade."

That "you got a trade" was kind of a fancy way of saying I'd taken a special course in cleaning and pressing at school. The idea was, I could enter into that field for a living, and baseball could always be something extra on the side.

"I think I can play for Piper Davis," I said.

"So does he," my dad said. "He's got a lot he wants to teach you. Hit a curve ball, quit crowding the plate, so forth and so on."

"Then what do you think?" I said.

"I think you like baseball," he said.

It was as simple as that.

No. Not quite that simple. Because the next night, for what was to be the last time, my dad and I played together on the same team. He was in center field. I was in left. He was something like 36, 37, at the time, but his condition was fine, and he could still go get them.

It was a game between a couple of factory teams, but they had some good ballplayers. And in the second inning, one of the hitters, a left-handed batter, looped a long, sinking liner to left-center, the wrong field for him, and I heard my father say, "All right, all right, let me take it!" But then I was aware that the ball was sinking and he was too far back, and I knew if I cut in front of him I could handle it, so I did, and caught it off the grass-tops.

And I knew also that I'd shown him up.

And he knew it.

I've never apologized to him for making the play.

He's never apologized to me for trying to call me off.

We both wanted the same thing—to get away from the situation where I had to play side by side in the same outfield with my own father.

Because even the great Kitty-Kat was beginning to slow down, the same as his son will slow down, and the only thing worse than being shown up by youth is being shown up by your own flesh and blood.

Because then you got to pretend you like it.

I think he had four or five years, maybe more, of part-time ball left in his system, my old man, but he didn't play them. I went with the Barons, and "One in a family is enough!" he'd say happily to anybody who asked, but I'd gone and knocked him out of the one thing he loved and lived for, and he knew it and I knew it. It's great for a man to see his son do something he always wanted to do but couldn't. It's great for a man to see his son want to follow in his father's footsteps.

But don't play in the same outfield together. It's like a father and a son chasing the same girl.

Things will never be the same between you again.

All I had to do was let him have that baseball for himself, out there that twilight in left-center field.

I could have said: "Take it—it's yours!"

But I didn't. And I can't buy it back.

# 6

THE GIANTS SENT me to Trenton, of the Interstate League, where Chick Genovese was manager and Bill McKechnie, Jr., was general manager, and I was a scared kid. Not from the baseball part of it. Class B was, like I said, a comedown from the kind of ball the Barons had played. But it was the first time I was away from home for any real period, and the first time most of my baseball "family" was white.

That was the summer of 1950. I was just turned 19.

I hit .353 in 81 games and had 55 runs batted in. Four of my 108 hits were home runs. "It don't matter if you hit home runs," Genovese said to me, "so long as the other side *thinks* you're going to. Because then the outfielders lay back, and when they're laying back the junky little humpbacked fly balls start dropping in for hits."

Two nights later he called me over again. "Are you comfortable playing in that close?" he asked.

"I'm trying to do what you said."

"What I said? What'd I say?"

"You said the outfield plays back on the big hitters, so that's when the short hits drop in."

"That's when the triples can go over your head, too," he said. "I was talking about you as a hitter, not you as a fielder."

He had got me to thinking, though, and I started going out into the outfield during batting practice, to see how close in I could actually play and still be able to break back for the long hit. The

72

most interesting thing I learned was that there could be 10 or 15 feet difference in how deep you played, not according to who the hitter was or what the situation was or who was pitching, but in terms of the ground—whether it was fast or slow, hard or soft, dry or wet. To this day, before the start of a game, I'll take the ball to the out-field and bounce it against the ground. The slower the ground, the closer in the center fielder should play, because otherwise the most common kind of hit to center field—a single—will be a double because it dies instead of bouncing out to where you are.

Man for man, situation for situation, I believe I play a closer center field than just about anybody else in the game, but that's just a guess. The ball park has a lot to do with it. In Wrigley Field in Chicago it looks like I play a deep center field, but that's because the fence is close in. Actually, measuring from second base out, I play a shorter center field there than in a lot of parks with more outfield room.

You take a lot of things into consideration, playing in the out-field, but, like anything else, you can overthink it. You can get too scientific. If you start playing deep or close on account of the speed of the hitter, for instance, you'd better stop and remember that before he can run he's got to hit first, and before you can throw the ball you got to pick it up. It's not just the distance between you and the fence behind you, either, because the closer in you play, the better chance a ball has of getting past you to either side. I take the speed of a runner into account before he comes up, not as to where to defend him but as to what I'll do with the ball once I get it. But if you're going to play a hitter at 260 feet because he's fast, and his range is 460 feet, you don't need a glove out there —you need a ladder.

A lot of people think the better an outfielder can throw, and the better his "jump" on the ball and his range, then the deeper he can play, and should. On the surface, this makes sense. But I think what people forget is that the farther a ball is hit, the more time it spends in the air. So, it seems to me, you've got more time to run out and still make the catch than you have to run the same distance *in*. Once again here, your throwing arm doesn't make much difference. You've still got to catch it before you can throw it. The base runners may know whether you can throw or not, but the ball doesn't.

Still and all, this is the way *I* play it, and some fine players have had other ideas. Take Bill Virdon, a real good center fielder. I don't believe anybody ever hit a ball over his head in all history. When I'd come up to bat at Forbes Field in Pittsburgh, he'd be playing me back of the monument. I've hit one I swore went 420 feet, only to see Virdon come *in* for the catch.

In fact, playing deep might be the perfect way to play a hitter who's swinging from his heels, because the home run he misses will be the long fly ball that just didn't go far enough.

In fact, if anything I say in this book sounds like advice, then the first piece of advice, ahead of anything else, is "*Don't copy.*" The best I can do is point out things that maybe not everybody's thought of. But kids who copy me by not getting down on one knee to block a ground ball in the outfield, or who try the "basket catch" that I use, or things like that, just for the sake of "being like Willie," are doing the worst thing they can do.

I know. I did the same thing. I copied DiMaggio. Once, when I did it, my arm nearly fell off.

Baseball men tell how, in the 1949 World Series, DiMag's arm was hurting him so bad it was, for all practical purposes, a dead arm. Yet he had to keep the Brooklyn club, with all its flashy base runners, from taking the extra base on him.

So, in fielding practice before the game, he'd cut loose with two of the damnedest throws anybody ever saw—one to third base, one to home. It killed him to do it, and his arm would be useless for the rest of the day. But the Dodgers respected his arm to begin with, and they didn't know it was hurting, and they'd seen those two throws and they decided they weren't going to run on *him*. And they didn't, the whole Series long.

I got the idea to do the same thing, a dozen years later, before a game with Milwaukee. I'd been kept out of the lineup the night before, and Manager Dark announced I was just being given a routine rest. But the rumor got out there was something wrong with my shoulder, which was true. I'd had a cold that had settled in there.

So next night I got the bright idea to get off a couple of great throws in fielding practice, just like DiMag had done. I did, and it like to kill me, and now everybody knew my arm was hurting. It never occurred to me that with DiMag in the World Series, there was no tomorrow, whereas with us we had more than half a season still to play, and risking them running on my arm while it was healing was a lot smarter than doing something that would make it take twice as long to heal.

But you learn. Like I say, I'm still learning. I don't say that just to sound modest. I'm still learning.

And it started, really, at Trenton in the Interstate League. I've said this was a step down from the brand of ball I'd been used to, and I've also said there isn't a great deal of difference between Triple-A and the majors—but I suppose here is the place to clear that up. What I was talking about was the *talent*. When it comes to what can be done with that talent, it's like night and day, going from the minors to the majors.

Genovese and McKechnie both spent extra time with me when I was at Trenton. Talking before a game, sitting on the bench, riding on the bus, they'd start firing the stuff at me.

"One-and-two, hitter's weakness is high inside, where do you pitch him?"

"You're on second, one out, long fly to center, center fielder's arm is average. Do you tag up? If not, how far off do you lead?"

"Last of the ninth, score tied, your pitcher coming up, two out. Do you let him bat or do you pinch-hit for him? What do you think about, before you come up with the answer?"

And on and on it went. No more than half the questions, seemed like, had anything to do with anything *I'd* ever have to worry about. At one point, I burst out at McKechnie, "Shoot, you got a *manager* to do that kind of worrying! That's what they pay him for!"

"Buck," he said softly, "someday you may be a manager."

"Where? Negro league someplace? Gonna be no Negro leagues anyhow, time you get through raiding 'em."

"You think I'm fooling with you," he said. "I'm not. I say the day can come when you'll be a manager."

"Sure. And what if it don't?"

"Then you will have been a better player, because the more you understand about this game, the quicker you'll put your ability to maximum use."

I still didn't believe him. "Tell me this: I'm never going to pitch. Right?"

"I didn't say that."

"No, you didn't. But *I'm* saying it."

"All right. You'll never be a pitcher. Now—what's your point?"

"Point's this," I said. "Why do you keep asking me if I'm the pitcher, what pitch do I throw in this situation or that situation, or to this hitter or that hitter?"

"Because," he said gently, "the only way to be a smart hitter is to try to think like a pitcher."

I started to learn.

I found out things I'd never dreamed of. Like—just one example —there are times when you're two runs behind, and you get up with nobody on and one out, you try to swing for the home run, not just to get on base. Sure, if you get the homer you're still behind, but if you've got a team that can play for one run, then the home run gives them the chance to do it. Some teams play better for one run than they do for two. The Dodgers nowadays, for example. Be one run ahead of them and they know how to tie you. Be two runs ahead of them and they're not equipped to fight you. One run behind, they're running. Two or more, they're not. And that team don't run, it don't win.

(An all-time illustration of this is our game of August 19, 1965, against the Dodgers. The team that won was going to be in first place that night. We led them 3-1 going into the sixth, and they weren't going anywhere. Then Drysdale homered for them to make it 3-2, and now, just a run behind, they were the Dodgers again—and they beat us 8-5 in 15 innings!)

You've all heard, when the team was behind, somebody yelling out, "A walk's as good as a hit!" But is it?

I started to learn.

And I think I did learn, and one reason was—like I said in talking about Little Leaguers—I was doing good myself. So when they talked to me afterward, it was suggestion, not criticism; or, if it was criticism, at least it wasn't blame.

I learned something else I didn't even know I was learning at the time, because things were easy on me in that Interstate League. Now I'm talking about off the field, not on it. In the years since, I've come to understand, from other people's experience as well as my own, the way a bad mental state, some outside depression, can hurt a player on the field. In those days, I was old enough to understand that "feeling good," and loving the game the way I did, things came easy. But I thought everybody loved the game, and I thought everybody automatically felt good. If you didn't feel good, you must have a cold or be sick or hurt or something.

I didn't understand what I understand now—that what you're *thinking*, what shape your *mind* is in, is what makes the biggest difference of all.

You can go too far that way too. Like I'll spell out in detail later on, not all slumps are "mental." Some things you do wrong you do wrong because something went wrong, or because you just plain did it wrong, and there doesn't have to be any advance state of mind have anything to do with it.

But none of that comes across to a 19-year-old kid. In the Interstate League in 1950, it was the fifth season after Jackie Robinson had first come into organized baseball, so fans didn't look at Negro players like they were freaks anymore. And it was in the North, and anywhere I went with the club I'd eat with them and use the same rest rooms, and I never had to sit on a bus while a couple of white players went in to bring out a takeout sandwich. I don't know what the hotel situation was because Class B teams don't stay at hotels. Most commonly the players head for the Y or boardinghouses, and a lot of times you sleep on the bus anyway.

Contrast this with what happened to Orlando Cepeda. Like mine, Cepeda's father was a great ballplayer. People used to be after him to leave Puerto Rico and go to the States and make some real money playing ball, and this he could have done, because Orlando's younger than me, and his father still had some good baseball mileage left in him after dark-skinned players had made the majors, so Cepeda's father could have gone all the way.

But his father refused to leave Puerto Rico. "I won't stand for the treatment," he said. And when Orlando was signed, the first club he played for in the United States was a team in Virginia, some-place like that, where they hated to see Negro mix with white and where the fans were segregated in the stands and where there were no Spanish-speaking Latins and the only people who'd take him in would be Negro folk, so he became kind of one of them. Except he couldn't even talk English, and to get something to eat he'd have to look and look till he found a cafeteria, so he could point to the food he wanted, because he didn't know how to order.

And so he was a bad baseball player, till after a month or so somebody got smart and switched him to a farm club up North, and the rest is history, because he batted .393 for Kokomo in '55, and .355 for Charlie Fox at St. Cloud in '56, and .309 for Minne-apolis in 1957, and by '58 he was ready.

I had one other advantage, for which I guess I can thank my Aunt Sarah and my whole upbringing, or maybe it's me myself too. But what I wanted to do most in the whole world was play baseball. And it showed. I was enthusiastic, and young, and I guess I kind of bubbled. The older guys treated me like a happy kid—which is what I was—and I didn't do much brooding or sulking, and—let's face it—I guess I talked too much.

And because it was fun for me, it was fun for the others too, and over the years this has cost me in more ways than one—my voice is pitched higher than most people's, so I've always sounded younger than I am. They say Mays is Peter Pan and eternal youth and still a boy at heart and loves the game and bubbles over because of it, which is fine till they throw at your head and you go down and everybody, even the umpire, laughs, because it was you they did it to and with you everything's fun.

But I'm not bitter about it. I wouldn't have had it any other way. If you've got enough enthusiasm so it infects other people, everybody's going to do better, and the fans are going to come out to see you. The Cardinals once offered the Giants a million dollars for me. They weren't serious. I mean, they may have been serious about making the offer, but they didn't seriously believe Horace Stoneham was about to say yes.

This is just plain dollars and cents. The Cardinals in 1963, when they finished second, drew 1,333,631 fans on the road. (Road attendance is a fairer figure than home attendance, because clubs with small home parks obviously can't be compared fairly in home attendance against clubs with home seating capacities of as much as 25,000 more.)

That same year, we finished third. They were five games closer to the top than we were, and they lasted in the race long after we were out of it. Yet our road attendance that year was 1,684,377—highest in the league, which it has been more years than not. Now subtract 1,333,631 from 1,684,377. You get a difference of 350,746. Multiply that by the average admission price of, say, $2.50, plus maybe a dollar for concession purchases inside the park. That becomes 350,746 times $3.50, or $1,227,611. This is what the Giants earned as a road attraction over and above what a better ball club could earn.

Pete Stoneham—that's Vice-President Charles H. Stoneham of

the Giants, Horace's son; everybody calls him Pete—once measured my value in a funny way. "Buck," he told me, "using the most conservative set of figures you could possible assign, I just figured out that over the years, you—as a drawing card—have personally put an additional $3,000,000 in the pockets of the parking lots on the road."

"They going to give me a bonus?" I said.

"I doubt it," he said.

Put it another way. Take that $3.50 figure I used a minute ago. Put 30,000 people in the ball park at $3.50 a head. That one game brings in $105,000. Last year my salary was $105,000. That's one game out of 162.

What's important to the arithmetic, too, is that I'm not a pitcher. The greatest crowd attraction, as a pitcher, in all baseball history would only average three days' work every two weeks. Pitchers get you into the World Series, but only one club in each league can make it to the World Series. The meat and potatoes at the gate is the everyday draw. When Dean was going to face Hubbell, the fans flocked to see the game. But how often did that happen? Five times a season, at the most?

It's been said of me that I have "that electric quality." I don't even know what that means, so I'm the last person in the world to try to describe it. But I can sense the truth of it. A Ruth drew people. A Speaker didn't. A Maury Wills draws. A Jim Wynn doesn't. Of course, if you're eccentric, dazzling, brilliant, colorful, you're a crowd draw. But when an Appling or a Musial can't account for extra fans at the gate, then is it basically a matter of talent? Something else must be at work too.

I think that something else is very simple. It has nothing to do with baseball. It's the communications business, instead. You get your reputation in one of the two "big towns" in this country— New York or Los Angeles—and people everywhere know about you. Play like Appling did for 20 years for the White Sox, and your chance is 'way down.

There's no color line in this. Sure, the Braves drew better when both Aaron and Mathews were in the lineup, because winning teams draw better and with Aaron and Mathews you got a chance. But as individuals, one Negro, the other white, the fan who finds out one of them isn't playing that day isn't going to change his mind and not go to the game.

There's an infrequent exception—a Ted Williams, a Ty Cobb. But most of all, if you ask me, it's whether you got that New York or—nowadays—L.A. reputation. Just for example, most of the TV shows originate in those two cities. So the studio audiences are mostly made up of local people. Who're they going to cheer the loudest for?

And cheering infects people too. And the fact that you have to go back all the way from 1965 to 1948 before you find a World Series—the most widely watched TV program of all—that didn't have either a New York or a Los Angeles team in it.

Winning, of course, means a lot too. Being in contention is important. Someday, some sociologist is going to come along and make something out of the fact that the teams that were slowest to bring Negro players onto their rosters were the teams that didn't win. The Red Sox, the Phils, the Detroits, just for example. There's nothing strange about that. In the early stages, the Negro man had to be very good or he didn't last. They weren't sticking with him, bringing him along.

As far as I know, Branch Rickey and the Dodgers pioneered bringing Negro players into the majors, and that extended to seasoning them in the minors. But the Giants are the first team, to my knowledge, that went in for bringing a Negro boy up, then sending him down, then bringing him up again. And this, to my mind, was the true completion of the idea of racial equality in baseball, because before Horace Stoneham, a Negro boy would have only one chance to fail. White boys could have more than one. There is no equality in the opportunity to succeed unless there's equality also in the opportunity not to succeed right away.

The old saying is, "If at first you don't succeed, try, try again."
It wasn't Branch Rickey and the Dodgers—it was Horace Stoneham
and the Giants who made that true for the Negro player in baseball.

So many players—Dick Ellsworth, Vern Law, Bob Friend, Nellie
Fox, and I could go on—came to greatness after years of trying and
improving. But how many Negro players did? They were either
established long before their first chance, like Satchel Paige, or
they made it on sheer talent their first shot, like Jackie Robinson.

I once asked Horace Stoneham, "If I hadn't made it in fifty-one,
what would have happened?"

"You would have made it in fifty-two," he said.

It's like freedom of religion. The right to pray is basic. But it also
has to include the right not to pray or, when you come down to
it, it's no right at all.

Branch Rickey deserves all the credit he can get, because he
established the right of the Negro man to play. And the Negro man
didn't have any choice about it either: he had better play good, or
we were all in trouble, and the whole thing would have been set
back.

But Horace Stoneham did something else, and in the glamour of
what Rickey accomplished, it went unnoticed. Nobody ever thinks
of the case of Henry Thompson. You might remember him as the
Giants' best player in the 1954 World Series (even though Dusty
Rhodes and, I'm afraid, Willie Mays got bigger headlines, it was
Mr. Henry who made that Series move, more than anybody else).
You might even remember that after his career with the Giants
was through, Henry got in some trouble—nonbaseball trouble—and
you might or might not know that it was Horace Stoneham who
helped him get clear of it.

But what NOBODY remembers is that Thompson broke into the
majors with the St. Louis Browns in 1947. He played something like
25 games for them. He was one of a couple of Negro boys they
brought up. I don't know what to say about the Browns' motives,
because I don't know that much about the background of the

story. I do know that St. Louis was a city that was "Southern" in character—it had separate rest rooms for white and Negro in the train station there, and the hotels were all segregated—and, being a river town and that far "South," St. Louis also had a good-sized Negro population. And since the Browns weren't drawing white fans, I'm told somebody got the idea they could attract Negro business by bringing in a couple of Negro players. So they did.

All well and good. But Henry Thompson didn't make it with them—like I say, he only lasted about 25 games—yet two years later, Horace Stoneham brought him up. Here was a Negro boy who'd "failed" being given a second chance.

Like I said earlier, pickets may be necessary, but people who do something else beside picketing may not be all wrong either.

# 7

THE STORY OF HOW I was brought up to the Giants, late in May of 1951, has been told time and again—what I said to Leo Durocher on the phone and what he said to me—but it bears retelling. Lord knows it's the truth.

Number-one thing to remember is the Giants weren't going real good in the National League that year. They'd lost their opening game, then won the second one, then lost 11 straight.

I'd met Owner Stoneham and Manager Durocher that spring, at Sanford, Florida, where both the Giants and their farm teams were training. It'd been a brief meeting, very polite and see-you-later kind of talk. I don't remember anything specific that was said between Stoneham and me. I remember Durocher saying, "We got quite a report on you from Trenton."

"What'd it say?" I asked.

"It said your hat keeps flying off," Leo said, and went away laughing.

My manager now was Tommy Heath, who's one of the real good ones, and the ball club was the Giants' Minneapolis farm club of the American Association.

They say the Minneapolis fans took me to their hearts. That's true. They did. It's hard to be disliked when you're hitting .477.

Which is what I was hitting with the Millers, for my first 35 games with them. I had a slugging average (that's total bases divided by times at bat) of .799. I'd made some good plays in the field, and one line drive I hit, at the old Borchert Field in Milwaukee, actually put a hole in the fence, and instead of repairing it they were going to paint a circle around it and keep it as a memento.

The people were nice, and I'd even started dating a Minneapolis girl, and this one day, late in May, we had a schedule break and were supposed to play an exhibition game in Sioux City, which was where another Giant farm club was.

So I did what I always did with time off. I went to a movie.

All I remember about it was, it must have been a double feature, because in between pictures the house lights went on and the manager of the theater come out on the stage and said, "If Willie Mays is here, his manager wants him at the hotel."

So I went back to the hotel, and Heath was in the room there, grinning and holding out his hand. "Congratulations!"

"For what?"

"You're going to the big leagues." He said it the way all baseball men say it, with the accent on the word *big*.

I looked at him. "Who says so?"

"Leo."

"Shoot," I said. "Man must be out of his mind."

"I just talked to him on the phone," Tommy said. "Not half an hour ago."

"Call him back."

"What do I have to call him back for?"

"Tell him I'm not coming, that's why."

"You're not . . ." He stared at me. "What the hell's the matter with you?"

"I'm happy here," I said. "Can't hit that big-league pitching no how."

"It's that girl," he said. "You're in love."

"Got nothing to do with any girls or love," I said.

"You know," he said, "I believe you're serious."

"Well told I'm serious!"

He stared at me some more. "All right," he said finally, "I'll call Leo back. But I'm not going to tell him. *You* tell him."

And he got Leo on the long-distance phone. "You won't believe this," he said to him, "but Buck's here and he says he don't wanna come."

From where I was sitting, it sounded like Donald Duck when he gets mad, on the other end of the phone. All I could make out for certain was: "Who's Buck?"

"Willie," Heath said into the phone. "Here. He'll tell you himself."

I picked up the phone and said: "Hello?"

Then for what seemed like the next 10 minutes I held it away from my ear. Finally, when the uproar seemed to stop for a second and it looked like I was supposed to say something, I said, "I can't play that kind of ball."

"What do you mean? What can't you do?"

"Hit."

"What are you hitting now?"

".477."

For all I know, that may have been the only moment in his life, before or after, that Leo Durocher was at a loss for words.

There was a terrible silence on the phone. I was almost ready to ask was he still there, when his voice come back on, this time kind of quiet and subdued-like. He said:

"Do you think you can hit .250 for me?"

".250?" I said. "I think so."

"Well," he said, and as he spoke his voice started getting louder again, "I could tell you my troubles, with the whole ——— ——— ——— ball club running in the ——— ——— ——— house, but the Giants don't have enough money to pay for how long the ——— phone call would take if I took the time. So GET UP HERE!!"

I hung up.

"I better get a plane," I said to Tommy Heath.

"The next plane," he suggested.

I got in touch with the girl in Minneapolis. "The Giants have called me up," I said.

"What does that mean?" she said.

"I make more money," I said. "Five thousand a year, I'll be making now."

"I'll never see you again," she said.

"I'll probably be back in a week," I said.

I left for New York so fast they had to send my clothes on later. I took a little canvas bag with my baseball shoes and glove, and I had my favorite bat (in those days, if I remember right, it was an Adirondack, 34 ounces, 35 inches), and the only thing else I remember was a kind of plaid golfer's cap, the kind those guys in the ads wear smoking a pipe and driving one of those old open touring cars.

That's how I showed up at the Giant offices, just off Sixth Avenue on 42nd Street in New York.

I guess I must have made a funny sight, in those midtown crowds with a basball bat and a touring cap. I know one woman in the elevator took a look at me, then another look, then said, "My God!" and turned away like people do in elevators, pretending she'd never seen me and we weren't in the same elevator togther.

They took me into Horace Stoneham's office, and he got up and came around the desk and said, "Glad you could make it so soon. But they're not glad where you came from."

I didn't know what he meant.

"The Minneapolis fans," he explained. "They're upset. I tell you what we're doing. We're putting an ad in the papers there, apologizing to the fans but telling them that you're the answer to what the Giants have got to have."

I still said nothing.

"It's unusual, I know," he said, "but . . ." He broke off. "Is something the matter?"

I found my voice. "Mr. Stoneham," I said, "I know it's unusual, but what if . . ."

"What if what?"

"What if I don't make it?"

Horace Stoneham has a way of talking very plain, very matter-of-fact, without being unkind about it. He gestured toward a Manila folder on his desk. It was bulging with papers inside. I looked, and I saw it had my name on the outside.

"You think we just picked your name out of a hat?" he snapped. "You think we brought you up because somebody saw your name in a headline one day in Louisville or Columbus or Milwaukee or Kansas City? You think nobody's been watching you? You think managers haven't sat up nights doing progress reports, that we haven't had you checked time and again by our own scouts? You think all this is just something somebody dreamed up in the middle of the night two days ago?"

I stood there and said nothing.

Now he pushed a buzzer somewhere under the edge of his desk, and said into the intercom, "Ask Doc to come in." He looked at me. "Got luggage?"

"No, sir," I said. "It's still back in Minneapolis. They're sending it on."

He nodded and pushed the buzzer again. "Ask Brannick to save out seventy, eighty dollars," he said into the intercom. Then to me: "Buy yourself a couple of things—underwear, shirts, socks—till your stuff gets here."

The door opened and a bouncy little red-faced man came in. It was Doc Bowman, the team trainer.

"Here he is," Stoneham said to him. "Take him with you." He stuck out his hand to me. "Good luck, Willie."

"Thank you, Mr. Stoneham." I shook his hand. "I hope I can get in a few games, get a few chances to help. I hope you won't be sorry."

"I won't be sorry," he said, and turned away. Then suddenly, he turned back. *"Get in a few games—get a few chances to help?"*

He shook his head, wonderingly. "Don't you know you're starting tonight?"

My tongue and the back of my mouth went dry. I said, "Starting? Where?"

Stoneham looked at me. Then he started to laugh. "Center field," he said. "Where else?" He nodded toward Doc Bowman. "Get him out of here, Doc."

The team was already in Philadelphia, where they were starting a three-game series against the Phils at Shibe Park that night. Doc Bowman had been left behind especially to shepherd me down to Philly.

It was a beautiful day. We had a Pullman, the only time in my life I'd ever been in one of those outside of seeing them in the movies. And we went through Trenton and over the railroad bridge over the Delaware there, and I thought of the summer before, playing ball in Trenton—this time the train didn't even stop there—and how Genovese and McKechnie could have been sitting up late at night, doing reports on how I was doing, and the questions they used to fire at me every chance they got and how they'd clucked and worried over me. And then we were out over the bridge, and out the window to the right, to the north, is another bridge, this one for cars, and it has a big sign on it that you can see from the train:

TRENTON MAKES, THE WORLD TAKES

The clicking of the wheels said You're-a-GIant You're-a-GIant You're-a-GIant You're-a-GIant. . . .

# 8

MONTE IRVIN was lying on one of the two beds in the hotel room, in his shirt-sleeves, reading a book. When the bellhop opened the door, Monte kind of blinked as he looked at me. Then he said:

"Roomie, where'd you get that cap?"

Then he blinked again and said:

"Roomie, where're your bags?"

Then he blinked again and said:

"Skip know you're checked in?"

Then he reached for the phone, and asked for another room number, and when it answered, he said into the phone, "Skip, three guesses what just checked in."

I could hear those same Donald Duck noises on the phone.

"C'mon," Irvin said to me then, "let's go see the man."

"Wait till I get rid of my cap," I said.

"Wear it," Monte said. "He's got to see this for himself."

We went out into the elevator and up a couple of floors and, the next thing I knew, I was being ushered into one of the biggest hotel suites I ever dreamed existed, and Leo Durocher was standing there with a deck of cards in his hand. Beyond him there was a closet and the door was open and I saw more suits and ties than I'd ever seen outside of a store.

"Whose money you taking, Skip?" Irvin said to him.

"My own," Durocher said. "It's a form of passionate solitaire. I figure the way we're going, I might as well practice new ways to lose too. Saints preserve us, where'd he get that cap?"

I said, "Why does everybody laugh at my cap?"

"What else we going to laugh at?" Irvin said.

I said, "I didn't bring any clothes. I got to get some underwear."

"Saints preserve us," Leo Durocher said again, though I had an idea it wasn't an expression he chose to use too often, "did you bring a bat?"

"Yes."

"Your glove?"

"Yes."

"Spikes?"

"Yes."

"Then you came to play," Leo said. "Son, I'm glad you're here." He seemed immensely cheerful. "See, this ball club's been having a little trouble. They have all the right ideas, but the ———— ———— can't hit the side of a barn worth a ———— ———— ————, and the pitchers ———— ———— ———— on me every chance they get, and when they do pick up the ball, which ain't often, it's like a week ago when my left fielder makes a great catch of a foul fly ball only he forgets the no-good ———— ———— tagged up at third with the winning run."

"Best thing he's seen is the umpiring," Irvin said to me happily.

I said to Leo, "Where'd you get all the suits?"

"Because I'm the only ———— in this organization with an ounce of brains," he said. "Ballplayer buys an expensive suit, then lets the hotel clean it for him. Hotels care about how quick they do a suit, not how good a job they do. This way I can change to a new suit and leave the ones I was wearing till I get home, so they can get a decent cleaning and pressing. Remember that." Now he reached for the phone and asked for a number, and when it answered, he said to the clubhouse man, "Logan? Captain Video just checked in. You got a uniform for him or has Dark torn them all up?"

(I found out Alvin Dark, the shortstop and team captain, took

losing real hard and sometimes got violent in the clubhouse afterward.)

Leo took it hard, too, but in a different way. Give him a sniff
at a pennant, and he's got to be the greatest manager anybody ever
played for. Let him lose interest, and he didn't care what happened.
He'd let other players manage for him. There's even a story that
a year or two before he'd intentionally benched players, in order
to lose games so as to impress the front office with the trades he
wanted them to make.

I've played for five managers in the big leagues: Leo, then Bill
Rigney, then (for just over half a season) Tom Sheehan, then Dark,
now Herman Franks. Each was a different kind of man, in his
temperament. Each was different in his baseball too. One of the
main differences is the way they'd play it when you were the home
team and the score was tied in the last of the ninth or in an extra
inning. It's a general thing, but I think it's not unfair for me to
say that Durocher and Franks—and Franks was a coach under
Durocher in '51 and for some seasons after that—anyway, in the
situation I just described, the two of them would tend to go for
broke and win it right there, even if it took lousing up the lineup
so if you didn't succeed right at that moment, your team in the field
and the bench would both be weaker from then on. Rigney, Sheehan, and Dark, on the other hand, would tend more to hoard their
strength for an emergency if they needed it, and take the home-
team advantage and make the other team be the one to make the
move.

Actually, the Giants, when I first joined them—actual date was
May 25, 1951—weren't as bad in the standings as everybody was
making out. After that 11-game losing streak at the start of the
season, they'd won 16 of their next 23. They were won-17, lost-19
in the standings. but they were laying fifth in the race, and that
was the part Durocher didn't like. Lots of baseball people feel like
they'd rather be six games out, but in second place, than five games
out with four other teams to pass. You can see why. If you're in

second place, your fate is much more in your own hands than if you have to hope everybody else in the league is going to lose the same day. And as the season moves along, the problem becomes worse and worse.

Let's take a fictional example of what I mean. Say the Dodgers are in first place, the Braves are one game back of them, and you're three behind, in third place. There are three games to go for each team, and the Dodgers and Braves are playing their remaining three against each other.

You'd say offhand that being three behind with three to go gives you a chance to tie, if the Dodgers lose all three. But if the Dodgers lose all three, the Braves win all three, so *they* win the pennant. Mathematically, three behind with three to go seems to give you a chance, but actually there's no chance at all.

On the other hand, be four behind with four to go, but be in second place, and you do have a chance.

The story is that when I joined the Giants, Durocher made his "big move" of the season, which was to take Bobby Thomson out of center field to make room for me and put Thomson on third base. Actually, that didn't happen right away. Thomson was taken out of center, but he went to left. Irvin was playing right.

I know Irvin was playing right field because I bumped into him chasing a ball hit by Eddie Waitkus that night against the Phillies. The thing should have been caught, but thanks to me it went for a double.

At the plate, I was 0-for-5.

We won the game, 8-5.

Second game of the series, I didn't get a hit. We won.

Third game of the series, I didn't get a hit. We won.

We got back to New York and I was 0-for-12, my first time out before the home fans.

They gave me a big hand when my name was announced in the batting order. I turned to Irvin in the dugout and said, "Is everybody crazy except me?"

He said, "They got it figured out. So long as you don't hit, we win. Only trouble will be if you ever get a hit." He was laughing.

I went up for the first time as a Giant at the Polo Grounds, facing a pretty fair left-handed pitcher named Spahn.

If you're going to guess when you go up to bat, might as well guess on the first pitch. And might as well guess a fast ball is what he's going to throw.

I did and he did and the ball went tracking out of there, 'way over the roof in left on one long line, still going up when it went up into the blackness of the night.

My first major-league hit—a home run off Spahn!

We lost the game 4-1.

I said to Irvin, "You were right."

I might add, I didn't get anymore hits that night. They say that homer off Spahn broke my beginner's jitters and set me off on a tear.

Truth is, a couple of more games and my batting average was .039. That home run had been my only hit in 26 at bats so far.

I actually sat in front of my locker and began to cry.

Herman Franks saw it. He sent Leo over. Durocher bent down over me and said, "Now, what the —— —— ——'s the matter with you?"

"Mr. Leo," I said, "send me back down. I *told* you I couldn't hit this pitching!"

"Look," he said to me, "you could have won me a ball game to-night, but you didn't. Ever occur to you tomorrow's another day? And you're going to be playing center field tomorrow, and the day after that, and the day after that. So get used to the idea!" He turned to leave, then turned back. "And by the way—who do you think you are? Hubbell?"

I stared at him. "Hubbell?"

"The way you wear the legs of your pants, down nearly to the ankles," he said. "Pull them up."

"Why?"

"Because," he said, "you're making the umpires think your strike zone's down where the knees of your pants are. They're hurting you on the low pitch. Pull up your pants. If you do, you'll get two hits tomorrow."

I pulled up my pants. I got two hits—a single and a triple as we beat the Pirates 14-3. Then, against the Cardinals, with Dave Koslo pitching a beautiful game, I got two doubles and scored the only run. We won 1-0.

The Giants were in third place now.

After that 1-for-26, I was 9-for-24, and now the home runs were beginning to come. At one point I had six consecutive homers— that is, out of six hits, all six were home runs.

More than that, I was learning baseball.

I thought I knew a lot. One game, there were men on first and second against us and the batter hit a grounder to Dark at short-stop, and he shoveled it to Eddie Stanky for the force at second. But instead of throwing to first to try for the double play, Stanky threw it to third and the man there was tagged out after he'd turned the base.

After the game, Dark said to me, "What'd you think of that play?"

"Lucky the way it came out," I said.

He looked at me, smiling a little. "Lucky?"

"Maybe Stanky don't pivot too good," I said, "so he's got to throw that ball to third instead."

"You ever see anybody else do it?"

"No," I confessed.

"How many outs were there?"

I thought back. "None."

"What'd the next batter do?"

"Singled."

"So if Stanky hadn't thrown to third, they would have had the run, right?"

"I guess so."

"But this way they didn't score, did they?"

Like I say, I was beginning to learn.

One night Monte Irvin stole home. I'd come to appreciate that stealing home with a left-handed hitter at bat was far more difficult than with a right-handed hitter, because with a right-handed hitter the catcher's view would be blocked. And Irvin did it with a left-handed hitter.

"You were taking a chance," I told him afterward. "Coming in like that with a left-handed hitter."

"Look," he said to me, "there's rules and there's rules. In this case it was a pull hitter so the third baseman was playing wide of the bag, and that's how I got my lead to begin with."

I'd never thought of that part of it.

There are an awful lot of "inside" things that fans like to show they know, but sometimes, like me, they get so they can get "too inside."

Example: When I was just a kid, I thought bases were stolen on the catcher. As I came up through the minor leagues, I learned bases are stolen on the pitcher instead, a lot of times. And so, like a lot of fans, I'd say knowingly, "Bases aren't stolen on the catcher— they're stolen on the pitcher."

It's true that if a pitcher can't hold you close, or hasn't got a good move to first, or takes too much time with his delivery, you can go on him. But I found out, from watching Whitey Lockman, that the way the first baseman holds the bag against the runner has a lot to do with it. The guy who just holds the inside corner is inviting the runner to get a bigger lead because he can get back head-first. The first baseman who looks like he's going to be in your way is going to make you come back feet first, because there's more force behind a foot than there is behind a hand, and if you come back hands first and he's there, then there's a chance you'll tag him instead of the base.

Furthermore, a bad throw from the catcher and it doesn't matter if you got a good break or not. So catchers *do* have something to do with it.

And there was Leo, teaching me how to draw a throw while

running the bases—in order to protect another runner. And Dark, showing me how to get hung up in a rundown so other runners could move up two bases in the time it took them to tag me. And Stanky, working with me on how to take the pitching sign from the shortstop or second baseman, because curve balls act on way when they're hit, and fast balls another, and change-ups another. The toughest play an outfielder has to make—the line drive hit straight at him—often is just a question of what the pitch was, as to how the ball will act. Fast ball tends to sail when it's hit. A line drive off a slower pitch will get less distance, tend to drop faster. Always remember, a baseball's essentially a rubber ball. Harder it's thrown up there, farther it's going to travel when it hits something—a bat, for instance. Doesn't have to be a bat. I once saw a guy get a single with his helmet, or at least the ball went to the outfield on the fly when he got hit. And you've all seen outfielders playing a carom off the wall. If the ball's traveling fast, they play it for the hard rebound; if not, they play it close.

Yet the more you learn, the more there is to learn, because every play has its exception, and some "inside" stuff isn't "inside" at all— or may be "too inside."

How many times have you sat in the stands and seen a runner break from first, and the hitter swings and fouls it off, and the runner has to return to first base, and you turn to who you're sitting with and say, "Gee, if he hadn't swung, that base runner would have had second standing up."

And, knowing baseball as a longtime fan, you then say to yourself, either, "These guys try the hit-and-run too much," or, "Somebody must have missed a sign."

Maybe some teams do try to hit-and-run too much, although sometimes that play is something that sort of comes and goes in waves with all teams, like when everybody's in a slump and the sluggers are pressing for the long ball, then the hit-and-run is a good play because it gets your attention back on meeting the ball.

And heaven knows, signs are missed in baseball.

But there can be so many other things here too.

Remember, to begin with, that a runner breaking from first with the pitch doesn't enter the field of vision of a left-handed hitter as fast as with a right-handed hitter. Time and again you've seen hitters deliberately swing at a bad pitch—even a pitchout—to protect the runner by lousing up the catcher. But if you study it, you'll find most of those hitters swing right-handed—because they can see what kind of a break the runner got; the left-handers can't.

But other things can happen. Maybe the runner's on his own and the hitter's just plain swinging. Maybe the hitter sees the runner going and says to himself, "I must have missed the hit-and-run sign," so he swings. In that case, that's not missing a sign—it's missing a nonsign.

If you ask me, stupid defense has loused up more clever plays than clever defense ever will. I don't mean by this that bad teams win. Talent's going to wind up winning ball games. But straight ability is one thing, and thinking is not always the same thing.

One of the greatest plays I ever saw was pulled by a man playing center field for the Giants, in 1965. His name wasn't Mays. We were ahead of Houston by something like nine runs in the first game of a doubleheader, and with Marichal pitching. So the manager pulled me and Hart and McCovey out of the game, and now maybe Juan let up a little and they got some hits, and we made a couple of bad plays, and now they had something like two men on and three runs in and nobody out and the next hitter slammed a sinking liner to center field.

Out in center field for us was a bonus rookie named Ken Henderson, and he came in and made just a great shoe-top catch of that tough ball. And he came up throwing—on the fly to home plate. And Nellie Fox, a great, cagey veteran, had been on third for Houston, and of course he was just trotting home after the catch, knowing no center fielder in his right mind would throw home, because here we still had something like a five-run lead at the end of the game, and we weren't as worried about an impossible throw to the

plate as we were about the routine throw back to the infield to keep
that other runner from moving up one or even two bases while that
useless throw was being made.

But Mr. Henderson was something like four years old when I was
in my first World Series, so he hadn't been around the big leagues,
and all he could say to himself was, "Throw it home." Which he
did. And our catcher put the ball on the shoulder of Mr. Fox as he
trotted by him, and it was a double play and we had ended the
threat. And there were the papers the next day saluting Henderson
for his "amazing" play—and the Giants had congratulated him too,
because it wasn't the time to criticize, although in years to come he
will learn, just like the rest of us, and come to learn that a *great*
throw isn't necessarily the *right* throw.

But that iced a ball game for us, and there was Fox, who hadn't
even bothered to look or slide, standing there, out at home with
egg all over his face. He'd been shown up by a teen-ager, and while
I won't say it cost them a ball game, it cost them their last chance
at a ball game.

One time, when he was younger, Felipe Alou made a great throw
to third to get a runner going from first on a single to right. He
threw it on the fly, missing the cutoff man and thus giving the hitter
a chance to go to second on the throw. Later in the same game, I
made an identical throw to home plate—that is, on the fly all the
way—after a single with a man on second, and gave the hitter the
same chance to move up on the throw.

It so happens Alou's throw was wrong and mine was right. It
could have been the other way—he could have been right and me
wrong; I could sit down and start dictating under the heading
MISTAKES I HAVE MADE and I'd fill a book longer than this one. But
I remember this game especially, because on the surface, Alou's
gamble seemed to make more sense than mine. His came when we
were ahead 2-0 with none out in the fourth. And he got his man.
Mine came when we were ahead 6-0 with two out in the sixth. And
I didn't get my man, because he decided to hold at third.

Yet look at it this way: with a 2-0 lead in the fourth, Alou was wrong, because if he missed his man—and nothing but a truly fabulous throw was going to get him—then we were handing the other side a setup for a big inning: men on second and third with none out. With a six-run lead in the sixth and two out, things were different with my throw to the plate.

Maybe I sound like I am contradicting myself here, for I am criticizing young Henderson for throwing to the plate with a big lead, yet excusing myself for the same play. The canny reader of course will say, "Ah, but there's a difference—Henderson's throw came with one out; Mays made his with two out."

That's not what the difference was. (In fact, I confess, as I think back a second time, I can't remember whether Henderson's catch before his throw came with none out or one out—all I do remember is the double-play throw to get Fox at home. And, as I say, it makes no difference.)

The difference wasn't a six-run lead or the point in the ball game or anything else. The difference was simply that in the Houston game, when Henderson made his throw to the plate, the other team was getting to us. In the other game, when I made my throw, I wasn't throwing to stop them from scoring a run—I was throwing to stop them from scoring THEIR FIRST RUN!

If you've got a big lead and the other team already has scored at least once during the game, what do you care about another run? But if you've got that same big lead and they haven't scored, now you *do* care, because a shutout may not mean much to you in center field, but it means a great deal to your pitcher. It will make him that much better next time out—or, at least, it's a factor that can work that way.

So it comes down to this: in the fourth inning, with nobody out, and you're ahead 2-0, you're trying to win, not save a shutout for your pitcher. At that stage, you can't even afford to think about it from that last standpoint.

But in the sixth, with two out, and you're ahead 6-0, you *can* afford to think about it.*

This is what I guess you'd call "inside" baseball, if you bothered to call it anything, but the larger point here is that you can arrive at any number of situations where you think too much for your own good. The solution isn't to be less thoughtful. In fact, there is no solution.

Stu Miller, who owns a lot of master points as a bridge player, told me one time that in tournament play the worst thing you could run into would be the team of "little old ladies," who didn't know how to play at all. They'd mix up the spades and clubs in their hands so they couldn't even read what they were holding, and then they'd go ahead and bid something like they really had it. Stu told me about one time where he had a good bid in clubs and his opponents were both bidding spades, and he got a little encouragement from his partner, so he went ahead and got the bid in clubs, and he went down. He'd figured from the bidding that his partner must hold at least one or two of the missing high clubs. It turned out the other side—two little old ladies—had the ace and king of clubs, but both of them had mixed them in with their spades by mistake. So now Miller found himself playing the hand and missing the ace and king of what had become the trump suit.

Miller once told me baseball was a lot like bridge. "Let's face it," he said, "you can see twenty games of basketball, and you've seen everything there is to see. But you can play bridge for twenty years, and something new will still come up. Same thing with baseball."

And he's right. Like I keep saying, I'm still learning.

Not everything I've learned deals exactly with baseball, either. I remember back in '51, we were going to the clubhouse in center

---

* This pitcher won the game 7-0. Next time out, he was knocked out of the box in the fifth inning. Both Alou's throw and mine had invited the hitter to move up to second on the sequence, but the fact is, neither hitter advanced past first.

field after hitting practice and Earl Rapp said to me, "Race you the rest of the way for five dollars."

"Let's go," I said, and we broke out running, and I beat him easy.

"Okay," he panted at me, "let's have the five."

"What do you mean? *You* owe *me* the five. *I* beat *you*."

"Wasn't anything about *beating* anybody," he said. "I just said I'd *race* you."

"Hey, Maglie!" I said. "What am I supposed to do?"

Maglie was standing there. "Pay him," he said.

I got it from the other clubs too. First time I ever saw Preacher Roe, he threw me what I got to swear was a spitball—I never did see an ordinary pitch behave that way—and the umpire called a strike, and Campanella, catching for the Dodgers, said, "How'd you like that pitch, Twenty-four?"

"He's pretty mean," I said.

"Wait till you get Newcombe tomorrow," Campy said. "He hates uppity young colored boys."

Something like four years later, I was going to pull maybe the greatest single piece of base-running—or sliding, or whatever you want to call it—of my whole baseball lifetime. I was coming home against the Dodgers and Campy had the ball, and what I did was actually dive over him and come down the other side with my hand touching the plate, and he never did touch me with the ball. I was kind of using his head as a fulcrum or something, and actually kind of ran up one side of him and down the other, and his hand with the ball kept aiming for me but never did touch me. And the umpire called me out.

Durocher came storming out of the dugout and, for one of the few times in my life, I put up a protest too. But the umpire had a point. He said to Leo: "You're telling me he did the impossible."

"He did."

"Well, I ain't fixin' to believe it," the umpire said.

Leo was a caution with the umpires. One time he got thrown out

of a game before the game even started. He'd been thrown out the
day before and this day the umpires came on the field, and Leo
spotted the one who'd tossed him out—I think it was Goetz—and he
shouted, "Hey, ————! Just say you were wrong yesterday. That's
all I want to hear!"

"I didn't have to listen to it yesterday and I don't have to listen
to it today," Goetz replied. "Get out again!"

Sam Jones told me he once got thrown out before a game. He was
warming up before the game began, and the umpire passed him and
said something and Sam told him what he could do and the umpire
told Sam he could do the same thing, in the shower.

In 1965, we had one game where Bob Shaw lasted two pitches
and got thrown out for saying something. One time Umpire Dascoli
threw Lockman out when Lockman didn't say anything.

"I didn't say anything," Lockman told him.

"I knew what you were fixing to say and it's the same thing,"
Dascoli told him. "Get out."

The worst umpiring I know of comes when they don't bear
down—when they're out of position to make a call, or where they
don't run into the outfield to see where a ball hits or whether it's
caught or fair or foul. I've seen two 500-foot home runs taken away
from McCovey because the umpires didn't hustle the way they
should have.

Also, I've seen strange things happen because one umpire called
it one way and another one another—but you can't get mad at them
because that happens once in a while. What you can get upset
about is when an umpire doesn't signal clearly whether he means
safe or out. I remember one time in Philadelphia—you may be
getting the idea by now that everything seems to happen in Philadelphia, which is true—when the whole Giant team started leaving
the field because we thought we'd made a double play to end the
inning, only the umpire at second base had never made a call on
the force-out there and it turned out he'd said under his breath
that the runner was safe. Only person in the ball park who heard

him was the runner. While we were leaving the field, he picked himself up and scored.

Once, in an exhibition game at Phoenix, we had an American League umpire working at third base, and he ruled a ball that Hank Sauer hit was foul, although Franks, who was coaching there, showed him the mark the ball had made when it hit fair on its way out along the left-field line.

Well, the umpire wouldn't change his mind—they never do on a play like that—but you could tell he knew he'd missed it. So pretty soon, somebody put a little pop fly back of third, and their third baseman caught it and flipped it routinely to his shortstop, who dropped it. Now the umpire ruled our hitter was safe because the man who'd caught the pop-up "didn't have possession long enough." That was about the silliest ruling I ever saw, but nobody argued it much, because everybody knew the umpire was just being human, and it's human when you blow a call to want to even it up and give it back to the other side next chance you get.

The only trouble with that is, when you get it happening on balls and strikes, you can get into a situation where instead of calling one wrong out of six, the umpire's calling two wrong out of six—the one he missed and the one he evens up with. They say two negatives don't make a postive, and to be equally unfair is not to be fair. Besides, it can spoil a pitcher's confidence in his strike zone and a hitter's ability to take a pitch, and the worst games you see are the ones where the umpire's always a pitch behind, trying to get himself even.

If he calls a pitch a ball one time and a worse pitch a strike the next, he isn't helping you by squaring accounts. All the players I know, pitchers most of all, would rather have an umpire miss a pitch once in a while than confuse everybody by being "fair" so he misses more than one.

Some umpires give you a lot of talk, like a running commentary on what you're doing. The Braves had a second baseman named Hartsfield one time who used to tell about an experience he had in the American Association, where he laid off a pitch and the umpire called it a strike and then said to him, "When you learn to hit that pitch, you'll go up to the big leagues."

"When you learn to call it," Hartsfield said to him, "we can take the same train."

Sometimes something happens so umpires can go out of their minds. We had a game against the Cubs one time where with two out and a man on first the batter swung and missed at a pitch for strike three, only it got by the catcher, and, as the runner started for first and the catcher turned to chase the ball, the umpire automatically put a new ball in his glove. I guess he may have thought it was a foul ball, although it wasn't.

Now we had two runners in motion and two balls in play, and in the middle of everything, Jocko Conlan, who's umpiring at second, puts up his hand and says, "Time!"

Then Scheffing, the Chicago manager, came out of the dugout and went up to Jocko and said to him, "What are *you* calling time for? The decision wasn't yours, and you're not the plate umpire in charge of the game."

"Manager," Jocko said to him, "I'm glad you said that, because it shows you're thinking, and I like managers who think. Only trouble is, in this case you haven't thought it out quite far enough. I've seen more baseball than the rest of these three guys put together—" he indicated the other umpires "—and in my studied opinion, the situation's so ———— ————* that we're going to stop it right here before it gets any worse!"

It's been said that an umpire always gets abuse, never praise, and of course some players will get on them worse than others. I don't. I feel they're skilled and they know their rules, and they do the best they know how. They've got the same human problems as anybody else, and the toughest job in baseball.

And—to repeat—they know their rules. I believe I "sense" the rules as well as anybody, and after 2,500 big-league games I guess I've

---

* By which he meant confused.

seen every one of them called. But I've never—here's a confession—
I've never been through the rule book from cover to cover. Not
because I'm lazy, but because some rules don't affect players one
way or the other. For instance, there's a rule that says that on
batter's interference with a man on third, with less than two out the
runner is out; with two out, the batter is out. (The reason for this,
I suppose, is that the book doesn't intend to "reward" the hitter by
letting him come to bat again next inning, which is what would
happen if it was the runner they called out with two out.) As you
can see, this is a rule that it's up to the umpires to call, but it makes
no nevermind to the players.

Besides, wasn't it Leo Durocher who always said: "Willie Mays
can do the five things you look for in a player—run, catch, throw,
hit for distance, hit for average—better than anybody I ever saw. So
he never had to be taught a thing."

It's a nice, flattering fib.

The things they had to teach me, especially back there in '51!
And this includes the rules of the game.

Generally speaking, what I've always done is, if I was in doubt
what the call was or the rule was, complete the play the best way
I knew how, assume the best, and then, if I was wrong, let the
umpire say so. If you're on first base and a guy hits one down the
first-base line and out toward the right-field corner, take off. Don't
worry about was it fair or foul. And don't let the other team's shortstop tell you it was foul, either. Go as far as you can, or till you hear
an umpire tell you to go back. In cases like that, it doesn't cost anything to be wrong.

But back in '51, I was on first base one time, and our hitter
walloped one to deepest right-center in the Polo Grounds, and I
took off and was nearly to third when they caught it. So I hustled
back to first and beat the throw, only to have them call me out anyway.

"What was wrong?" Fitzsimmons, our first base coach, asked the
umpire. "He beat the throw back."

"He also come back through the pitcher's mound," the umpire said.

That was the first time I'd honestly known that you have to touch the same bases in order going back as you touched going forward. I simply hadn't known that rule.

I've heard it said that I sparked the ball club in '51 because I had a great quality of "innocence." "Ignorance" might be just as good a word for it.

But the fans went for it, and so did the other players. You couldn't get me mad—I was having too much fun playing baseball in the big leagues. Here I was, earning $5,000 for doing the one thing in the world I wanted to do most. For traveling first class and staying at the best hotels and eating the kind of food that up till then had only been a rumor.

Some of the guys took me to a place in Boston one time and ordered me a clambake, and it came in this big iron pot with seaweed inside, and I didn't know what was coming off, till I started dipping those clams and that lobster claw meat in the butter, and I almost cried, it was so great.

And the New York sports writers, the ones who covered our club day in and day out, were about as fine to me as writers can be—because they were patient with me, same as Leo and the rest of the Giants. Some of the things I did wrong, they ignored; others, they'd play it up in a nice way—like a habit I had of never being able to catch a guy's name the first time I met him, so the second time I'd say "Say Hey!" to him, and it became a kind of greeting with me, but what it really was, was a cover-up for the fact I couldn't remember his name. So they started calling me the "Say Hey" kid, and the nickname still sticks even though by now I haven't used the expression for years.

And they played up the fact that I was always running out from under my cap—somebody wrote that I'd actually stopped while chasing a fly ball to grab back my hat from midair, then had gone on to make the catch (I don't remember it, and I'd have to doubt it).

And when I started living in Harlem, near the Polo Grounds, with a Birmingham family there, they took pictures of me playing stickball in the streets, late afternoons after a day game, with the kids on the block.

Stickball is pretty much a New York game. You play it with a broomstick and a handball. Home plate and second base are manhole covers—they call them "sewers"—and the fenders of parked cars are first and third. You measure a long ball by "sewers"—a guy who can hit for four sewers is a monster.

It isn't bad for your eyes, either, because it's a little ball and a thin stick you got to hit with, and when it comes in—they pitch it on one bounce—it can really travel. The only better eye-sharpener I know of is a good game of pool. It relaxes you and sharpens you at the same time, and I can't think of anything else that can do both those things. Even so, I feel bad everytime I talk about it, because somebody's going to say, "See—Mays is advising kids to go to the pool hall."

I even had a "day" at the Polo Grounds in '51. A bunch of Trenton fans came in and gave me some things—a picture and a watch, things like that. I had a "day" at the Polo Grounds in '63, too, after the Giants had moved to San Francisco and the Mets were playing there.

In San Francisco, they don't go in for things like that so much. They gave me a banquet, for charity, at the Fairmont Hotel in 1964, but on the field the only "day" I can remember was for Stu Miller, back in 1961, and the papers, or at least one or two of the writers, got on them for it—you know, the old story of why donate something to a baseball player who earns more than you do to begin with—so things are different there. I still feel funny about having my biggest "day" in New York when I was with the visiting team, but that's how it happened.

So I guess I was innocent—or ignorant, one or the other or maybe both. But I was playing well too, and the ball club was winning, back there in '51. The Polo Grounds was suited to my range in the outfield, because it had the biggest center field in baseball, and the Giants as a club were suited to my speed as a runner, because just about every one of them could get at least a piece of the ball to protect you when they had to. People like Stanky, Dark, Mueller, Lockman—these were magicians with a bat. Matter of fact, they used to call Mueller "Mandrake," the way he could do things with a pitch.

Late in June of '51 we toured the Western cities, and at one point I had a 10-game hitting streak. All in all, for that Western swing, I had four home runs and 16 RBI's, and now, back home, Leo made the move—putting Thomson on third—so now the lineup was set. Westrum catching, Lockman at first, Stanky at second, Dark at short, Thomson at third, Mueller in right, me in center, Irvin in left. Main starters as pitchers were Maglie, Jansen, Koslo, Hearn, George Spencer.

We were in second place now, but there was hardly any sighting on the Dodgers—they were almost out of view, they were so far ahead.

Yet somehow Durocher wasn't giving up—and everybody knew he was at his best when he smelled a chance. He must have smelled something. One game, the Dodgers were beating the pants off us, and just to rub it in they had Robinson squeeze a runner home.

"That was a pretty bush thing to do," a writer said to Leo after the game. "Squeezing for an extra run with a lead like that. Are you mad?"

"Mad?" Durocher said. "I'm delighted!"

"Delighted? Why?"

"I've got their ———— ———— bunt sign, that's why!" Leo said.

And I remember seeing Pee Wee Reese on a TV show. He was the Dodger shortstop and captain. "I keep telling everybody look out for the Giants," he said, "but nobody'll believe me."

That broke them up. The MC and the audience all laughed. Everybody laughed except Pee Wee.

Maybe he knew something too.

All I know is, on August 11 we were shut out by the Phillies, while Brooklyn was beating Boston 8-1 in the first game of a double-header. At that exact moment, as a lot of people took the trouble to figure out afterward, the standings were:

|  | W | L | G.B. |
|---|---|---|---|
| Brooklyn | 70 | 35 | — |
| New York | 59 | 51 | 13 1/2 |

If anything could make that look worse, it was the "loss" column. We were 13 1/2 back overall, but were 16 down on the lost side. That meant we'd played more games than them. Games we could never get back because they were on the lost side. If we now won 11 in a row and they now lost 11 in a row, we'd be even with them at 70 victories apiece. But they'd still have lost five games fewer than us.

And they weren't about to lose 11 in a row.

Nor were we about to win 11 in a row.

We were about to win 16 in a row!

# 9

BROOKLYN LOST THE second game of their doubleheader that day with the Braves, and next day we beat the Phils 3-2. Then Al Corwin—the newcomer I mentioned awhile back when I was talking about cutting up the World Series shares—pitched a four-hitter, and we beat the Phils 2-1 for a doubleheader sweep.

A headline in the next day's paper said:

### RELAXED GIANTS MAY HAVE FUN AT LAST

Yes, I'd call it fun. Jansen beat the Phils 5-2 for his 15th win, and then we swept three from the Dodgers at the Polo Grounds. It was in that game that I made the play that *Time* magazine later called "The Throw." We were tied 1-1 with Billy Cox, a fast man, on third base for them with one out in the top of the eighth. Furillo was at bat and he hit a kind of looping fly ball to my left, in right-center field. It wasn't too short a ball, but it wasn't too far out for a good throw. The thing everybody talked about later was that, being to my left, it was away from my throwing arm. I would have had to stop and set, and that would give Cox the time he needed to score.

What I did, though, was catch the ball and kind of let its force in my glove help spin me completely around. There was no trouble locating the plate, because Lockman had lined himself up, like a cutoff man except of course no cutoff was going to happen in that

111

situation. And I let fly and Westrum had the ball in time to nab Cox sliding into the plate.

"He'll have to do it again before I believe it," Brooklyn manager Dressen growled afterward. It was a tribute, and it was headlines the next day because we went on to win the game when I led off the last of the eighth with a single and Westrum homered so we won 3-1.

Have you noticed how often the guy who makes the big play in the field happens to be first up next inning? I think there's a reason for it, but I'm afraid it unglamorizes the glamour. First place, a lot of times he *isn't* first up next inning. You only notice it when he is. And, second place, one thing that can make a big play a big play is that it gets you out of an inning, which I guess is why so many of them seem to happen with two out.

Maglie won his 17th as we beat the Dodgers the final game of the series. Then Spencer beat the Phillies 8-5 and Jansen shut out Roberts 2-0 and somebody got hold of the Brooklyn score. They'd lost to Boston, 13-4.

I think, looking back, that it was that Brooklyn-Boston score, more than any one thing, that suddenly got it through to us that we had a chance in the pennant race. To beat them a tight series and then have them go stumbling out into the night and get rocked 13-4 —well, we went out next day to play the Phils again, and some-how—words won't explain it—we were a confident, cocky ball club.

So cocky we were behind 4-0 in the seventh inning.

So confident we scored five times and won it 5-4.

Then the Western clubs came in, and we're trailing the Reds 4-2 going into the last of the eighth. So Westrum, Stanky, and Lock-man homered—Wes hit his with two on—and we wound up winning 7-4.

One kind of overconfidence—the letdown you get after you win by a big score—was something we weren't in danger of here. It was as if we were flirting with defeat, trying to see how close we could

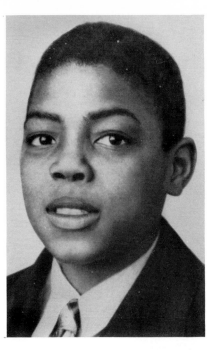

Willie Mays — 13-year-old schoolboy. *(Courtesy United Press International)*

Mays's boyhood home in Birmingham, Alabama. *(Courtesy Lee Mendelson Film Productions, Inc.)*

Willie Mays, as a teen-ager, playing for the Black Barons. *(Courtesy Lee Mendelson Film Productions, Inc.)*

Willie receives pregame instruction from Leo Durocher before playing his first major-league game, May 25, 1951. *(Courtesy Wide World Photos)*

Mays steals second against Yankees in 1951 World Series. *(Courtesy United Press International)*

Waiting for a preinduction physical examination, October 23, 1951. *(Courtesy Wide World Photos)*

FACING PAGE: The Mays stance (1954). *(Courtesy Brown Brothers)*

Close-order drill at Camp Kilmer, New Jersey, May 29, 1952 (Mays, second from left). *(Courtesy Wide World Photos)*

Left to right: Al Dark, Monte Irvin, Wes Westrum, and Willie Mays—all hit home runs to help 1954 pennant-bound Giants beat Brooklyn 10-2. (*Courtesy Wide World Photos*)

Mays catching long drive by Vic Wertz in 1954 World Series. (*Courtesy Wide World Photos*)

Willie Mays, his former wife, Marghuerite, and his five-week-old son, Michael, March, 1959. (*Courtesy Wide World Photos*)

Typical Mays slide on the base paths. (*Courtesy Wide World Photos*)

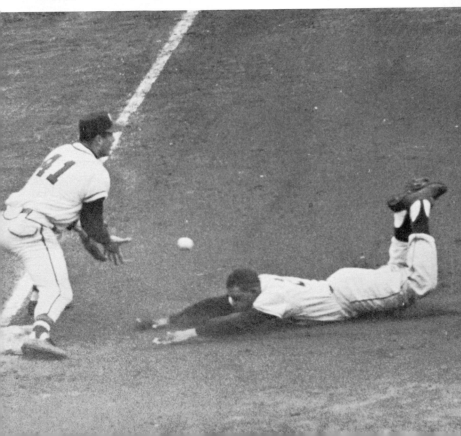

Ted Williams, Stan Musial, and Willie Mays—three superstars congregate at the 1959 All-Star game. (*Courtesy United Press International*)

Mays recuperates in hospital after one of his recurring fainting spells, September, 1962. (*Courtesy Wide World Photos*)

come. We beat Concinnati 4-3, then trailed the Cardinals 5-4 going into the last of the ninth, scored twice, and won it 6-5.

Then a doubleheader with the Cubs. We won the first game 5-4. Are there any scores outside of one-run scores? Oh, sure. We had a "laugher" in the second game of that doubleheader, winning it 5-1.

And now another doubleheader with the Cubs. We were tied 3-3 in the top of the 12th, first game. They scored once in the 12th. We scored twice and won it, 5-4.

In the second game, Corwin went all the way and we won it, 6-3.

Sixteen in a row.

And the worst—two doubleheaders on consecutive days—was behind us now. Coming in to play us were the Pittsburgh Pirates, who were the easiest team in the league.

Naturally, we lost.

But we'd set the baseball world on fire. We heard they even had trouble with the fans at the tennis championships at Forest Hills, because they were smuggling radios into the stands, to keep up with the Giant scores.

"I'm just as happy you lost," Eddie Logan, the clubhouse man, said after the Pittsburgh game. "Now maybe you can send your socks to the laundry. It was getting a little gamey in here."

"How 'bout your own socks?" Dark asked him. "You going to send them to the laundry too?"

"Don't have to," Logan said. "By now, all I got to do is point 'em in the right direction. They'll walk there on their own."

We'd cut eight games off the Dodger lead with that winning streak, and now, the first week in September, here we went again. Maglie won his 18th, beating the Dodgers 8-1 on September 1. We pulled a triple play and Mueller hit three homers. Next day we beat 'em 11-2. Mueller hit two more homers.

Obviously, somebody besides Willie Mays was helping "carry the Giants on his back." I think my contribution was a good one, but it was mainly speed and fielding. The throw on Cox was only one of half a dozen big plays I'd had. But looking back over the years now, it would be hard to rate any of them, including the Cox play, as a "greatest." The Cox thing was you-do-or-you-don't. But we won, and that gave it extra importance. That's true so often in baseball. I remember a throw on Cunningham that got him at the plate from the right-field fence in St. Louis, but we went on to lose the game. I remember another throw, on Bill Bruton, that didn't get him. I'd gone deep for a fly ball and Bruton, a fast man, was tagged up on third, and we were behind anyway and there was nobody else on, so it was a what-the-hell throw and it sailed into Westrum's mitt and Westrum's glove was on Bruton's shoulder and Bruton's foot was coming down on the plate and the umpire—I think it was Robb— waited a long time before he called it, and after the inning Wes told me, "He finally said 'Safe.' Then he muttered to himself: 'He's *gotta* be safe! *Nobody* throws Bruton out from there!' "

In the 1962 World Series, I made what I would call my finest all-time throw. Nobody remembers it. In Yankee Stadium, Skowron had hit one to the monument in left-center, 460 feet away. I went back, dug the ball out of the corner, and let fly at Pagan, our short-stop. Pagan, figuring Skowron for a triple, took the ball and looked at third. If he'd thrown instead of looked, we would have had him. Actually, he should have had a triple anyway. He didn't expect a throw like that, so he let up the last half of the way between second and third. But on that play, I just threw the twine off the ball. Like I say, it didn't get anybody and nobody remembers it. But to me, it would be just about the best one I ever made.

But the best throw I've ever made isn't the best throw I've ever seen. That one took place in 1965. For years, other outfielders have commented about the way I deliberately stay back of a fly ball when I'm going to have to make a throw after the catch. That way, rush-ing in for the catch at the last minute, I have not only my arm, but full body momentum, behind the throw.

Some outfielders agree with this. Others say it can lead to a hasty mistake, like throwing it before you have it, or losing something off your aim.

Jim Wynn, the Houston center fielder, happens to agree with me. He was back pretty far for a fly ball with Jesus Alou on third for us, and he drifted even farther back, then rushed the ball at the last minute and caught and threw, and you never saw a thrown baseball go so far so fast so true. It was just like the play I'd made on Bruton that time, except in this case the man was out. Not only out, but out by plenty.

And I'll swear Wynn had a special grin for me when he trotted off the field.

Of course, you find, more and more as the years go by, that peo-people compare what you do with other things you used to do. I'm supposed to have said one time, "I don't rate 'em—I just catch 'em." I doubt I ever said it quite that way. But I do believe every play deserves to be measured by itself, and its own situation. There's only so much comparing you can do; pretty quick it becomes meaningless. One thing I didn't say about the Wynn throw, for instance— it was made against a rough, quartering Candlestick wind. In one way, that made it an even greater throw. Yet who knows? Without a wind, maybe his aim would have been off! (Or, on the other hand, maybe including everything else, he gauged the wind in the split second and took it into account. The good center fielder in Candlestick is part outfielder, part weatherman—that I do know.)

That was one thing, at least, that didn't come up during my first season as a Giant in 1951. If I made a good play, they said it was a good play. Wasn't anybody around to say, "No, he made the same play even better four years ago against St. Louis." There *is* no same play in baseball.

In a way, it was bad, back in '51, because I was just turned 20, and all this excitement and headlines had me believing I must be a little bigger than life-size. What saved me from a swelled head, I think, was one wonderful thing—wonderful for me, maybe not for the ball club:

My own mistakes.

Like against the Phillies that first week in September, when I belted Roberts for an inside-the-park home run.

Only I forgot to touch third.

We lost it, 6-3, and in mid-September we went into Brooklyn for our final two games of the regular season against the Dodgers, and Newcombe beat us 9-0 with a two-hitter, and by now there was no special halo around the ears of Willie Mays anymore. We were 6½ out with barely more than two weeks to go and that, children, was it. School was out.

Maglie went out to pitch that last game against the Dodgers, the day after Newcombe beat us. There'd been standing room only, the Newcombe game. Now the stands were barely more than half filled. One game, but it had made all the difference.

They called Maglie "the barber" because even when he shaved it always looked like he had five o'clock shadow. He looked like the meanest man in the world, but he was one of the nicest. He had one speciality: beating the Dodgers in Ebbets Feld. How *any* pitcher ever won in Ebbets Feld, I'll never know. The only regret I have, out of all my years in baseball, is that I never got to play there regularly. One season I hit nine home runs there in 11 games. You had to *love* that park. Not only were the fences short all around, but the upper deck in center field hung in over the lower deck, so you could hit a routine fly to center, and the center fielder would be back there camped under it, and all of a sudden it would be in some fan's lap, 40 feet above him, for a home run.

Duke Snider wept when the Dodgers moved from Brooklyn to L.A. They were taking the shortest right field away from him and trading it for the longest. Alston, the manager, broke the news to him. "I know you've been hitting home runs, Duke," he said. "You think you can learn to hit singles?" It was like asking a steak man if he could learn to like frankfurters.

And pitching in Ebbets Feld—well, put it this way: an awful lot of hitters used to get thrown at there. Maybe it was an accident, or maybe pitchers can stand just so much. The time at bat after he hit four home runs and a double in one game, Joe Adcock was hit with a pitch and it put him in the hospital. Ebbets Field is also where Medwick got beaned that time.

For years, I was the one Giant who got thrown at the most, yet the one Giant who wouldn't wear a batting helmet. I'd wear a liner inside the cap instead. I felt easier up there, without that bulky object around my ears.

Finally, I think it was in 1962, Manager Dark put it on the basis of a flat order, so I started wearing one. In '65, Manager Franks let me start the season without one, but I kind of went back to wearing one myself. As I was getting older, all the fast-ball pitchers in the league seemed to be getting younger. And wearing a helmet, it turned out, wasn't so much that it got in your way as it was a question of getting used to it. Some players, like Cepeda, who once got skulled by a thrown ball while running between first and second, wear them all the way around the bases, not just at bat.

I guess if I'd played in Ebbets Field all the time, I would have gone to a helmet a lot earlier. Like I say, it wasn't a good park for a pitcher's blood pressure.

Yet Maglie had a way of beating the Dodgers there, and if there was ever a blood feud, it was the one between him and them. I once asked him, "What's the secret—how do you pitch in that park?"

"Very carefully," he replied.

Actually, Maglie was one of those very few pitchers who never learned how to warm up. No, scratch that. I don't mean he never learned how. What I mean instead is that no matter how he'd warm up before a game—short or long, easy or hard—seemed like he needed an actual inning or two of a game to get his real stuff going. Some pitchers, like a Marichal, go out there and paralyze the other side the first inning, and it's a great psychological weapon. For instance, one game against the Houstons, with Farrell—a good pitcher—going for them, at Candlestick Park, Marichal struck out the side in the top of the first. Then in the bottom half we got a walk and an ordinary ground ball bounced over the first baseman's head for a double, and now we had men on second and third and nobody out, and you could just see the Houston club give way like a balloon where somebody untied the knot. They just knew they were beat.

A Maglie, on the other hand—something like Bob Shaw nowadays—would have to struggle through that first couple of innings. In its way, this was just as bed mentally on the other team as the Marichal type, because they'd be pressing to get to him early, knowing that if they didn't get him out of there right now, he'd mow 'em down the rest of the way.

And this one game at Ebbets Field back in 1951—our last game against the Dodgers on the regular schedule that year, with them now 6½ ahead in the standings in mid-September—well, it was too late—everybody knew that—but nobody told this to Maglie. Or to Irvin, who hit a home run. Or to Thomson, playing a new position at third base and with us leading 2-1 in the last of the eighth, they had the greatest runner in the game—Jackie Robinson—jockeying off third with one out, and Andy Pafko, a big hitter, at bat. Pafko hit a smash down the third-base line. Thomson gloved it, tagged Robinson, and threw to first for the double play, so fast it made your head go around, and that, dear friends, was that.

We had to keep on winning.

We kept on winning.

September 25, we beat the Phillies 5-1—our 34th win in 41 games —and the Dodgers lost a doubleheader to the Braves!

We had closed the gap to one game behind.

We had to keep on winning.

We kept on winning.

Going into the final Saturday of the season, we were tied for the lead. That day, we beat the Braves 3-0. Maglie won his 23rd. On one base-running sequence, I stole second, then third. I was beginning to learn that a lot of times it's easier to steal third than it is to steal second, because of the bigger lead and bigger jump you can get.

Brooklyn beat Philadelphia that final Saturday, too, but we didn't care. Things were in our own hands now—all we had to do was win—and the next day, the final day of the regular season, we did win, beating Boston 3-2, and the scoreboard showed the Dodgers were getting the whey kicked out of them by the Phils.

People ask me if it's true I give advice to left and right fielders playing along side of me. The answer of course is yes. Other fielders gave me advice when I first came up; now it's my turn. But we use signals and quiet things—I don't like to make a public exhibition out of it.

I must say, though, that on that final out of that last game at Boston in '51, I had some advice for another fielder, and I shouted it at the top of my lungs.

It was a routine fly ball to Irvin in left. I came charging all the way over from center as he camped under it. Then, it occurred to me to yell a mild suggestion to Monte—so I did.

"Catch it," I advised him. "Catch it or I'll kill you!"

# 10

WE WERE ON the train, going back from Boston to New York, when the news reached us that first through an impossible bases-loaded catch of a line drive, then with a home run in the top of the 14th, Jackie Robinson had led Brooklyn to an incredible come-from-behind win over the Phils.

We'd won 37 of our last 44 games, dating from August 12. Over the same stretch, the Dodgers had won 26 out of 48. So they played .540 baseball for what was close to the last one-third of the season. To catch them, we'd had to play .840 baseball. Which we did.

Now there'd be a play-off. We won the toss, meaning the first game at Ebbets Field but the next one and the if-necessary one after that both at the Polo Grounds.

I'd hit 20 home runs since coming up on May 25. Irvin had 23 on the season and Thomson had 30. But my hot splurge had come earlier. Now it was the two of them who were carrying us most of all with the bat. They each homered in that first play-off game, and Westrum threw out a couple of their pussycats trying to steal, and that was it. We won 3-1, back of a five-hitter by Hearn.

Durocher was feisty now. Ever see a riverboat gambler where he's playing five-card stud and his first hole card gives him a pair of aces? Rather than go to Maglie, who'd worked Saturday—this was only Tuesday—Durocher could afford to play the second game loose, almost anticipating the start of the World Series. Besides, the Dodgers were worse off for pitchers than we were. They had to start a kid we'd never seen before, name of Clem Labine.

And they beat us 10-0.

Which set the stage for Wednesday's game, and I began this book with what happened then. The only thing I can remember that I didn't tell about already was after the game, they gave me a glass of champagne—the first I'd ever tasted.

If the newspapermen had been looking for me, which they weren't, they would have found me bent over a bowl in the shower room, throwing up.

I didn't hear this, but they also tell me one reporter said to Durocher, quite seriously, "What was the turning point of the game?"

As for Bobby Thomson, he got off one of the best lines of all. "It was a play we worked out long ago," he said. "We decided to win the pennant this way to create excitement, restore fan interest in the game. You know how it is."

We took the Yankees six games in the World Series. Actually, we were leading two games to one, and Stengel's pitching rotation was down to the point to where he had to use Sain in the fourth game, which we thought gave us a real chance, because Sain had come over from the Braves and we were familiar with his pitching.

But that game got rained out, so we never did see Sain except for one very short relief bit, so they went on to win it. In the fourth game, DiMaggio hit a two-run homer and we lost it 6-2. In fact, from that DiMaggio homer on, we never saw the lead in the Series again.

The biggest crowd I ever saw—70,000 people—was at Yankee Stadium for the opening game of the Series, which was played the day after (barely 20 hours, really) Thomson's play-off miracle. The first inning, Henry Thompson, filling in for the injured Mueller in right field, walked, went to second as Irvin singled to left, and scored on a Lockman double. Then the mighty Thomson stepped to the plate, and this tremendous roar went up, a hangover from the day before, and even Reynolds, the pitcher, was staring at him like he was from outer space or something.

At third base, Irvin grinned at Durocher, who was coaching there, and said, "Yeah?"

"Yeah," Durocher said.

So Monte stole home.

Then Dark hit a three-run homer in the sixth, and we won it 5-1.

I'm not going to replay that World Series game by game, for one very good reason—there's very little about it that I remember. I do remember Mickey Mantle, their prize rookie that year, twisting his knee in the second game, while going for a fly ball, and that was the last we saw of him. It also was the beginning of a career-long plague of injuries that hurt the playing lifetime of a man who has to be called the greatest switch-hitter of all time.

And it was the end for Joe DiMaggio.

He was my idol, as you know, but I'd never seen him in the flesh. Before the first game of the Series, a photographer came up to me and said, "We want a picture of you with DiMag."

I said, "What does he want to be in a picture with me for?"

I'll never forget the late inning in the final game of the Series, when Stengel sent in a pinch runner for DiMag, who was on third base. As he went to the dugout, those fans came to their feet and gave him a tremendous ovation. I used to think they realized he'd never play again—he announced his retirement that winter—but maybe I was overthinking it.

There are different kinds of applause you get from the stands. There's the roar when your name is announced, and the sound they make when you come to bat, especially in a big situation. And the cheer for the big hit or the big play on the bases, and the applause after the good play in the field.

But nothing has the wonderful sound to it of the ovation when you leave a ball game, not after a great play, not because something's expected of you, but simply a standing, concerted round of applause that says, "We're glad you were here . . . we're glad we got to see you all those times."

It's quieter than the other kinds of cheering, but it has a meaning all its own.

I've heard it three times in my lifetime—heard it, that is, for me.

Once was after my last time at bat at the Polo Grounds in 1957, last game of the season, with the club scheduled to move to San Francisco for the next season. I didn't do anything—hit into a routine out—but I got that hand from the fans—that standing, prolonged handclapping and cheering as I returned to the bench.

Once again, in 1959, I heard it—this time from the San Francisco fans. It was late in the season and I'd got four hits that day at Seals Stadium and Rig was going to let me rest out the last inning, so he sent in a pinch runner for me. And the fans let me hear it. In a way, it's the nicest fan sound of all, because they're not expecting anything.

And I heard it after my last at bat in '65, when I hit my 52nd home run of the year.

I've been on airplanes where they made an unusually smooth landing—not in the face of any trouble or anything like that, but just a great flight and then a beautiful landing—and I've joined in with the other passengers, clapping my hands. I think it's the same thing. It's appreciation for a job well done, and for a happy time that you were given by somebody else.

They tell me the last game Ted Williams played, the manager *made* him go out into left field, then immediately sent out another player to take his place, so Ted would have to jog in from the field to the dugout and the fans could give him this salute.

All I know is, it's a wonderful thing to hear. Maybe the most wonderful of all.

It doesn't happen often, but it isn't supposed to happen often. Sometimes, events keep it from happening. I know I would have heard it from the fans in the last game of the '62 World Series, except it was the last of the ninth and I was on second base and we were a run behind when McCovey hit a terrific line shot that Richardson, playing him out of position, caught for the final out. So that applause was there for you, but the situation didn't give the fans a chance to let you know.

They talk about Babe Ruth "calling his shot" on that World Series homer that time, pointing to the stands before he hit the ball there. I'd like to have heard the fans on that one.

The only time I ever "called" a home run, the fans didn't know anything about it. This is one of my favorite stories, yet I don't think it's ever really been told before.

It was late in 1963, and a television company headed by Lee Mendelson, a San Francisco producer, was making a show called "A Man Named Mays" that ran twice on NBC, and one of the parts of the show was an interview with me as I drove my car toward the ball park for that night's game at Candlestick.

The car was so loaded with cameras and sound equipment and everything else that I thought we were going to blow up at any minute. But I was supposed to talk as I drove, so I did, and one of the things I said was that I thought I'd hit the 400th home run of my career that night. I knew who was pitching against us and I could sense what the weather would be, and I even pinpointed the inning—"It'll be before the fifth," I said. "After that, the wind comes up on a night like this."

And in the fourth inning, sure enough, I hit the home run.

I saw Mendelson after the game, and I was laughing. "You get that all right on film?" I asked him.

"Which?" he said. "The interview or the home run?"

"Both," I said.

He nodded. "We got both."

"Then you ought to be happy," I said.

"I'm miserable," he said. "Here we've got you calling your four hundreth home run in advance, and no if's, and's, or but's about it. And there's no way we can use it."

"No way you can use it . . . ?" I stared at him. "I thought you said it came out all right."

"It did," he said. "But it won't look that way if we use it in the show."

"Why not?"

"It'll have to look staged," he said sadly. "Phony. Fixed." He nodded at himself. "It'll look like you hit the home run first and we rigged the interview afterward. It can't come out looking any other way. Sure, you called it. But try telling that to thirty million people on TV. I'm sorry, Buck. But all we can do is throw it out and forget it."

# 11

I BOUGHT MY DAD a car with part of my '51 World Series share, and a portable phonograph for me. And back home in Birmingham I was a hero—particularly to my draft board, which saw a lot of me, in the way of what you might call command performance. I was called up in October, but there was an aptitude test to take and then the question of dependents, because I was contributing to the support of my Aunt Sarah and my brothers and sisters.

In the end, they decided they were going to draft me, but I didn't actually go in till the end of May, 1952, which meant I got to start the season with the Giants.

I count 1954 as my first full season with the New York club, and one of the reasons is that when you add my 1951 and 1952 seasons together, you get a total of 155 games and 591 at bats, which has been typical of all my seasons since. Also, the games I missed in '51 and '52 weren't due to anything involving my being with the club—I wasn't injured, or being benched, or rested, or anything like that. I just wasn't with the Giants, period. For that reason, when people talk to me about my "per season average" for things like runs scored, RBI's, thing like that, I think it's just as fair to regard those two seasons as one. Not that it helps my hitting any. I was .274 in '51 and, for the 34 games of '52, I was .236—30 for 127, and 20 of those 30 hits were singles. The only thing halfway decent about my hitting to that point was my runs batted in—23 in 34 games—but the thing of it was the Giants had won 27 of those first 34 games in '52, and I think then and there was born the myth that has flapped around my ears ever since—*Without Mays, the Giants can't win.*

The team was in fifth place when I joined the club in '51. They went on to win the pennant. They were in first place when I left in '52. They finished second. I was in the Army all of the '53 season. The Giants finished fifth, a full 35 games off the pace. I came back at the start of '54. The Giants won the pennant. Not till 1955 would I play for them and see them fail to win, but by then the myth had taken hold, and started to be, "If Mays has a bad day, the Giants lose," or, "If Mays rests, the Giants lose." I'm not being supermodest for a single instant when I say it's not so—fact is, as I'll detail here, it's caused me some of the strangest grief a ballplayer ever had.

And not so much in those early seasons, when the fact was the Giants did win with me and didn't win without me (though that was due to other factors as much as to any one man).

It actually got worse after it was proved they could lose with me as well as without me.

Even worse when we moved to San Francisco.

Worst of all, it seemed, last season.

After 38 games of the 1965 season, Manager Franks gave me a day off . . . a Monday afternoon game against the Braves at Candlestick. Actually, I went up to pinch-hit in the ninth, when we were a run behind at 4-3 and had the tying run on second with two out. But with first base open they walked me intentionally, so I didn't get to swing.

Next morning's main sports headline in the San Francisco *Chronicle* said:

GIANTS LOSE, 4-3; MAYS ON BENCH

The story began:

They gave Willie Mays almost a full day of rest yesterday, and the Giants fell asleep.

With the Great One lounging on the bench, resting shoulders and arms that were beginning to show the wear and tear of a .379 batting average, the Giants bowed to the Milwaukee Braves, 4-3.

The headline on a separate clubhouse story in the same paper said:

### MAYS: 'A HORSE DOESN'T RUN EVERY DAY'

They quoted me as saying, "I'm not hurt, but why can't I have a day off without nine guys coming around to ask why?"

That's an accurate quote. And I still don't know the answer to my question. How many ballplayers can you think of who become the main headlines in the paper every time they *don't* play?

There was even a story, which became current the time I collapsed on the bench in Cincinnati toward the end of the '62 pennant race, that the Giants had never won a game in which I didn't play. This may actually have been true at the time as far as the *San Francisco* Giants were concerned—they might not have won a game with me out of the lineup since coming to the Coast—but that doesn't have much meaning either, because I didn't miss that many games in those early years.

The fact is, I haven't missed many games, period. That's one of the things that gets me about those headlines. A fan reads the story and says to himself, "Poor guy. Hitting .379 and making $100,000 a year but he can't play baseball two hours a day. Needs his rest."

In 1964, I tied a National League record for playing 150 games or more in consecutive seasons. The record was 11. That meant all 11 of my full years in the majors up till then.

In 1965, I played in 157 games, so now I hold the record on my own.

Does this mean I just play parts of a lot of games, like starting and leaving early, or coming in at the last minute like in that Milwaukee game? Well, the figures also show that I've averaged more than 540 official times at bat per season over my major-league career. But for the first seven seasons in San Francisco, which is where all this resting talk started up, my average of official times at bat per season wasn't 540—it was 590! Somehow, somebody's got to have it figured that the more I rest the more I come to bat.

I pity my manager more than I pity me when I bring this subject up. Sure, I'm the one who makes the headlines when I rest, but he's the one who has to make the decision. He knows me, knows not only that I can use a breather every now and again like everybody else but even maybe a little more so—on account of my age, and because I'm more tense—or maybe *in*tense—on the field than some other players. He knows my efficiency is down when I get real tired. He knows just a quick rest—sometimes just one full game—can sometimes have a way of restoring me, even sending me off on a tear.

Still and all, what if he rests me and the Giants lose? All ball clubs lose games, and sometimes a defeat in the right place can mean more victories later, for any number of reasons—a player gained from a rest, or you spotted something in one of your players or the other team's, or a couple of guys got shook up in the right way and snapped out of some bad habit that was hurting you. But the fans have a way of noticing it especially when you lose. If I rest and we win, people don't take on about it.

But now: I rest and we lose. First off, they want to know is Mays hurt. Second, especially if you're on the road but to some measure at home too, there is always the bunch of fans who came out to see their one game that year—typically, and even worse, coming in a chartered bus from 400 miles away or something. They came to see Mays and for no good reason Mays didn't play. Hell has no fury like the fan scorned in a manner like that.

A baseball manager is many things, and one of these is a link between the players and the front office—and another, a kind of public-relations man for the club. He stands to gain no friends by playing me, but he stands to lose them by not playing me.

Take a maybe exaggerated, but still absolutely true, example of this. We're in spring training in Phoenix. So far we've played two Saturday exhibition games in Tucson, where the Indians train. We've yet to play the Angels at Palm Springs. Now it's a Wednesday. We've got a split-squad date—two games that day. Half our squad will go to Tucson, the other half to Palm Springs, where we've got our first date of the season with the Angels. The game there is being televised back to Los Angeles.

You're the Giant manager. Ordinarily, you might give Mays the day off on a given Wednesday in mid-March. Will you give him the day off today? No. Will you have him play with the half of the team that goes to Tucson? No. Mays is going to go against the Angels at Palm Springs, and probably will work at least seven innings. Ridiculous? Not at all. If I can make a "split squad" out of myself, as Mays the manager I have to tell Mays the player to go to Palm Springs too.

And what, finally, about the nagging things in the back of the manager's mind—the big question? Mays, he says to himself, catches, runs, throws, hits for distance, hits for average. I'm the manager. I may not know what all my players can do, and they still may not surprise me. But I know what Mays can do, and yet he never fails to surprise me. Sound crazy? You can look it up. There it is. So if he doesn't hit it out, he can still hit it. If he doesn't hit it, he can still reach base. If he doesn't reach base, he can still catch it. If he doesn't catch it, he can still throw it. He can be in his worst slump, his most tired-out condition, in all history, and still win me a ball game. Rest him?

Maybe this wouldn't be a problem with a second-division ball club. But every Giant club since we came West has been a contender.

And all this assumes that there really isn't something physically wrong with me. Pity the poor manager who knows I've got a sore arm and doesn't want the news to leak out, on account of if it does they'll be running on me. When *he* rests me for a ball game, what does he tell the press about it?

This actually happened, in Milwaukee in 1961, with the result that in one of the San Francisco papers the next day a columnist, who didn't know about my arm, wrote:

> The point wasn't that Mays shouldn't be given a rest. It just wasn't the right time or place.

Four years later, when Herman Franks rested me in that game I've already described here, where we lost 4-3, another Bay-area columnist said:

> Surely you wouldn't say 40 ball games, less than one fourth of the schedule of 161 [sic] games, calls for a rest. And no one in his right sense would want to lift the star player from the lineup when the club is facing one of its strongest competitors.

So you can see, when you come right down to it, that it's the manager who gets it, more than me. No matter when or where or what the circumstances, the result always comes out the same. "Maybe it's all right to rest Willie—but not now." Sometimes I get to wondering: when *is* now?

So the manager catches it, more than me. Yet I catch it too. After we lost that 4-3 game, one of the afternoon papers the next day (we were playing a night game that night) had as its main headline:

HOLIDAY OVER, MAYS REJOINS GIANT LINEUP TONIGHT

And the subhead:

S. F. LOSES WITH
STAR IN DUGOUT

(Funny thing: I didn't start and we lost 4-3. Next night I started and we lost 14-1. Somebody using straight logic could have pointed out therefore that the Giants were 12 runs better off without me than with me.)

Of course it is a tribute to me that such disappointment, concern, attention, even bitterness can arise when I don't play. But behind this tribute is, I think, a common brand of thinking that says it is not asking too much of a $100,000 ballplayer that he play in every scheduled game. And even the fact that they make a point out of it when I don't play—even the ones who don't use the sarcastic phrases and words like "holiday"—is a form of criticism. To the bigots, a day off for me is a field day for them. Lazy—uppity—not a team man—too good for us poor whites who pay to see him—you name it, you'll hear it. By itself such criticism doesn't bother me. But I wonder if the headline writers stop to think all the time how they help feed this kind of thing.

I talked about this with a baseball writer once. "Most fans have longer working hours than you," he said to me. "Even writers covering the team, like myself. Five months of the year, you're off."

"What does that prove?" I said.

"It proves," he said, "that you get better than a hundred thousand dollars for maybe five hundred actual working hours a year, and that work consists of playing a game, and it comes down to that you get two hundred dollars an hour for playing a game, and when you just take a day off people are going to be bound to resent it."

"Do you resent it?" I asked him.

"Ah, Buck, don't be ridiculous," he said.

"I'm not being ridiculous," I said. "You just finished saying you work longer hours than me. But you took a vote in your chapter of the baseball writers the other day on whether the name of the official scorer should be announced and put in the box score, and you voted against it."

"What's that got to do with anything?"

"Just maybe that when you blow one in your job, you don't want forty-five thousand people sitting there—and maybe ten million more on television—knowing it was you."

He thought for a minute about that. Then he said, "No, that's still unfair. You're saying there's something different between your job and mine because you're in the public eye. But I'm in the public eye too. I've got a by-line and up to maybe half a million readers a day."

"And you've got an editor too," I said, "to catch your mistakes. Nobody ever caught one of mine."

Again he thought. Then he said, "How many mistakes do you make?"

"Too many," I said.

"But because you're trying," he said. "People realize that."

"Do you call it trying when you get picked off second with the bases loaded? When you're the tying run and walk off the field because you thought three were out? When you drop the simplest fly ball in history? When you swing at intentional ball four and pop it up?"

He began to laugh, because I have done all those things and he knew it. "Actually, though," he said to me now, "the reason I voted against publicizing the name of the official scorer was first because the fans ought to judge the decision in terms of what they saw, not who made it; and second because most scoring decisions, like earned runs, assists, credits for runs batted in, aren't announced on the spot to the fans anyway, and I think it gives a wrong impression of what the scorer actually does to announce him when most of the decisions he makes are going to be what you might call private anyway. If a real crucial call comes along, the fans are going to find out who made it regardless."

"That's fine," I said, "but if that's your choice, then all it means is you've got a choice. I don't."

It was a kind of meaningless discussion, and I guess neither of us made our points the way you could if you sat down and prepared for it in advance. But when they talk about your $100,000-plus salary, somebody should remember you didn't get to make that kind of money by resting. And that when you do rest, the purpose of it is to help you help the team—not that one day, but baseball doesn't consist of any one day.

It should be remembered, too, that the day of the iron man is gone. It is gone with the dead ball, the eight-team league, day-games-only, the easy and luxurious Pullman jumps. It is gone on account of bigger population and television and the dropping off of the minor leagues as a training ground.

Yet if all those are worse conditions, it is gone on account of better conditions too, because today the player doesn't have the old-time worry about protecting his job or being paid by the game or by the size of the crowd.

And have baseball skills suffered on this account?

In the relatively brief span of years that I have played, other outfielders, playing at the same time as me, have been Joe DiMaggio, Ted Williams, Mickey Mantle, Henry Aaron, Stan Musial.

I don't think too many in that list are going to miss the Hall of Fame, do you?

Not one of them was an "iron man."

Is there a time in baseball history, do you suppose, when you could choose from among *so many* outfielders, just for sheer plain brilliance at what they did for a living?

Early in May of 1965, I became 34 years old. In big-league baseball this is advanced middle age.

I have tuned in weekly television shows where it was announced that the master of ceremonies, who was younger than I was, was taking that week off for a "well-deserved rest." And you know what happened when that announcement was made?

The audience applauded.

Take not just myself, but Joe. D. and Ted and Mickey and Henry and Stan the Man. Think up any number of hospitals you want. Multiply that by the numbers of kids in those hospitals. The ones who are dying because medical science doesn't know how to stop it. The ones who have been hit by automobiles. Any other categories you like.

Then take a Joe D. or a Williams or a Mantle or an Aaron or a Musial. Join me in there with them. You don't read this in the papers. Pick not just the six of us, but 500 major-league ballplayers. This is the only place in this book I will refer to this.

It doesn't get out in the papers when players go visit in hospitals a lot of times, for two reasons. Number one is, we don't want the publicity. The one thing I've never seen happen in my life is a ballplayer who hired a press agent to set up hospital visits for him —or a ballplayer who said he'd go only if there were photographers going too.

The second reason is that there are not enough ballplayers to go around. For every kid you visit—who may never walk again, who may never move again, who may actually be dying and there's nothing anybody can do about it—there is another kid in another hospital somewhere just as bad off, maybe worse, whose parents read that you visited somewhere else, and all it does is hurt these people, because they're in no shape to understand why it was somebody else's kid and not theirs. They're so close to it, so heartsick themselves, that it's as wrong as it is useless to go up to them and say, "Look, there's only so much Willie Mays or Stan Musial or Ted Williams to go around."

My own hospital visits take place as much out of season as in. Maybe even more so, because people know there's no baseball schedule to get in the way so the number of requests becomes greater. And this may work out the right way, because the reason they want you there is that the kids look up to you, and the reason the kids look up to you is that you do well at baseball, and one of

the ways to make sure you do well at baseball is not to be sad
and down and depressed in your mind, and when you have come
away from a hospital room where the kid was in a coma and you
were the first person he recognized or spoke to since the accident
and his parents and the nurses broke down and cried in the room
because of what happened—and maybe because they knew only a
miracle would ever make the kid well again, or even keep him
from dying—then you have seen this with your own eyes, and you
know that either they think you were this miracle—or you know
they knew you weren't, but still the kid was happy to see you.
Sometimes, afterward by yourself, you cry some too.

And most times you don't go to hospitals just to see one kid.
It starts out that way, but then the floor nurse or somebody says,
"Mr. Mays, if you could just drop in to this other room down the
hall for a minute—there's a boy there who . . ." And then the nurse
there says, "The ward is right here, Mr. Mays. We've got three
youngsters who . . ."

And of course you go.

I don't want to talk about this much more. In fact, I don't
much want to talk about it at all. When you add it to everything
else, like your age and the strain of trying to live up to your own
standards in public day in and day out, I think, though, that a lot
of times the headlines that rag you because you didn't start that
day's game don't really stop to think about everything that's involved. Put it this way: the least famous ballplayer gets more requests to visit kids in the hospital than the most famous headline
writer.

I guess I run the risk of being charged that I'm too sensitive
about this. It's the old Hollywood line: never mind what they
say—the only time you got to worry is when they stop writing
about you.

But by now, I just don't care. They tell me I don't have to defend
myself. If that's true, then it also means, I think, that if from time
to time I want to defend myself, I've got that right too.

The funny side of it is that when they're after you for "rest-ing," they don't even see the occasional thing that could make them right.

That same week in May of '65 when I got my first rest of the season, and I had this cold and it was so my hands were shaking when I came to bat, I played a full game against the Cardinals and Curt Simmons was pitching for them and I got one long fly ball in the first inning and then nothing after that. It got so bad that the last time up, I put up a foul pop, and I was so disgusted, not looking better than that against this pitcher, that, for the first time in my life, I walked away from home plate without following the flight of the ball.

The catcher nearly dropped it. He held onto it, though, so I was out anyway.

But the ball wasn't foul when it came down. It was fair, right in front of the plate.

"Too bad you weren't looking, Twenty-four," Franks said to me, when I got back to the bench. "That ball came down fair."

The worst critic I've got in the press box didn't understand that for what it was. That I'd just walked away from a play. Otherwise he would have written next day wondering if I'd been fined.

Which wouldn't have been a bad guess. You can have reasons and you can have excuses. I had many reasons for what I did. But there was no excuse.

Maybe, even so, I am being sensitive. The honest-to-God truth is it doesn't bother me that much. It looks here like it does. But like I've said before, talking at book-length about myself isn't a usual thing for me either. The choice is to talk about these things or not to talk about them, and if I ruled things out that don't particularly bother me, this would be a lot shorter book than it is. The publishers said talk about all the things, and I'm setting out to do what they said. And there's nothing wrong with what they asked. Maybe it's like a house fly. Ordinarily, if somebody said to you, "What bothered you yesterday?" you'd think of the major

things or nothing at all. But if they said, "Take yourself minute by
minute yesterday—what bothered you?"—then you might remember
that you spent 12 minutes going after a fly with a rolled-up newspaper. And maybe that 12 minutes is more time than you spent
the whole day on any other single problem.

So, as you get into detail, you bring up things that ordinarily
you wouldn't think of. And when you rank one set of details against
another, then the one single problem that takes the longest to tell
and took the longest to solve—12 minutes with that fly—is bound
to look bigger, as a problem, than you or I know sensibly it ever
was. I don't know any way out of that, and I don't particularly
want to know. If you want to hit me as supersensitive in an area
just because it got more pages than something else, then I'm not
fixing to fight you about it.

Besides, there's "rest" and then there's "rest." You can be tired,
or you can be aching, and need a breather, and the fans won't
realize it a lot of times. To me it's the same as being actually hurt,
as far as how much you can really and truly help the ball club. But
when you are actually hurt, the time off you get may be the same
as far as you know, but the fans take it easier on you, because they
can see it for themselves.

Like in June of 1965, I pulled a leg muscle and was hobbled
pretty good, and they were putting me in right field and left field
a couple of games instead of center, and a couple of games I didn't
start at all.

Even then, it gets more attention than you'd rightly expect.
But you get some understanding with it. Here's a piece that Bob
Stevens of the *Chronicle* wrote, about a day I didn't start, a week
or so before the All-Star break in '65:

> Manager Herman Franks of the Giants looked across the
> clubhouse just before yesterday's game with the Cubs and
> shook his head.

"I'm scared," he said. "Just plumb damn scared. Feel a little sick, too."

Across the room, slumped in front of his locker, his back turned to the usual pre-game bustle, was the object of Franks' worry.

There was no spark in Willie Mays' eyes as he tried to read a paper. There was no bounce in Willie Mays' step as he suddenly wheeled and arose and headed toward the water cooler. There was no smile.

He was hurting—physically and mentally. A pulled groin muscle was tearing his insides out, and that cannot be challenged. Friday, for the first time in his career, the incomparable centerfielder of the Giants looked bad going back on a routine fly ball. He stumbled. His poetry in motion was gone. He didn't pound his glove.

He just plodded after the ball, got it and returned it to the infield. His throw was lacklustre, his return to his normal defensive post was made with head down, with feet dragging. "I just don't know what to do," continued Herman after Willie returned to his clubhouse stool. "I wish he wasn't here. I wish I couldn't see him. Because I shouldn't play him. But he's here and—damn, should I risk it or not?"

In Franks' lap was the lineup card. It read, Schofield, ss; M. Alou, lf; McCovey, 1b; Mays, cf . . . etc.

"I'd rather lose three games with him out of there," said Franks, "than play him and lose him for a month. Maybe longer. And if that happens we've had it. Yet, Willie insisted he play yesterday, which was against my better judgment, and he's ready to go today.

"I'll ask him, that's what I'll do. I'll ask him again, and again try to talk him out of it. Hey, Willie: c'mere, will ya a minute?"

Mays slouched over to Franks and they whispered.

"OK, Herm," said Mays. "If you say so."

Mays then went over to where Bob Shaw, who was to pitch, and second baseman Hal Lanier were dressing. The three of them talked awhile and Mays went back into the tiny manager's office in Wrigley Field.

"They just made the decision," said Mays. "They want me to play. How about playing me at first base? Don't have to move around so much there."

"Absolutely not," said Franks. "One quick move, another muscle tear, and we can close up shop for the rest of the summer."

"OK, Herm," sighed Willie. "You're the boss."

Mays headed for the trainer's room and a rubdown and Franks turned to coach Charlie Fox.

"Scratch Willie," said Herman, "and do it quickly so I won't change my mind. He wants to play. Shaw wants him to play. But I'd be a damn fool to play him."

Franks got up and began circling the clubhouse, nervously. He almost collided with Shaw.

"Sure," said Franks. "You'd like Willie in there for you, Bob. So would we all. But it just isn't worth the risk."

"You're right," said Shaw.

"Damn right I'm right," growled Franks, still trying to convince himself. "So he plays today and we win and he breaks down and we don't have him for another month. Makes sense, doesn't it, Bob?" "Yep," said Shaw.

Mays returned from the trainer's quarters, slumped down in his locker, resumed his reading. Franks looked over at him, gave one more glance to the batting order, shook his head and started for the dugout.

"I think I'm going to be sick," he said.

Like I say, you get some understanding in an article like that, but at the same time you can't get away from the feeling that the whole thing is getting more attention than it deserves. I probably "rested" more in the first three months of the 1965 season than I ever did over a similar period in previous seasons. Yet in our first 85 games of '65, I failed to start eight, and seven of those eight I was either actually sick or hurt, and four of those eight I got in before the game was over anyway.

The Saturday before the '65 All-Star game I banged my hip pretty good in a collision with the Philadelphia catcher. We both wound up in the hospital for X rays. It was in the first inning, and I left the game, but I could have—and would have—played the rest of it, but we got four runs and Marichal was pitching, and if you give Marichal a four-run lead you ain't about to lose. Gene Mauch said afterward, "The guy comes into home four feet in the air, kicks my catcher in the face, and still manages to touch home plate. He'll limp to the Hall of Fame." It was a nice tribute, but it wasn't quite what he said the moment the collision happened. At that time, he was telling the umpires I hadn't touched the plate at all.

But I did touch the plate, and both the catcher and I were lying there stunned, and he had to be carried off on a stretcher and the fans all booed. I guess they were booing me, although in Philadelphia you never can tell. When I got to the hospital I found out about him first, and he was all right, and the first or second game he was back in action after the All-Star break he got himself four hits.

Maybe I should say here, in case anybody's wondering, that I play to win. Physical contact is a part of baseball. In fact, I sometimes go out of my way to find that contact. If I'm coming into third base and there's a throw coming, and I've got the throw beat —maybe not by much, but I've got it beat—then I want my coach there to signal me where to slide. A lot of guys want to slide away from the ball, but in cases like that, I'm the opposite. I want to slide where the ball is. If I slide away from it, I can't kick it loose, can I?

But legitimate contact is one thing, and a man throwing at your head or your body is something else. I have never—I can say this honestly—invited contact with the number-one purpose of trying to hurt the other man. I wish all pitchers could say the same. Yet even here, it isn't all on one side or the other. To throw a duster is one thing. To retaliate is something else. I know some pitchers who if they actually hurt you with a pitch, they'd break down and cry, and they'd mean it too—the crying, I mean. They know what's in their hearts and I know what's in their hearts, and a lot of times I know they don't mean to do any real damage. And they know it. The trouble is, the ball doesn't always know it.

Every once in a while you read the bleeding-heart business where it's the Negro players who get thrown at most of the time. That may be. Good hitters do get thrown at more than bad hitters, and when you take the percentage of Negro players in the National League, then look at the percentage on the All-Star team each year, you have to conclude that some of the Negro players can hit pretty good. Some, like Frank Robinson, crowd the plate with their stance. Others, like Jim Hart, are supposed to be weak on the inside pitch. Others are a fraction slow getting out of the way. There are a lot of reasons why you can get hit.

It's also my feeling that right-handed hitters get thrown at more than left-handers. The obvious reason for this is that all catchers throw right-handed, which means their glove is to the side of the plate that's inside to a right-handed hitter, and I think it can be psychological with a pitcher. He may not think of it in so many words, but he must figure unconsciously that fewer pitches will get away from the catcher on his glove side than on his bare-hand side, so they can take more chances.

It can be a question, too, of who's coming up behind you and who's pitching for you that day. If the man behind you is a good hitter who's hitting good at the time, the pitcher may not be able to afford putting you on base. And if your pitcher has a reputation for protecting you by retaliating when their pitcher comes up, they may think twice too.

I remember one time Drysdale put me down and Marichal said next time he did it he was going to throw at his head. I know Marichal meant it. Anyway, before the next time they faced each other the league had a talk with them, and it came out in the papers there'd be a $1,000 fine if it happened. Which is a joke, because you know the club's going to pay the fine for the pitcher. That is, they let him pay the fine himself, then quietly give him the money. So I don't think a pitcher is worried about losing money, at least not so much as he worries about getting thrown at himself. Anyway, next time we met, Drysdale didn't put me down, and that was that.

Which isn't to say he may not do it next time. Obviously there's times when you can throw at a man and times when you can't. If you're tied in the last of the ninth and the bases are loaded and the count's 3-and-2, the pitcher isn't going to be throwing at you.

It was for this reason, among others, that in one of those four games I was talking about in the first three months of '65—where I didn't start, but got in at the end—they pinch-hit me for Hart with bases loaded and two out in the last of the ninth of a tie game against the Cardinals.

Ordinarily, when you're the home team and you've got the score tied and Jim Hart at bat, you don't take him out of the lineup and replace him with another right-handed hitter. The worst that happens is that he's out and you go into the 10th, so you save your Mays to pinch-hit farther down in the order, or if you fall behind in the score.

I might say at this point that 11 of my first 22 homers in '65 came on my first time at bat, which is a figure that means something, because over the years it's also true that I have a good pinch-hitting record.

Put those two facts together and you'll see that they spell the same thing. In fact, as I remember, when I hit home runs in six consecutive games, back in '54 I think it was, all six of them came on my first at bat in the game. And I haven't pinch-hit too much, but I can remember at least three pinch homers. Like I say, it all adds up. Some players need to see the pitcher, or have a few innings under their belt, before they can do their best hitting. This has never been true of me.

But when Herman Franks pinch-hit me for Hart, which on the face of it doesn't look like a sound move under the circumstances, the fact was that Gibson was pitching, and Gibson is the pitcher who broke Hart's shoulder with an inside pitch the year Hart came up. Now, with bases loaded, you knew Gibson wasn't going to be hitting a man intentionally so as to lose the game by forcing over the run. Still and all, Hart was supposed to have the weakness on the inside strike, and Gibson may have been the man who created that weakness in him to begin with. So Franks figured Gibson wouldn't want to throw me anything over the middle but could work the inside corner on Hart in a way he couldn't get away with if it was me. Also, like I said earlier in the book. Herman's a gambler. So he pinch-hit me.

What happened? I put up a silly fly ball to left field and the left fielder dropped it for an "impossible" error and the winning run came in.

Afterward, one of the St. Louis writers said, kind of bitter, "That Mays—he can beat you in so many ways!"

Anyway, there was that Saturday game at Philadelphia where both the catcher and I wound up leaving the field, and my right hip was bruised pretty good. But the next day, Sunday, it rained, and then we had the All-Star break. Mauch, who was managing the '65 National League All-Star team, batted me leadoff in the order. He said it was because he wanted me to get the most possible number of times at bat, and it worked out that way—I came up five times—but I know too that in the back of his mind he knew I was hurt and if it turned out I wasn't healing right, he could always get me up right away and then take me out, and the lead-off spot was best in the lineup for him if that's the way things turned out. We were visiting team, so this way I'd make my appearance in the box score and still not be in anybody's way if I couldn't play anymore after that. Turned out I went the whole game, and led off with a homer, and scored the winning run late in the game, so it was a good day, but I know what part of Mauch's thinking was and I'm grateful to him for it.

What with the All-Star rest, though—and by "rest" I mean the surrounding days off, because the collision at home plate happened on a Saturday and it rained Sunday and our next scheduled game wasn't till the next Friday night—I got some rest and a chance to have the hip heal. Otherwise, the eight games of our first 85 that I didn't start, and the four I didn't play in at all, might have been more in number.

Even at that, I'm not going to say I've turned lazy in my old age. In one way, when you've turned 34, you *are* old age where baseball is involved. The fact is that, excluding pitchers and the occasional acknowledged part-timer like a Duke Snider, I believe I've been the oldest playing Giant since before I was 30!

I'm just not ashamed that I sat out four games of our first 85 during the 1965 season. And one thing I will never understand is the critic who says that all Mays is interested in is hitting home runs and resting. If you hit a home run, you're not resting. If you're resting, you don't hit home runs. At this rate, I've got to get into heaven—my sins cancel each other out.

# 12

ALL THIS HAD to have a beginning somewhere, and I guess it got its start back there in May of '52, when I left for the Army with a lousy .236 batting average for 34 games that year, but the Giants were in first place.

Fact is, they were to finish second that season, only four games out, in which case you can't very well say my absence made too much difference. Somebody else's absence meant a great deal more, if you ask me.

We'd been in an exhibition game that spring at Denver, against the Indians, and Irvin was on first and went around to third when I hit a single behind him. And he slid in there and broke his ankle.

I guess a couple of guys got to him before I did, but I was there —as fast as I ever ran in my life—and when I saw what had happened to him, I broke out crying. This was not only a fine ballplayer—this was my friend, my roommate, the guy who looked out for me. I knew the right thing was to drive a Pontiac. How'd I know? Because Irvin drove a Pontiac. If he wanted to play Boss of the Room, we played Boss of the Room. If he wanted to eat somewhere that's where we ate. If I wanted to take out a girl on a date, she knew she'd have to meet him first, get his okay.

One time we got to Cincinnati and there was a phone message for me. All it left was a girl's first name and a number. Irvin got the message and threw it out and didn't tell me about it for three weeks.

146

(Dark and Stanky, who used to room together, once had two girls come and knock on the door of their hotel room. You never saw a door slammed in two girls' faces so fast in your life. You don't have to be a monk about it, but I'll always remember Bob Hope's line in one of those *Road* pictures with Crosby, and I've always subscribed to it: "I'm not a-lookin' for trouble, but if trouble comes a-lookin' for me, I'm a-gonna be mighty hard to find!")

Anyway, Irvin had led the league in 1951 in runs batted in, and we won 96 games over the regular 154-game stretch. In 1952, without him, the Giants won 92 games over the same number of games. Yet nobody ever brought up his name. Everybody said, "They miss Mays . . . they miss Mays . . . they miss Mays. . . ."

The strange thing was, I'm not just talking about the fans. The Giants got so they were talking the same way. I always thought ballplayers see things one way and writers and fans see it another, but Cookie Lavagetto, who's seen twice the baseball I have, tells me he thinks the writers and fans can see things a certain way till it gets to the point where the ballplayers start thinking the same way. I think maybe he's got a point.

The worst bunch of all was the pitchers. Anything that went to the outfield, in '52 and '53 when I wasn't there, anything that went in for the long hit, they'd come in to the bench after the inning saying, "Willie would've had it." It's a nice compliment, but maybe they were bailing out just a little too. After all, I wasn't there to prove I *wouldn't* have had it.

And the feeling on the club was different—so I'm told. At one point in September, the '52 club was actually closer to the Dodgers than the '51 club had been—but there wasn't the same "feel." In those final couple of weeks, Durocher actually started a rookie, even though a top man—Hearn—was rested and ready to go, and a couple of writers came awful close to accusing Leo of not trying to win.

In '53 it was even worse. Nothing went right. Like I said, the ball

club finished 35 games out, and at the end there Leo was letting
his players take turns managing the club.

Me, meanwhile, I was at Camp Eustis, Virginia. In the Army you
do what your company commander says. My company commander
said I should play baseball. He didn't make a special case out of
me. He told Vern Law and Karl Olson the same thing, and they
were on our team. We didn't demand special duty in Korea, so we
wound up playing baseball. If we had demanded special duty
in Korea, we still would have wound up playing baseball. If you
didn't feel like soldiering, they didn't mind, but if you didn't feel
like playing that day, the got mad as hell. I'm just saying what
it was. I'm not mad at them. If everything in an army was the way
it should be, there wouldn't be any army to begin with, because
people would be too fair to need wars or protection. I guess that
applies to my draft board too. I had 11 dependents, but I was
healthy, and I suppose they thought they'd look bad if they de-
ferred Willie Mays. To my knowledge, in any event, Selective Service in Washington doesn't take what the draft board in Birmingham
does as a model for what should be done everywhere.

So I have no pride in my Army career. But I have no apologies
for it either. I did what the man said, and when they needed my
car they could have that too. So everybody came through just fine,
and I played in something like 180 games in the service.

Also, I played basketball in the service, and one time I sprained
my ankle while I was doing it. Another time, playing baseball, I
stole a base with our team 'way out in front.

I remember those two occasions, because each time—don't tell
me how he found out, but he knew—I got a call from Donald
Duck. Durocher was on the other end, sputtering and fuming and
asking me was I out of my ———— ———— mind.

What I didn't tell him on the phone, either time, was that I
was working on something. They'd assigned me to the physical-
training department at Camp Eustis, and put me on instruction
work, and there was this one boy there who thought the way to

catch a fly ball was to hold his glove like he was taking out an old railroad watch and looking at it.

I said to him, "You gotta be crazy."

"Why?" he said.

"Because," I said, "only way to catch a routine fly ball is hold the glove up in front of your eyes."

"Why?"

"Because," I said, "that way you never lose sight of the ball."

"I don't understand that," he said.

"Here, let me show you," I said. "Throw me some high flies."

I trotted out about 100 feet away from him, and he threw me a routine fly ball. I caught it with my glove up in front of me.

"See?" I said.

"Try it my way," he called, and threw me another.

I tried it his way, with my glove down around my belly button, and I caught it that way too.

"Doesn't make any difference, does it?" he said.

"Sure it makes a difference."

"Try it again. Show me."

He threw it again. I caught it again.

This time I noticed something. If I caught it out in front of my face, like I always had before, my body could be in any one of a number of positions—my feet, too.

But if I caught it down by my belt buckle, my body automatically took up what for me was the rightest, most comfortable stance.

"Throw me another!" I called.

I tried it again. I tried six of them. Next game we played, I tried it. And there was no getting around it. For me, the one way I I knew was the wrong way was the most comfortable, the most perfect. I could never be off balance, catching a ball that way.

I still knew it was wrong—for other people. I still realized, obviously, that there were balls you *couldn't* catch that way—

line drives, deep balls to either side, short flies, balls over your head.

But the fact remained, a lot of balls *could* be caught that way. And then and there was born the Mays "basket catch."

It was only later that I came to understand that there was some show business connected with it too. Because, I tried to tell the guy to begin with, if you catch it that way your eye isn't on the ball when it comes down into the mitt. That gives it a sense of risk, of danger. And for most players, that's exactly what's wrong with it.

For me, though, I've dropped two balls that way in my major-league career. Through some freak, I feel surer that way than the more accepted way. Some prize baseball statistician told me last year my "error factor" on plays where I used that catch was something of the nature of .0006 percent.

To my knowledge, there's only one other guy in the world who's using that kind of catch today, with the specific approval of a baseball instructor.

That's the guy I was instructing that day at Eustis.

I rejoined the Giants on my discharge from the Army, at Phoenix, where they were training, in March of 1954.

The Giants sent Frank Forbes, a Negro scout for the club, down to pick me up at the gate of Camp Eustis and drive me to Washington, from where we'd get a plan to Phoenix. It was an unexpectedly cold day, and Forbes lent me his overcoat, then stuffed a couple of newspapers inside his shirt to keep himself warm. So, dressed that way, the two of us drove up to the Washington airport. That was the same day some revolutionists had shot up the House of Representatives. A couple of police gave us a funny time for a couple of minutes.

(My greatest "brush" with the police, though, happened years later, in San Francisco, when Lee Mendelson, that television producer I was talking about, waited at the wheel of my car for me one day when I went into the bank for a minute. A cop came along and said to Mendelson, "All right—move it." "But I'm waiting for Willie Mays," he said. "I don't care if you're waiting for Jesus Christ," the cop said. "Move the car.")

We landed at Phoenix at dinnertime and checked in at the Adams Hotel, and I was tired, and had supper in the room and went right to sleep. Next morning I drove out to the old ball park there on Mohave Street, south of the tracks about two miles along Central Avenue from the hotel.

I walked into the clubhouse, and all the guys were there, only none of them seemed to notice me.

"Name?" Logan, the clubhouse man, said to me.

"New man?" Doc Bowman said.

"Hey!" I yelled. "I'm here!"

"We'll give you a uniform," Logan said. "Let's see—what's your name—Mays?" He consulted a clipboard. "All right. You're number twenty-four. Get dressed and go out and hit. Extra men hit first."

"*Extra* men . . . ?"

"You weren't here last year, were you?"

"Hey, Logan! It's *me!*"

He consulted the clipboard again. "You're supposed to be out there hitting right now. You're late. Skipper isn't going to like that."

I was getting undressed and getting dressed and shouting all at once. I even left my shorts on and put my jockstrap on over them. A couple of the other guys were laughing. I was screaming.

Sal Maglie came clomping into the room. He had a rubber shirt on and the sweat was pouring off of him. He threw me a brief look, then turned to Logan. "Who's this? Some new busher?"

"Maglie!" I yelled. "It's *me!*"

He shrugged and turned away.

I tied my shoes and grabbed my bat and went out of there, down the wooden-cleat runway, like at a bathhouse at the beach, and out onto the field.

Durocher was standing at the batting cage.

He stared at me.

"What's your number?"

"Twenty-four."

"You hit in a minute."

"Listen, Leo," I said, "what the hell goes on here?"

But he wasn't paying any attention.

Whoever was hitting got out of the cage, and I busted my way in. I dug in, lined up on the first pitch.

And I hit it.

I hit it downtown.

The thing cleared a palm tree back of the fence in left-center.

Westrum was doing the catching.

"Hey," he said, mildly, "you're supposed to bunt the first one."

"You're supposed to get out of the cage, too, so I *can* bunt it," I said.

"Oh, I love a fresh-ass busher," he said.

Just back of the cage, I became aware, there was a hot, loud argument going on.

"I say you can drink in this weather and you can play ball in this weather. Only problem is doing both."

It was a ballplayer I'd never seen before.

I got back in the batter's box. "Curve ball."

The pitcher threw a curve.

I hit it downtown. Out past the other palm tree, the one closer to the line.

"If you want to drink," this player behind me was saying, "drink. You want to play, play. The trick is doing both, like I say."

I said to Westrum, "Who's that?"

He said, "Who're you?"

"Willie Mays."

"He's Dusty Rhodes."

Then the photographers and the newspapermen were there, and so was Irvin—a healed, healthy, happy Irvin—and Durocher and

Maglie and Jansen and Dark, and Mueller and the others (no Bobby Thomson, though—him, they'd traded to what used to be Boston but what now was Milwaukee).

And Mr. Henry. Henry Thompson. "Henry!" I appealed to him. "It's spring! Same as ever!"

He nodded. "That's right. Spring. Same as ever. Eight ———— ———— out for my job!"

I was home.

# 13

THE 1954 GIANTS.

The greatest club that ever took the field, anywhere, anytime.

Don't shoot me with any of that sentimental jazz that I never saw the '29 Seals, or the Redbirds in the Association or the Bears in the International League. Don't tell me I didn't see the 1938 Yankees.

All we won, that year in 1954, was 97 games.

But our pitchers had 19 shutouts, and 22 more games in which the other team was held to one run.

As a staff, they turned in 64 games in which the other club was held to two runs or fewer.

Pitching's the main thing, of course, but maybe I can use a few statistics on hitting here too. The top two hitters in the league for '54, one at .345 and the other at .342, were both Giants.

Pinch hitting? I wish I had the full set of statistics on it. All I can remember is not the singles or doubles or triples or walks, but the pinch home runs.

Pinch home runs?

The Giants of 1954 had *10* pinch homers!

Nine of them won ball games.

I can remember that bullpen—Wilhelm and Grissom and McCall —like it was yesterday.

I can remember Dark, kicking the dirt back of a runner at second base. Fans think this is just a meaningless thing. No way to pick the man off second. And that's true—you can't pick him off second.

154

But you can have him leaning that way, and if the next man gets a single, then the way that runner on second was leaning is the difference between whether he scores on the hit or only gets to third. (In that case, he only got to third. We were ahead 1-0 at the time. And that was the final score of the game.)

Out of our season's series with each of the other clubs in the National League, we beat the Phils 16 out of 22, 15 each from the Cubs and Reds, 14 from the Pirates, 12 each from the Braves and Cards. We beat the Dodgers 13 out of 22. In other words, in a league where anybody could and did beat anybody else, we beat everybody.

The Cleveland Indians, that year's American League pennant winners, won a record 111 games in their league. But in that league there were only two other teams—the Yankees and the White Sox —who finished above .500, and the best the Indians could do with them on the season was an 11-11 split with each.

(Don't forget, too, the Yanks and White Sox were in opposite divisions of the league, one East, one West. What does that mean? It means that the Indians never had to play the two of them one after another, without any kind of break. So Cleveland could suit up its pitching without any problems.)

Funniest of all, the Indians were training in Tucson while we were training in Phoenix, so we played them all the time. Sometimes, in exhibition games, you're leveling. Sometimes you're not. All I know is, whenever we were leveling, we kicked the living george harrison out of them.

All of this leads up to something else: by the time the two of us squared off in the World Series, they were officially 8-5 favorites, besides being favored for each single game of the Series. Unofficially, the odds were 2-1. Between friends, it was as much as 13-5.

Underdogs like that, we not only beat them, we beat them four straight. We beat them without ever looking back. You could almost say, and with truth, we beat them without trying.

In a way, I believe it was the worst setback baseball had received since the Black Sox scandal. Because the smart money was betting the Giants. It wasn't *planned* money, it wasn't *fixed* money, but if you took what was in front of your eyes and took the Giants to win the Series at 13-5, and the Giants to win each game of the Series, at 7-5 each, then you weren't going to wind up losing money.

That season, Durocher could and did gamble—like a madman, except he had the horses. He pinch-hit Rhodes one time in the 13th, pinch-hit him for our last catcher, and when Rhodes said, "What if we're still tied going into the 14th—who catches?" Durocher said one word: "You." Rhodes singled home the winning run.

Durocher let Wilhelm bat for himself, another game. This caused a violent conference on the part of the other team. Everybody thought (and so the radio and the newspapers reported) that the extended discussion was to go over the double steal, because we had men on first and third at the time. Truth is, the double steal had nothing to do with it. The other team was conferring for the simple reason that they'd never seen Wilhelm bat before, and they didn't know how to pitch to him. Wilhelm singled home the winning run.

And Durocher came to me, after I'd had 36 home runs and it was still July, and he said one of the strangest things I ever heard.

"Buck," he said, "I want you to stop hitting homers."

I stared at him.

"I mean it," he said. "What are you hitting now?"

".316," I said.

"You can put thirty points on that average between now and the end of the season," he said.

"The hell I can."

"The hell you can't. Stop hitting homers—I mean, stop swinging for them. The reason you're hitting .316 instead of .340 is that the ones that don't get out of the park are being caught. Ever think of that?"

I kept staring at him. "What do I do instead?"

"Go to right field."

"What'll that do?"

"When you hear what I've got to say next, it'll do plenty."

"What've you got to say next?"

"I'm moving you up to third in the batting order. Now you can get on. You can run. You can spread the defense. And God knows there's hitters coming up behind you that can get you around. It means more runs for us, Willie. That's why I'm asking it."

Neither one of us brought up the possibiliy that if I'd kept on swinging for homers I could have broken Babe Ruth's record. We didn't bring it up not because we were trying to suppress it, but because neither of us had ever seriously considered it to begin with —even though the newspapermen, who by now were jumping into the shower with me for extra interviews, had written about little else since June.

I said, "Okay, Skip. I'll try it."

I tried it. And from that point on, I hit only five homers the rest of the season—and one of those was inside the park, and two others were after we knew we had the pennant.

It's true in a way to say that homers come when you're not swinging for them. But it's equally true to say that homers come when you *are* swinging for them. That 1954 record of mine is, to my mind, all-time proof that there's a difference. Thirty-six till the man said stop trying. Then, from there on, just five, only two of which really counted. Actually, only one of them counted. The other was the homer I've already told about, off Haddix's change-up, and that was in a game where we were hopelessly behind.

And Leo was right. My batting average did go up.

To the point where, although we clinched the pennant with a week still to go, he had to keep playing me. Mueller and I, and Snider of the Dodgers, were locked in a fight for the National League batting title, and it wouldn't have looked good if anybody rested.

Going into the final Sunday of the season, the hitting situation was:

|         | AB  | H   | B.A.  |
|---------|-----|-----|-------|
| Mueller | 613 | 210 | .3426 |
| Snider  | 581 | 199 | .3425 |
| Mays    | 561 | 192 | .3422 |

Why had I come up fewer times than the other two? A simple case of batting-order mathematics. It wasn't till late in the season that Durocher moved me up to third in the order. Like I've covered earlier in this book, the sooner you bat the more chances you get.

Anyway, that last day I was 3-for-4 off of Roberts; Mueller was 2-for-6; Snider was 0-for-3 against Jake Thies of Pittsburgh. So the final reading was:

|         | AB  | H   | B.A. |
|---------|-----|-----|------|
| Mays    | 565 | 195 | .345 |
| Mueller | 619 | 212 | .342 |
| Snider  | 584 | 199 | .341 |

We came back from Philadelphia, and I was booked on two television shows in the same hour—"The Ed Sullivan Show" and "The Colgate Hour" on a rival network. All I remember is shuttling from the two studios, and Sullivan asking me, "What does it feel like beating out your own teammate for the National League batting crown?"

To which, I replied: "If it hadn't of been me I would have wanted it to be him."

Ask a stupid question, get a stupid answer. Isn't that how the old saying goes?

That was a club, the '54 Giants—Lockman at first, Davey Williams at second, Dark at short, Hank Thompson at third; Mueller in right, me in center, Irvin in left. Of the three of us in the outfield, Mueller was perhaps the best hitter that year, but the least accomplished fielder. The word from Leo was, anything I could handle out there, I should take, whether it was in Mueller's territory or not. And Mueller knew it, and he wasn't pleased—why should he have been?—the way he lost out on the hitting championship the last day of the season.

Anyway, next day, when we assembled at the Polo Grounds for an informal practice and having the team picture took, he passed me in the clubhouse while I was tying my shoe and said, sort of out of the side of his mouth, "Hey, Willie, is it true you're the greatest center fielder in history?"

"Greatest right fielder too," I said, and went on tying my shoe.

Nobody hated anybody else on that '54 Giant club. But it wasn't exactly a Jeannette MacDonald–Nelson Eddy picture either. Fact is, there were at least four guys who disliked Durocher. But he got them to play for him.

Like I say, that '54 Giant club was something. Westrum, the catcher, hit under .200 for the year, but there wasn't a better man at the position, all around—and I mean hitting, too, when it counted —in all baseball.

As for pitching—well, for openers there was a guy who'd pitched against me in the Army, name of John Antonelli. And Maglie. And Ruben Gomez. And Hearn. And a left-hander named Don Liddle. And the others, including the three relief pitchers I've already mentioned—Whilhelm, McCall, and Grissom.

The pinch hitters were mainly Rhodes and Bobby Hofman, but Bill Taylor and Hoot Evers—the latter only lasted a couple of weeks with us, but he won us a couple of ball games—were in there too.

New York City staged a ticker-tape parade up lower Broadway for that club. The Yankees in all their lives, with all the pennants they'd ever won, never got a ticker-tape parade—let alone one that took place not after they won the Series, but before!

Dark and I rode together in the lead car of the parade, him as team captain, me as batting champion, and I'll never forget Leo on the steps of City Hall, when they gave him the microphone.

"I never threw a ball all year," he said. "I never picked one up. I never hit one. The credit goes to these men, not to me."

And the people cheered him, and we loved him, even though under our breaths we were still kidding, like we had been all season.

"Knock with five, Leo," one of us said, and somebody else: "If you didn't do nothing, why are you making a speech?"

So rough and tough—and damn good—was that team of '54 that even the mistakes paid off.

Take the first game of the World Series, for instance. In one of the very first innings, Mueller, in right field, picked up a single somebody'd hit and tried the old Mel Ott trick of throwing *back* of the runner, sending the ball back to first after he'd made his turn. For some reason—mainly, I think, the shape of the ball park—this is a play that used to work best of all at the Polo Grounds.

Anyway, everything was fine except Mueller threw the ball away and the runner wound up on second on the error.

You'd think this might have encouraged the Indians, but I'll swear all it did was make them cautious. They weren't much by way of being a running team anyway, and you could just see them saying to themselves, "If Mueller'll try that kind of a play what'll those other two outfielders try?"

Maybe I'm overguessing it. I do know that was the last extra base an Indian took the whole series long. . . . I mean by gambling or overturning or something like that. If the Giants had got $250 for every Cleveland runner left on base in just the four games of that Series, it would have been the richest winner's share in all history.

It was in that first game of the '54 Series, too, that I made what people have called, ever since, "The Catch." This was the one on Vic Wertz. Like "The Throw" on Cox that time in '51, this was

what you could call a "money play"—even more so, for this one happened in the World Series, and I guess up to 50 million people
saw it.

Also—let's face it—the '54 Series was almost completely lacking
in suspense. After that first game, we just kept pulling farther and
farther in front. It got so when they went to put together the
annual movie of the World Series, to show at clubs and lodges
and banquets and the like, they kept cutting back to the shot of
me catching the ball off of Wertz, not because it was that great a
play but because there wasn't anything else, in the way of a single
high point, to show.

It was a 2-2 ball game going into the top of the eighth. Doby
walked to lead it off for them, then Rosen beat out an infield hit.

Wertz was up next for them. He'd already had a triple and two
singles, so Leo brought in the left-handed Liddle to pitch to him,
and no doubt of it—Wertz hit the ball a long way. But it was to
straight center in the Polo Grounds, and you could hit 'em a long
way to straight center at the Polo Grounds.

I turned my back and ran, looked over my shoulder once to gauge
the flight of the ball, then kept running. I caught it the way a football end catches a long leading pass. Then I spun and threw
—yes, my cap fell off—and Davey Williams had come out to
take the relay, and on the sequence Doby managed to tag and go to
third, while Rosen didn't go anywhere. If anything, I think the throw
was the remarkable thing, because the ball did get back there in a
hurry, and I was a good 450 feet out when I caught it.

As for there being anything difficult about the catch, though,
the answer is there wasn't. Any ball you go a long way for is exciting to the fans in the stands, because they're not looking at you
when you get your jump on it—at that moment, they're looking at
the hitter. But I'd gotten the good jump, and I had running room,
and the ball stayed up for me. I didn't have to pick it off the grass,
I didn't have to avoid another fielder, I didn't have to crash the

wall, I didn't have to jump in the air, I didn't have to gauge the wind (there was none) or some eccentric thing the ball itself did (it didn't rise, fall, curve, swerve, or bend too much).

I doubt there's a day goes by in the big leagues but some out-fielder doesn't make a more difficult play than I did on that Wertz ball. What's always amused me slightly is that two innings later, in the 10th—we did get out of that eighth inning unscored on, another reason people remember my catch; if they'd gone on and made a batch of runs anyway, nobody'd recall it today—anyway, in the 10th, Wertz got himself his fourth hit of the day, a wicked line shot to left-center. By now Grissom was pitching, and on the pitch before, Wertz came as close to a wrong-field homer as you can come and not get it: he slammed it a country mile upstairs to left, foul by inches. And me, like a complete fool, I still didn't guess what Grissom was doing, making Wertz want to go to the off field, so I didn't move over from right-center, and when he did hit the ball to left-center, I was just plain out of position. Maglie bawled the socks off of me after the game for it and all I could say was, "You're right, Sal; you're right."

The ball, anyway, was headed for the deepest left-center corner, over by the bullpen, which was inside-the-park-homer territory for a lot of hitters at the Polo Grounds, and with just plain speed I got there in time to cut it off backhanded on a wicked low skip and hold him to a double. And that was a *real* play, one I'm proud of even though it was my own fault for not moving closer to left when I saw how Grissom was pitching him. Yet nobody noticed it, and that led to another Mays "observation"—a quote of mine—and this one, I *did* say: "It ain't nothing 'less you catch it."

We got out of that inning, too, and in the bottom of the 10th I came up with one out and nobody on. Cleveland had changed catchers that inning, and I noticed that when the new one threw to second before we came up, the throw went in on the bounce. At that point, I asked Leo would it be all right if I stole if I got on. (Not all bases are stolen on the pitcher—remember what we were saying some pages back?) He said, "Yeah," and I got a walk and went down to second, and sure enough, the throw bounced in and I had it beat. Now Lopez decided to put the force on by walking Thompson intentionally, plus it would give him the right-handed Irvin for Lemon to pitch to. So—as he'd done time after time during the regular season—Durocher decked Irvin and called on Rhodes to bat for him.

(First time Leo'd done that, it cost the Dodgers a ball game, and afterward Campanella said in the papers, "Any club that's gotta pinch-hit for Irvin must be hurting." Sure, Campy, sure. We were hurting all over that way.)

And Rhodes pulled a real dinky fly ball that clanged off the facade in right field—your daughter throws a ball farther than he hit that one—and Napp, the umpire at second base, waved his hand around his head like he was going to lasso a horse, meaning home run, and we had it won, 5-2.

Next day, Al Smith hit Antonelli's first pitch for a home run, and Cleveland was to leave 13 men on base, just as they did the first game. Which doesn't mean Antonelli was pitching a bad game. He struck out nine, and I heard afterward that Joe DiMaggio— gray at the temples now, dignified, polished—took a look at the pitch John used to strike out Westlake in the fifth inning and turned to Tom Meany, who was sitting with him, and struck the side of his face with his hand and said, *"Mama mia!"*

Some magazine had come out with what they said was the top-secret scouting "book" on the World Series hitters. They should have seen the book we *really* had. I remember what it said about Doby, for instance. "Throw the first one at his knees. If that don't work, throw the next one at his neck. After that he won't bother you." And we did and he didn't.

Meanwhile, we were 12 up, 12 down against Early Wynn till the bottom of the fifth. Then I got a walk, Thompson singled to center to send me to third, here came Rhodes batting for Irvin ("They must be hurting," Campy had said) and he singled to center. We got another run that inning to lead 2-1, and Rhodes, who was left in the game, hit a homer next time up, so we won it 3-1. This wasn't any Chinese homer either. He busted it.

At Cleveland, third game, I singled home a run for us in the first inning, and of those 71,555 people there, I think there wasn't one who didn't know what was going to happen in this World Series.

Came the top of the third—we were ahead 1-0—and Dark singled to center. Mueller sent him to third with a hit-and-run single to *left* field! I bounced one to Rosen at third and Dark hung himself up long enough so on the sequence Mueller got to third and I got to second. That called for the automatic walk to Thompson to load the bases. Here came Dusty Rhodes to hit for Irvin ("They must be hurting," Campy had said) and singled for two runs.

We won it 6-2. To this point, we'd scored 14 runs to their five. They'd had 37 base runers to our 28.

I remember three things about the fourth game of that Series. First, I remember the second inning. Because Thompson led it off with a walk, and now everybody in the place looked into the Giant dugout to see whether Rhodes would be coming up for Irvin. By "everybody," I include Irvin himself.

But nothing happened. So Monte shrugged, went up to bat for himself, and doubled to left-center.

Top of the fifth, we're leading 3-0, Dark and Mueller single, I walk, Thompson walks to force over a run. Again everybody including Irvin looks for Rhodes, but Leo just sits there grinning. Irvin bats for Irvin and hits a two-run single. By the time the inning's over, we're ahead 7-0.

We got a little careless after that—maybe we were *too* relaxed. They got four runs, and now it was 7-4 in the last of the eighth, with Wilhelm, the knuckleballer, throwing for us by now. He started off the inning by striking out Avila, the American League batting champion. At the point were Avila swung and missed, the ball was in the strike zone. Then suddenly the ball did something. Don't ask me what, but in the space of about 12 inches it suddenly rose straight up, then sailed straight back over Westrum's shoulder. Avila ran to first, and they couldn't even give Wes an error on it. It had to be scored as a wild pitch—that's how crazy the ball acted.

At this point, Doby flied out to me in center and Rosen singled to left, but the pitches were acting as crazy as you ever saw, and now Westrum called time and signaled to Leo to come out of the dugout.

Out came Leo. "What's the matter?" he said to Wes. "You want a new pitcher?"

"No," said Westrum, "I want a new catcher. I'm not going to set any record for passed balls in a World Series. He's not only throwing the knuckler, I think he's spitting on it!"

Durocher and Dark started to break up laughing. Then Leo signaled to the bullpen, and Antonelli come in, struck out the next two men to end the inning, polished them off in the ninth, and that was that.

The newspapermen were disappointed we didn't whoop it up more than we did in the clubhouse.

The one final thing I remember was on the plane headed back for New York. Somebody handed me a glass and said, "Say when, Willie."

"What is it?" I said.

"Champagne," he said.

"When," I said.

"What's wrong with you?" he said.

"I had it two weeks ago when we clinched the pennant," I said.

"You got to learn to like it," the man said.

"No I don't," I said. "Maybe if I play for the Yankees I got to learn to like it."

"Why you got to be so cynical?" he said.

"Go get your card punched by Dark," I said. "At least I tried the stuff. All he'll drink is Pepsi-Cola."

"I think he's got stock in Pepsi-Cola."

"Then get me stock in Piper-Heidsieck."

# 14

I WAS NAMED most valuable athlete of 1954 in the Associated Press poll—the same year man broke the four-minute mile for the first time. I was the National League's most valuable. I won trophies and belts and watches and who knows what else. I made the banquet circuit and the television circuit, sometimes together with Leo—who by now had a Dusty Rhodes routine that I've heard 200 times, but it still flattens me when Leo does it (I'm not sure it quite flattened Dusty)—and sometimes by myself. The Giants put my salary up past $25,000 for 1955—not bad for a man entering his second full season in the majors.

And everywhere I went they wanted to hear the same thing.

What about the catch on Wertz?

The Catch. The Catch.

"I don't rate 'em—I just catch 'em." That's what I'm supposed to have said. I never did say it, but now I almost wish I had.

In no special order, let me say I made one off Willie Jones, one off Bobby Morgan, one off Roberto Clemente—I ran three miles for that one, and cracked off the wall too—and a truly great one off Tommy Davis in L.A., only Duffalo (our pitcher) had thrown a bad pitch so Davis hit it to the wrong field. I actually went out of the ball park at Candlestick to pull a homer back in off of Musial (one of the writers described it as climbing 11 feet up an eight-foot fence, which is close to what it actually was).

All these in different years, at different times, in different situations. DiMaggio told me one of his greatest catches was off Campanella in an exhibition game, yet it hurt him—what they said about it, I mean.

"It was just before my last season," Joe D. told me. "They wrote it was a hell of a catch for an old man. Let me tell you something, Will, it was a hell of a catch for anybody."

I made a catch off Amaro in Philadelphia in '64 that made the fans there come roaring to their feet. Another, same road trip, in Cincinnati, and the roaring was even louder. You know you've done something, when you hear it from the enemy fans.

And I could go on and on, but it wouldn't mean anything. Let me say just this: I can remember one ball I caught that I never hoped to catch. Maybe that should define it as "greatest." It was off Ed Bouchee of the Cubs, at Candlestick in 1960. He hit a sharp liner, good depth, to right-center. I ran to cut it off, knowing that, the way we were playing him, I could afford that luxury. If it was past me, the right fielder, going deeper, would play it off the fence.

And it was past me—not only past me, but bending ever farther away from me in the wind.

At the last minute, I literally stuck out the glove and snatched it out of the air when it was past me. My whole body had cooperated. Charley Doherty, the San Francisco *Examiner* photographer, has a picture of that catch, and it shows me coming down on my left foot at the moment of the catch—which, going to my own left, gives me up to a yard's extra reach.

This, again, is what they call instinct. I have it. You do too. Remember when you were a kid and tried the running broad jump? You *instinctively* hit the push-off board with your favorite foot, no matter how far away you started from, no matter how fast you ran, no matter which foot you started on. It's nothing special. More people have it than realize it.

If I have to pick a number-one catch—and I'd rather not—I've got to go for that one on Bouchee. All the others, no matter how vital the situation or how terrible the complications, have come down to being there when the ball was. This one, though—the ball was there first and I still caught it.

The nicest tribute ever paid to my fielding ability came, I think, from Clete Boyer, the Yankee third baseman in the '62 World Series. Here again is a case of a play nobody remembers. He hit a slicing shot to right-center and I caught it, and that was that. But later, he said an awful nice thing. The papers quoted him on it. He said, "I hit the ball and I said to myself, 'What's the condition of the outfield?' By that, I was measuring how far it would roll when it hit and whether I'd get a double out of it or a triple. And then, running toward first base, I said to myself, 'Oh, hell, *he's* out there.' And without even looking, I slowed down. And when I looked up, he was lobbing the ball back to the infield after the catch. And none of those San Francisco fans even gave him a cheer, outside of what you'd normally hear for any outfield put-out. I guess they expected it same way I did."

I feel myself that my fielding has always been my greatest contribution. This may sound ridiculous from somebody who's zeroing in on Mel Ott's home-run record, from the first man in history who ever hit at least 30 homers and stole 30 bases in the same season (I've done that twice), from the only man who ever stole 200 bases and hit 200 homers (I passed both those levels years ago), from the all time slugging-average leader, present or past, in National League history, from the man who Ty Cobb said "restored the art of base-running to the game."

But I can't run if I'm not getting on base. When I'm getting on base, I can catch the ball. When I'm not getting on base, I can still catch the ball. Manager Bill Rigney, talking to his rookie infielders in the spring of '57, paid me a tribute too. He said to them, "If they hit it to Twenty-four, you go to a base. Be there, in case he throws it to you. Never mind wondering whether he *should* throw it to you. Just be there."

I believe I can help the ball club in center field whether I'm hitting or not. I've become a step slower over the years, probably, but I think I've more than made up for that in knowing where to play hitters, how to gauge weather and wind and ground conditions and base runners' habits, and all the rest of it. Actually, at one all-out burst of speed, I'm not sure I *am* any slower than before. The difference now is, I rate myself.

Through 1964, I used to take outfield practice, then infield practice, before a game. In 1965, I didn't take either. There was a time when I'd challenge any ball that was hit. Now, if we're ahead six runs or behind six runs, I play it easier. There was a time when I wanted any ball I could get to. Now, I want to let the other fielders handle it if they've got a chance at it—particularly the kids. Maybe not always in a key moment in a key ball game—then I may still want the ball for myself, not because I've earned that right or because I can handle it best of all, but also because I don't want a kid dropping a key ball that I could have had. When I was young, other outfielders protected me. It's my job now.

Having used both Rawlings and MacGregor gloves, I am not going to pretend there is one make, and only one, that suits me best. I wear my glove almost off my hand, because the farther it is off your hand, the farther your reach. But that goes to the question of how much control you have. I think youngsters should practice fingertip control. But it should never be a question of keeping your hand out of the glove simply to keep the ball from hurting when it hits. You can quickly learn to "give" so even the hardest shot won't damage your hand—not when you're out in the outfield. The deciding factor should be, instead, how far out you can hold it and still have it act the way a glove should.

# 15

IN 1954, MY second "mother" died . . . my Aunt Sarah. My own mother had died in childbirth the year before. Now, the family she left was in charge of the oldest daughter, my half-sister Anna Pearl. I got to spend some time with them following the close of the '54 season. But baseball was my living, and where the chance was to make an additional living, there I went.

And it took me to Puerto Rico, where Herman Franks was managing the Santurce team in the winter league there. It was fun, even though they take their baseball more seriously down there. One newspaper story about Puerto Rican baseball said, "Razor-blade salesmen hand out free samples in the grandstand, even though Puerto Rican fans have never been known to shave between innings."

The only headlines I made back home, from Puerto Rico, was when I got into an argument with Ruben Gomez, the Giant pitcher who was on the same club with me, as to whose turn it was in the batting cage. They played it up, the U.S. press, like the greatest donnybrook of all time. Actually, it was next to nothing. We had a good club, and everybody wanted to win—and when you've got people like Gomez and Roberto Clemente on your side in the Puerto Rican league, you've got a chance to win, and we did win. Most of all, though, I remember saying to Franks: "When are you going to manage in the big leagues?"

"You think I can?" he asked.

171

"Sure you can," I said. "Only thing, they always go for somebody who's already managed someplace."

"I've already managed someplace," he said.

"Sure," I said. "Here."

He shook his head. "No. I mean in the big leagues."

"You've managed in the big leagues? What club?"

"Giants."

"*Giants?* Leo manages the Giants."

"Not when they run him, he don't."

It was true. I'd never though of it. As a Giant coach under Durocher, Franks had already probably managed more big-league innings than half a dozen actual big-league managers you could name from those who've come and gone over the years. Because every time Leo got kicked out, Franks became the manager. And every time you looked around, Leo was getting kicked out.

In the 1955 season, I hit 51 home runs—my career high for a single season, and a figure that tied me with big Mize for the Giant record. My slugging average was .659. And I also charged a ball hit by Duke Snider, and missed the try for the shoestring catch— and didn't chase it.

If the illusion ever existed, or even if exists today, that the New York writers thought I couldn't do anything wrong, the next day's papers would be of interest to all. Typical was what was written by Joe King, of the New York *World-Telegram and The Sun:*

Maybe success did come too fast for the young man. Maybe the dramatic Negro boy the Giants plucked out of deep South obscurity has failed to appreciate that last year was a freak and that baseball is a job you work at 60 minutes an hour, and that the prima donnas are hated worse than any other by the fans. That's what Willie was yesterday—a prima donna.

Also, in 1955, I was benched by Manager Durocher because I was going bad—the only time in my life I've been sidelined for that specific reason. I'd been slumping and pressing for a week or so, and it got to a point, in a game at Milwaukee, where I tried to tag up on first and go to second base after the catch of a routine fly ball to left field.

When Leo saw that, he sat me down.

For one game.

But it was what I needed.

In the next several pages, I want to talk about this—about slumping and pressing.

I'm supposed to be famous for them.

By now, I should be an expert on them.

Yet every time I look around, every extra month I play, I learn something new about them.

And what I learn gets me nowheres nearer solving them than I was before.

What happens with slumps? What causes them? How much about them is "mental"? I suppose I could say that if I knew the answers to questions about that, I'd never have a slump. But the thing is, I think I *do* know some of the answers—and the slumps come anyway.

Everybody says I get "mental" about slumps. If that's true, it's the most normal thing in the world. Look at it this way: suppose you're going good, and in a given game you fly out, then hit a home run next time up, then hit another homer the time after that, then finally line one at the third baseman, who makes a great catch to rob you. Now, it may be you hit that last ball best of all, but with two home runs you've had a good day and—assuming for the sake of this argument that the outcome of the game didn't hang on it—you'll manage to forget that last time at bat pretty quick. If you think of it at all, you'll shrug it off as part of the game, and be comforted that you're "seeing" the ball so well.

But if you haven't been going good, and in that same game you strike out twice and foul out once, and then the last time up you hit that same ball at that same third baseman and he robs you with that same great play—well, now, isn't this going to be mental? The one time you swung good in a week and you're out anyway. Will tomorrow's box score show that great catch? No. It'll show you 0-for-4, that's what it'll show. The story in the paper? It might mention that catch if there's room, but there's nothing newsworthy about a third baseman catching a line drive. The same writers who wouldn't have mentioned it the day you hit the two homers probably won't mention it now. And they're right. They've got other things to write about. The only thing newsworthy now will be something like, "For the third straight day, Mays failed to get the ball out of the infield." And they'd be right in handling it that way, too.

Yet in handling it that way, obviously *they're* conscious of your slump. Why should it be strange for you to be conscious of it yourself?

It seems that with me, my worst slumps have seemed to come right after really big hot streaks. I guess a lot of this is "mental" too, even in just describing it, because if you hit nearly .400 for August and .330 for September, is September a slump? Or take what really happened to me one season: I set the record for the longest Giant hitting streak of the year that season—it was something like 20 games—yet during that streak my average fell nearly 20 points and I didn't have a single extra-base hit! The record book says it was a streak. I call it a slump.

Your physical condition—anything from an injury to a bad cold to just plain fatigue—can have something to do with what happens to you too. After all, if you're not up to par, your mind knows it, and if your mind knows it, then there you are being "mental" again.

One particular thing that's said about me is that I make up my mind in advance that I am a "streaky" player, therefore I expect to slump, therefore I do slump. Therefore, even, the slump lasts longer than it should.

I don't know what to say about that. I know that all my career I have hit in cycles, but so have a lot of other hitters. In fact, most better-than-.300 hitters do. Now, are we going to say that I expect to hit in cycles because I always have, or that I hit in cycles because I expect to? Which chicken came before which egg?

Yet—as I say—I think I know some of the answers. In fact, I can right here and now chart for you the way a hot streak turns into a slump—and there's not a single thing "mental" about it.

Let's say I'm going real good. A sure indicator on this, by the way, will be to watch my strikeouts. If I'm striking out fewer than, say, eight times in 100 at bats, it must mean I'm seeing the ball. If I'm seeing the ball I must be hitting.

Now, this hot streak is going to get better before it gets worse, because before they start walking me, the pitchers are going to try some other things first. And if I'm hitting the pitches I'm not supposed to hit, they will try other pitches. The book says never change up on me, but if I'm hitting everything else, then time and again the pitcher will figure he's got nothing to lose and throws me the change, on the guess that at least I don't expect to see it.

So now I'm not only seeing the ball good but getting my pitch to go with it!

Now the next step is they're not going to give me anything good to hit, period. So they start throwing me bad balls, and you can clock this stage of it from the daily records too: a period sets in here where I start drawing bases on balls. I'll go four, five days of getting two and three walks a game.

So my chances to add to the number of hits is cut down, and the next step is for the pitchers to get a little bolder and try for the corners of the plate. They're not good pitches, but some of them do catch the strike zone, and once again you can clock it: I begin to strike out—not swinging, but taking the third strike. I think it's a bad ball, but the umpire says no.

Okay. What sort of pitches are these? Breaking balls, mostly. Sliders, curves, scroogies. So now, I have to set myself for this kind of a pitch. And the one pitch that started my streak going— the fast ball—is now going to be the pitch that I'm not timed to meet, because I'm set for something not as fast. Once again, you can confirm what happens: I strike out swinging or I hit foul pop-ups, mainly directly back of home or to the right side (which is the latest you can swing and still make contact with the ball).

And the slump is on, and all this suggests an interesting thing —something people don't always think of a lot of the time: in my opinion, it's wrong to say, like people always do, that slumps come on because the hitter's unconsciously doing something different. Seems like my slumps, anyway, come on because I'm *not* doing anything different. And there's nothing mental about that either. The pitcher knows what the pitch is suposed to be and the hitter doesn't. So naturally it's the pitcher who's going to change and do something different, not the hitter. Best the hitter can do is follow along.

I would say then that most of the time you don't *cause* a slump by doing something different at bat. It's when you're *in* the slump that you start changing, start pressing, and maybe this *prolongs* it. It may be good advice to tell a hitter, "Don't press, don't change," but when you're the hitter and you're 0-for-20 and you left maybe eight men on base last game and the club lost by one run, that good advice doesn't mean much on the ball field.

Sometimes, even in the worst of my slumps, I've had to laugh at the way my friends approach me and try to help me. They come up to me whistling, like nothing's wrong, except it's the kind of whistle you save for passing by the graveyard at midnight. Once, in '63, when I was going real bad, a good friend of mine called up and hemmed and hawed over the phone for 20 minutes and finally said, "Say, Buck, you noticed the new fashion in baseball?"

"What new fashion?"

"Wearing glasses. Everybody's doing it."

"Everybody? Like who?"

"Frank Howard."

"He ain't hitting either," I said.

I'm sure *confidence* plays a part in getting a hitter out of a slump, but what it is that gives you that confidence, brings it back to you, I don't know. I say I'm "sure" confidence plays a part. Maybe I'm not even sure of that. The most confident-looking guy the Giants have had in recent years, going up to take his turn at bat, was Ron Herbel, the pitcher, and, as the saying goes, I don't think he'll ever get a hit.

Sure, you start changing, and you start pressing, and you go worse than ever. And what brings you out of it?

I just don't know. It could be a lot of things. We might play two series in a row against teams whose catchers are giving away their signs to my first-base coach . . . who relays them to me. I've owed Wes Westrum a couple of suits of clothes in my time, just for tipping me to pitches. Some hitters don't want to know the pitch in advance. I heard a story that Joe Medwick, one of the fine hitters with the Gas House Gang Cardinals, got himself beaned that time because he was tipped to a curve ball and it never curved. For myself, if I can get tipped to a pitch, most times I welcome it.

There's one theory I know of, that some fans say explains how hitters come out of slumps. The theory goes like this: a few hits start to fall in—I get lucky—or I beat out a few to the infield. Now, the pitcher who's working against me knows I didn't hit the ball good. But the other pitchers around the league don't. And they see in the box score that Mays got a home run (a pop fly that the wind blew out of the park just inside the foul pole) and three singles (one a swinging bunt, one a little fly ball that fell in, one a grounder I topped and beat out). Next day I get three more hits (a grounder between two fielders, a hit off the pitcher's shin that if he wasn't in the way would have gone straight to the shortstop for a routine out, a pop fly that should have been caught but the scorer ruled a hit instead of an error).

Now—this is how the theory goes—those other pitchers around the league, they don't know Mays is looking as bad as ever. All they know is suddenly he's got seven hits, and he must be out of his slump. So—the theory says—now the pitchers lose *their* confidence, and decide I'm on a tear again so I'll hit anything they throw, which gives me *my* confidence back again.

That's all right as a theory, maybe, but it doesn't work. If it did work, wouldn't they go back right now to feeding me bad pitches? And besides, the theory overlooks the fact that these pitchers check with other pitchers, the ones who actually were working when I got those lucky hits. Don't ask me how, but the great American pitchers' union has the fastest grapevine in creation.

I don't know what it takes. I suppose I can say that over the years, I've done better in April and May than in other months, but if that statistic is there at all, it isn't by a big margin—and besides, there's a reason for it, which is that in April you get the kids on the mound and in the field, and the hot weather hasn't set in for the breaking-ball pitchers, and managers can afford to lose a game while they're experimenting with one thing and another, and taking everything together, the hitters are in charge.

None of this, of course, is day-in, day-out gospel. I once got three home runs in one game at St. Louis. I hadn't hit anything for two weeks before that and I didn't hit anything for two weeks after.

And funny things happen. Some years ago, when the Orioles were training at Scottsdale, Arizona, Paul Richards had a young pitcher that he wanted to get a look at, and the youngster struck me out with a fast ball. Next time around, Joe Ginsberg, who was catching for them, signaled the kid for a different pitch, but the kid kept shaking him off. Finally, Ginsberg just plain threw his hands up in the air, in total resignation, and squatted down. Everybody in the ball park knew that this youngster figured he knew how to strike out Willie Mays, so he was bound to throw the same pitch he struck me out on before. I don't have to tell you what happened.

In fact, somebody asked me afterward if I didn't think I'd been "cruel" to this rookie by creaming that pitch the way I did.

My answer then is a way I feel about baseball. The best thing you can do for a youngster is let him see for himself how mistakes can cost him—particularly when he goes against the advice of men who've been around the game for years. It's just dream talk in the papers when you read that a kid gets shipped back to the minors for making a mistake. Mistakes are what you learn by. There are only two tests: (1), the mistake ought not to be a show of laziness, like not running out a ball; (2), you can't go on repeating them. But this business about the kindly old veteran purposely making the kid look good not only doesn't happen, but no veteran with any true kindness would ever do something like that. Good advice will stop a lot of mistakes from ever happening, but the kindest thing you can do for a newcomer who disregards advice is show him as fast as possible what the consequences will be.

I don't mean to sound holy about all this. I like to win and I like to hit. I don't go up to bat saying to myself, "This is a kid and he's going to make a mistake pitching to me and if I hit it, it's for his own good." One of the things you have to consider is he might get me out on the same pitch again, just like he did last time. Then they'd say, "Mays deliberately made the kid look good," when the truth is Mays was trying to hit the ball downtown. Then if the next time I *do* hit a home run off that pitch, who's going to interpret it how?

The point is, baseball works certain ways, and when you've played 2,000 major-league ball games, you're going to see all the things there are to see and still know there are more to come. There are good stories that go along with this. Two of them, both concerning Dizzy Dean, are worth repeating here.

The first story is the famous one that Tom Sheehan tells about how Diz made a bet he'd strike out Vince DiMaggio every time he came up that game. And he struck him out the first three times, and the last time he had a two-strike count on him and now Vince put up a little foul pop-up that the catcher, Bruce Ogrodowski, was ready for, only Diz came racing off the mound yelling at him: "Drop it! Drop it!" So the surprised Ogrodowski dropped it, and then Dean struck out Vince on the next pitch.

The other goes back to the Cardinals–Detroit World Series of 1934, where Dean pitched the final and deciding game and won by a score of 11-0. In that Series, the book on Hank Greenberg of the Tigers was don't feed him a low inside fast ball. But with a big lead, Dean threw him that pitch, and Greenberg doubled it down the left-field line.

Now the Cardinal manager, Frank Frisch, came running in from second base, where he was playing, and said to Dean, "Why'd you throw him that pitch?"

"I just wanted to see what he'd do with it," Dean said.

"Well," Frisch said, "now you've seen. And if you try any more clowning, you're out of the game."

"Frankie," Dean is supposed to have replied, "you're not going to take me out of this game and you know it. Go back to second base."

We all have these anecdotes. As I say, if you play long enough, you see everything and you still manage to be surprised all over again by something that happens the next day. And I suppose Dean was helping Vince DiMaggio out by giving him another swing, and helping Greenberg out by feeding him the pitch he liked to hit. But you notice an interesting thing: it didn't cost ol' Diz, either time.

Where newcomers, youngsters, rookies, are concerned, help is one thing. Pity is another. Because pity isn't help.

Giving a youngster a chance is something else. I have slid far harder into second base than I had to, considering the score and the circumstances, to take out the pivot man and keep the rookie who was hitting behind me from having it go down in the book that he grounded into a double play. I have shied off easy fly balls so a young fielder, coming back into my territory, could handle the chance himself. In run-down plays I have gotten myself trapped to take the heat off a younger boy. *But there was a time when older players did these things for me!* They weren't out to show me what great guys they were. In fact, they were simply showing me things so I could learn to do them myself. This doesn't have to be confined just to the execution of plays. It can be confidence itself.

But when everything's said and done, the newcomer will rise or fall on, or off, his own two feet. The only thing the veteran can do is teach him some things a lot sooner than he'd learn them on his own.

So of course veterans help rookies. They help them every way they can. But one way to help is to let the youngster see the result of his own mistake.

And when that mistake is a pitching mistake, sometimes that's how the hitter on the other side comes out of a slump!

Now, I have tried to give some actual examples here, at the same time saying you can't really give actual examples, because there are too many ways. You will find me saying this time and again in this book. I'm not trying to quibble or get around giving answers. People think that a specialist in a business must be able to answer their questions about that business. Either that or come up with what looks like an answer. If a surgeon mysteriously loses a patient on the operating table or a stock broker's advice goes lousy, I guess they'd better have some answers anyway. But if you want to call me an expert on baseball and you now come to me and say, "Why is it that there was never a pennant play-off in either major league for half a century and then suddenly there were three play-offs in the space of five years?" then my answer is not only I don't know, but I don't know twice. Maybe your broker doesn't know why the market went down that day, but months or years later he can see a reason for it, or at least think one up. Now, I've got an idea I've seen more major-league baseball than most people, but a lot of times I can't tell you right then and I can't tell you later either. The answer is this: I don't know.

I will say this about slumps—a lot of players, when they're not hitting, fall off in other respects too. Their throwing and their fielding and their base-running and their alertness all seem to go down at the same time their batting average does.

I'm sure they don't do it consciously, which must mean they're being "mental" too, in a way, but I'll try to be "mental" in my own way, and so when my hitting is off I will try to be doing something else. The basic thing is to want to win ball games, and if you hurt the club everywhere on the field, not just at bat, you might as well sit down for a while. So I do consciously—*mentally*—try to do something extra in some other department when I'm not hitting. Even try to get on base on an error—did you ever stop to think the *hitter* may have something to do with that? A little extra hustle, a slide into first base, whatever it is that can upset the defense, make them want to throw the ball before they've got it . . . there's a little bit of that too.

Yet even in that, I can only talk in *general* terms. I'll make the wrong play when I'm slumping too, and that play will look twice as bad when you're not helping the club with the bat. There, in itself, is a reason to want to *win*. Because if you're not hitting and you *lose*, it's twice as bad on you *mentally*.

These are good rules to have, I think, and I try to follow them. But I'll never forget Joe DiMaggio telling me about a terrible hitting slump he was in with the Yankees one time. He was something like 0-for-17 or 20, and finally he beat out a ground ball to deep short for a single.

"I felt like a weight had come off my back," he told me. "Just that one cheap, wrong hit, but here I'd been wondering if I'd ever get a hit again, and now I'd gone and got one. It was that one single that did it—that one lousy grounder to the left side. But as I stepped off first base to take my lead, I heaved the greatest sigh of straight relief you ever saw. I knew the worst was over."

"And were you right?" I said.

"Yup," he said, "I was right."

"What happened after that?"

"Well," he said, "the slump was gone. Somehow, I had my confidence back and I started hitting again. I'd used different bats and all kinds of advice and movies of what I might be doing wrong, but that one cheap hit was what did it for me." And here, Joe D. broke into a grin. "But if, when you say 'What happened after that?' you mean what happened *right away*—well, I took my lead, breathed that tremendous sigh of relief, and the pitcher picked me off."

And I remember also, in the summer of 1965, talking to Bob Aspromonte, the Houston third baseman. I was going bad—at one stretch there I was 0-for-24—and he said, "Heck, Buck, don't worry about it. I'm 0-for-July."

I was almost 0-for-July myself, in '65. Yet it was the strangest slump I'd ever had. I'm not even sure it was a slump. I was hitting the ball as good as ever, not striking out much, and the ball club was playing good and winning its share of games. I started July with the league lead in home runs and a plus-.300 average and I ended July with the league lead in home runs and a plus-.300 average. I hit some shots that month as good as I've ever hit a ball (Tommy Harper of Cincinnati took a home run away from me with a catch I still don't believe, and it seemed like at least once a game some outfielder was climbing the wall or some infielder was throwing himself full length to pick off something I hit.)

Yet it was as bad a slump as I ever had, as far as the figures go. But I didn't feel bad about it, the team didn't feel bad about it, and in August I was to hit 17 home runs for the National League record for one month. In August, for the fourth time (another record) I was named the league's "Player of the Month." It was the first time in the history of that award that the voting was unanimous.

Obviously, I hit pretty good in August. Yet there was one spell there, just around the middle of the month, that the Phils came in for a three-game series at Candlestick and I looked so bad (striking out three times against Herbert in one game, for example) that I heard later their players went down to L.A. from San Francisco and told the Dodgers they didn't think Mays would ever get another hit.

I'm getting ahead of my story here, I know, but putting all these things together in this one place in the book may be the best way to show maybe the difference between the "Fan's-eye view" of hitting slumps and the way they really are. The point is, you can go into a real slump at the plate. Or you can get a combination of not feeling too good one day, and two hot pitchers against you the next two days, and half a dozen great fielding plays against you, and some close calls from the umpire, and nothing falling in for you, where you're hitting the ball as good as ever—maybe even better—yet the figures show you're in a worse slump than when you're in a *real* slump.

How can you tell an "unreal slump" from a "real slump"? Generally, if it's just a question of a stretch of bad luck, the "unreal" ones don't last as long as the "real" ones. But by the time you've played 2,000 games, an awful lot has happened to you, and it isn't impossible for you to be hitting the ball good and still go "0-for-July." I know. I did it.

Then all of sudden, the balls started falling in. And out. I'll talk about that part later on in this story.

# 16

IN 1956, MY ADDRESS changed. I'd been living, since the '54 season, in a Harlem rooming house run by a charming watchdog of a landlady named Mrs. Gooseby, but in the meantime I'd met a woman named Marghuerite Wendell. She'd been twice married—Wendell was the name of her second husband, a doctor. Her first husband was one of the original Ink Spots, a man named Kennedy.

It was in '56 that Marghuerite and I were married. She had a daughter by her first marriage, and in '59, in San Francisco, she and I were to go to an adoption agency, and that is how my son Michael came to live with us.

He was three days old when we adopted him.

I don't know what the chemistry was, but from the first moment I set eyes on him, I knew this was it. And it's been that way ever since.

People wonder what it must be like for a boy like Michael, having a Willie Mays for a father. They never wonder what it must be like for me, having a Michael Mays for a son.

All I can say is, he changed my life, my purpose, my outlook. I'll never forget one time, a couple of years ago, when a photographer came to my house in San Francisco to take some pictures for some magazine or TV show or something. I came downstairs and found him in the living room, reading a textbook on real-estate law.

When I came in the room, he dropped the book like it was contaminated. In a way it was funny. Everybody thinks all I read is Batman. In the past, that was more true than not. But in the "P.M." (post-Michael) of my life, I've taken to home study, mainly in the banking and insurance fields, and in early '65, I opened my own insurance firm, the Willie Mays Agency, Inc., in a deal with Pennsylvania Life Insurance Company.

The object is not just to sell insurance, but to establish careers for others—particularly ballplayers—who suffer from the common curse of the professional athlete: short career span and little training for something else once their playing days are over.

Pennsylvania Life had done a survey in this field that pointed up some unusual things. First, the average professional athlete earns less than $10,000 at the height of his playing career. Second, at 35, just when men in other fields are beginning to taste financial success, the average athlete is on his way down, looking for other work yet without the training for it.

You might think a ballplayer would make the greatest kind of insurance salesman of all, merely from his ability to sell policies to other ballplayers. But that's not the idea. Sure, we buy our own product, but there aren't that many athletes to go around, and I got a mental image of all of them selling insurance to each other.

The idea instead has to be to select certain athletes, then train them in an intensive schooling period in insurance sales. And by no means do they have to wait till their careers are over. If they're mature and want to work, then whether they're stars or not, we want to talk to them right now.

So the function of the agency isn't just to sell insurance, but to sell other athletes, in baseball and other sports too, on a job opportunity for themselves, one they can build with once their playing days are over.

The Pennsylvania Life figures show that a new man in this field can expect to earn $6,000 his first year, and that $6,000 would be in addition to the sports salary he's making at the time. Then, as his sports income start going down, his broadened insurance accounts will keep that income going up.

As for the question of who buys insurance, the answer, of course, is everybody. Surely it doesn't hurt if the man selling the policy is a familiar sports name—did you ever think the way to get Willie Mays into your living room was to want to talk insurance with him?— but we're firm on one point, which is that insurance isn't just for the purpose of selling somebody some kind of policy. This is the thing I stress most when I talk to other players about their maybe wanting to come into the business. Insurance, as I look at it, is less a sales business than it is a service business, and what makes a successful and responsible insurance man is not how much he can sell you but his ability to plan for your needs first and keep watching over them afterward.

My marriage itself didn't work out. I don't blame anybody but ourselves for what went wrong—basically, Marghuerite had trouble adjusting to my way of living, and I guess I didn't adjust to hers— but being a celebrity is no help in this direction. For a while we had an apartment on Spruce Street in San Francisco, off of California Street, and if the people in the apartment downstairs had an argument, like all married folk do, then that'd be all there was to it. But if my wife and I had a spat, it'd be all over the papers next day. One time Marghuerite had a fall on a flight of stairs, and sure enough it came out I must have been striking her. ("He hit her like he owned her," was one line that appeared in print somewhere.)

So that didn't make anything any easier, and we finally agreed on a divorce, after nearly six years of marriage. As of the moment, custody of Michael is officially in Marghuerite's hands, but he spent the entire off-season with me in San Francisco last year, when he was in kindergarten, and I want him with me every chance I get.

To give you one example of the lengths people will go to, in 1956, the year I got married, my batting average was under .300—it was .296—and the papers said it was my getting married that had caused this "downfall"! (But that was also the year I became the first man ever to steal 30 bases and hit 30 homers in the same season—not record-breaking figures by themselves; but as a combination of things, speed and power, that you don't customarily find in the same player, it was an accomplishment I'm especially glad of.)

So I hit .296 in '56, the result of 171 hits in 578 at bats and everybody said this was what getting married had done to Mays.

In 1964, I got off to the greatest start in my career. At one point, a month after the season started, I was batting .497. My slugging average at that time was *more than 1.000!*

But by season's end, I'd had 171 hits in 578 at bats, for the same .296 I'd had in '56, based on the same number of hits in the same number of at bats, and I'll swear, judge, I didn't get married to anybody in '64.

The year '56 too was the first year Bill Rigney managed the Giants. Durocher and Horace Stoneham had had a falling out—as much personal as it was professional, we'd heard—so Rig, who'd played for us as a utility infielder and then became manager at Minneapolis, took over.

Temperamentally, he was a lot different than Leo. Whatever might be bothering Leo, he'd let you know about it, but Rig instead was the kind of guy who'd bottle a lot up inside himself—he's got a prize ulcer to show for it too. He had one thing, though—a lot more patience than Leo, and he'd work a lot with the youngsters and steady them and bring them along.

The people who weren't blaming my marriage for my .296 average in '56 blamed the change in managers instead. Once again here, I'm not going to try to account for what really caused a bad year, since I don't concede it *was* a bad year to begin with. But it was common to hear people say, "Mays needed babying, somebody who thought he was the greatest thing that ever came along the pike, and who'd keep shouting it from the rooftops. Willie's got to have praise. Durocher knew that. Rigney goes around saying there are other guys on the ball club too."

There is some general truth in there, particularly to the part about me wanting to be praised, because it's always seemed to me that when the fans cheered, I did better. I believe this is true of every ballplayer who ever lived.

But what they never thought of was that I wasn't the kid I had been and this was 1956, not '51 or '54, and the Giants weren't winning a pennant every time I threw my glove down on the field. Obviously things were different, and if Rigney reflected it, so did I. I wasn't playing stickball on the streets of Harlem anymore either.

But to draw from that the idea that Rig secretly disliked me or that I secretly disliked him, which is what a lot of people did, is just to set up a lie. I played for Rig as hard as I ever played for any manager, and in '60, when the wolves got his job in San Francisco, I was spokesman for the players in his behalf.

It was a disgrace, the way they went after Rig and got him. Maybe you've never heard of firing a manager for being in second place in June, but that's what they did to Rigney. Most of us supposed it was stirred up by two or three San Francisco sports writers or editors, partly out of a drive to get a hometown man, Lefty O'Doul, named manager of the team, and partly because the San Francisco papers like to stir things up—sometimes, I think, just for the living hell of it. Like one time, one of them had headlines on page one that the club was playing "The Star-Spangled Banner" before night games but not flying the flag. Actually, the flag is only supposed to be flown at night for special patriotic occasions, or during an actual battle in a war, but that didn't stop this paper. Just to make their point, they got a bunch of crippled guys from a veterans' hospital somewhere and brought them to the ball park next day to present an American flag to Mr. Stoneham.

How he ever sat back and took it, I'll never know. When they had the pressure on Rigney, they started printing untruths, like "rumors" that I wouldn't play for him. That was when I spoke out. It's bad enough when people don't have their facts straight, but when they go and change the facts just to fit what it is they want said and done, then you have to wonder.

Stoneham of course had a new ball club in San Francisco, and as everybody pointed out, he'd moved because the Giants were no longer making their way in New York. What San Franciscans never stopped to think about, though, was that because the Giants had to move from New York didn't mean San Francisco was the only place they could possibly go. You get the idea that San Francisco picked the Giants. My understanding is that the Giants picked San Francisco.

Either way, Mr. Stoneham of course wanted to try to get along in the new town, and, like I say, he put up with a lot. Some lawyer sued him because there wasn't any heat in the stands at Candlestick, and won the suit. In fact, just about everything wrong with Candlestick has been blamed on the Giants at one time or another, even though actually the ball club is a tenant of a stadium the city itself built, and a lot of needed repairs weren't made because for years after it was built, Candlestick was tied up in litigation of one kind or another, with the city not talking to the contractor and the contractor not talking to the architect and so forth and so on.

My reception wasn't exactly the fondest in history either, when we moved out there.

# 17

ABRAHAM LINCOLN SAID you can fool some of the people all of the time, and all of the people some of the time, but you can't fool all of the people all of the time. I say if there's enough fooling, it doesn't make much difference.

When the Giants first moved to San Francisco for the 1958 season, I found I was disliked because I was from New York, and because I was a Negro, and because I was a threat to the legend of DiMaggio, and—of all things—because I didn't do much bunting.

There probably weren't a real big number of fans who resented me for any single reason, but there were enough reasons so there didn't have to be. Paste them all together and they could have populated a big-league ball park—and, it seemed to me, frequently did. Ours.

As I say, there were different reasons, but if you've ever been booed by 40,000 people, you know it has a way of sounding the same no matter what the reason.

The New York thing and the Negro thing and the DiMaggio thing, all those I could more or less understand. By "understand," I mean they didn't have to pick me up off the floor on account of being surprised. The bunting business, though, was harder to figure. I think I know now what it was; but at first I didn't.

Put it this way: these San Franciscans had been brought up all their lives on minor-league baseball. A fast brand of it, yes, but still the minors. And in all their experience, the faster a man was, the

191

more he bunted. To them, it made sense: to bunt to get on, you have to be fast—so if you're fast, you bunt.

What they had not found in the minor leagues was what you do find in the majors—the man who has speed and power both, in which case obviously he wants to use his speed not to make it to first on a bunt but to make it to second on a single or to third on a double. The reason you don't see this combination of speed and power in the minors is that the men who have it move right up to the majors. Thus your Willie Davises and Mickey Mantles.

I will bunt for the base hit for a variety of reasons—if the wind is real wrong, or if I haven't been hitting this pitcher, or leading off when the score and inning mean we have to have a base runner and they're playing me so a bunt looks like a better shot than trying to foul off enough to get a walk. Once in a long while, I've done it just to keep the defense honest, because when the third baseman's playing deep and you bunt safely against him, maybe the word will get around and the next third baseman will play a step or two closer on you—and then you might just hit one right past him.

But add them all together and I still don't bunt as much in a season as Maury Wills, who in this department happens to be a sheer genius, might do in a single week. On the other hand, Maury doesn't hit the long ball. If he'd moved to the Coast with an average of better than 37 homers a season, as I did, then for all his genius the L.A. fans wouldn't have seen him bunting too much either.

Yet, as I now realize, this was something brand-new for San Francisco fans. I don't fault them for it, now that I understand it. If a player has to learn baseball all over when he comes up to the majors, surely this must apply to writers and fans too.

In those first years on the Coast, though, this was one of the things they were down on me for. They put two and two together and got a quick satisfying five. I wasn't bunting because it was beneath me. I was swinging for the home run every time. I wasn't a team man. It was obvious to them that I would have been safe more often than I was out if I'd bunted. What they didn't know was that I would have been fined more often than I was safe.

Remember the famous Boudreau shift against Ted Williams? Three men, all on the grass, on the right side, and the third baseman playing a deep shortstop. Teams we play have used the same alignment against Willie McCovey. A Williams or a McCovey could bunt—they didn't even have to bunt well—and walk to first. The other team is giving them first base if that's all they want to try for.

And the interesting thing is, the fans don't expect a Williams or a McCovey to bunt. They go for it only in the case of a hitter with speed. They are looking for the close play, because of course it carries its own brand of excitement. But they forget sometimes that the close play is not the object of the game. You win by one run if you can. But if you can win by 10 runs, there's nothing in your contract that says that's illegal either.

And because of this, the fact is that, in addition to everything else, I was branded, when I first came West, as being not a team man. Being from New York and being a Negro and playing the same position as Joe D. didn't hurt the way that last thing did. I actually played five weeks of the 1959 season with a broken hand and got booed for swinging away, when bunting would have been the one thing that didn't bring pain with it.

They say prejudice springs out of ignorance. In that case, you tell me—what does ignorance spring out of?

I don't mean to try philosophy. I think the facts are there. Of all the Giants who'd come from New York—and I mean manager and coaches as well as players—who took the field for their first San Francisco game in 1958, only one regular—me—was still there opening day of '61. Some had left in the usual baseball give-and-take, sure. But some of them had just plain been run. John Antonelli, for one. He'd made the mistake of criticizing San Francisco's weather. Herman Franks, for another. He'd made the mistake of coaching at

third at Seals Stadium, where the fans sat close enough to read
him off, chapter and verse. Bill Rigney himself. He'd made the mistake of getting too close to a pennant with two teams ('58 and '59)
that only a fine manager could have whipped to that point to begin
with.

If you want a contrast, look at the Dodgers down south. They
moved from New York same year we did. But they had the good
sense to finish next to last their first season on the Coast. After that,
only way they could go was up. And opening day of '61, there were
still a dozen holdovers from the Brooklyn club that came West in
'58. Including the manager and the top pitcher, and as this is
written, they're still in business there.

Besides, thanks to Wills & Co., the Coast fans there had their
favorite play—the bunt—coming out of their ears. In the majors a
lot of times, separate teams can take wholly different approaches
to the game. In the minors you don't have 25 men to make
moves with, and the day-in-day-out execution of plays isn't as
expert, so all the teams tend to play it pretty much like all the
other teams. That was another thing that was new to the Coast
fans: seeing two teams in the same league that could play it so
different and still both be right.

I'll tell you how bad the bunt thing got in San Francisco:

We were on a road trip, and in this one game at Chicago it was
a hitter's afternoon, with everybody getting base hits and scoring,
and the score was tied in the top of the seventh and I came to bat
with bases loaded and nobody out and McCovey and Cepeda due up
next after me.

Of course I was swinging away, but I didn't get it out of the
infield and I think they got out of the inning with us scoring one
or none. I even forget who went on to win the game, although I
think it was them.

The point is, next day, one of the baseball columnists back home
in the Bay area wrote a piece wanting to know was I really too
proud to bunt!!

Here we had a chance to get ourselves four runs or more and I'm accused of being too proud to play for one run. This in the midst of a sluggers' game with the heart of the visiting team's batting order coming up and the sluggers on the other side still having at least three innings of their own coming up against you.

Sound foolish? I haven't even got to the worst part. The worst part was, here was this writer calling for what isn't even a major-league play. If one run is what he really wanted, the bases-loaded bunt in that situation was about the worst way to try to get it.

You do see it once in a while, under very specialized conditions, and even then only when you figure the batter is twice as good a bunter as his chance of getting you even a fly ball. But one of the things they pay big-league infielders for is to pick up the ball.

Now, if you bunt at the ball, you can miss it, or foul it, or pop it up, or bunt it fair. If you bunt it fair, the defense has a force at the plate—no tag necessary with bases loaded—and the guy on third has no choice at all. He has to run.

So if you want to squeeze a run home with bases loaded, in the big leagues it doesn't take just a bunt—it takes a perfect bunt. And the defense, starting with the pitcher, just might not cooperate.

Finally, when you do it with none out, you invite the costliest double play possible under the situation—the bunt in the air where the man from third is out too.

So your manager needs a perfect play to get one run where any number of less-than-perfect plays might get him a bundle.

I use this illustration here not because of the charge that I was too proud to bunt—though I start to laugh every time I remember it: somebody sent us the clipping and the whole club was rolling on the floor of the plane reading it afterward. The point is, we were a big-league team with a minor-league audience.

They meant well. But they had to learn, like anybody else. And meanwhile, not really meaning to, they did some real and lasting damage.

I was doing a lot of running on the bases there in '58, and in

'59 up till the time McCovey joined us. Then I cut down on it. The reason for this had nothing to do with me; it had to do instead with the man following me in the batting order.

If you add up my singles, and walks, and getting there on an error or a tipped bat or being hit by a pitch, I'll be on first base better than 150 times a season, and most of those times there won't be a runner on second ahead of me.

With Cepeda when he was new, Rigney wanted me running a lot after I got to first. The idea was that Orlando, hitting behind me, did a lot better with the fast ball in those days than he did with the breaking stuff or the change. Now, if the runner on first is a threat to steal second, the catcher in the back of his mind is going to be calling for more fast balls, because that's the best pitch for him when he has to get rid of the ball in a hurry.

But when McCovey joined us, I had an opposite role to play when I got to first, because now he was the one batting behind me. Stretch was a dead pull hitter. Now the basic thing for me was to stay on first and make the first baseman anchor there to keep holding me on, because this gave McCovey a big hole on the right side to hit through.

In other words, the hitter behind me was getting his best shot either when I was or wasn't running, depending not on who I was— I was still Willie Mays—but on who he was. Obviously, you don't play it that way every time, game in and game out. But it was deliberate, and it happened enough times so that sure enough, a local writer did a piece on how I was slowing down and used my declining stolen-base figure to prove it.

When I say this kind of thing did damage, I mean it. To begin with, it hurt Cepeda, and Orlando was far too fine a ballplayer, even his first year, to have to try to deal with this too.

He not only had a good year in '58, which he earned, but the fans—seeing in him not only a "native son" (it was his first big-league season, so he sure wasn't one of those overrated New York imports), but a man who could match the great Mays with the bat (and I think he could)—anyway, they blew poor Chico up to greater-than-life size. I hit .347 that first year; he hit .312; I had more home runs, more triples, more stolen bases, more runs scored, more runs batted in. After the season, the *Examiner* conducted a "Most Valuable Giant" poll and Cepeda walked away with it. I don't even remember if I finished second; if I did, it was close with somebody else. And I don't cite the figures above to try to prove I had a better year than he did in '58. That's a comparison you can't make. I'd been around the big leagues—he hadn't. Chico had about as fine a rookie year as you can have.

But they blew him up far more than that—far more, what with all their civic pride and private reasons, than the fans had ever blown me up in New York.

And it damaged Orlando Cepeda. He didn't turn 21 till September of that first year. Yet they glorified him not only for the tremendous work he did, but for the bad things too. When he'd run right through Herman Franks' stop sign at third and into a suicide out at the plate, they got mad at Franks—and fondly nick-named Orlando the "Baby Bull."

Chico wouldn't have been human if at the age of 20 he hadn't been flattered, even misled, by attentions like these. And it cost him.

I remember one time early in the 1961 season when he was at bat and we needed him on first base any way he could get there. And he got himself hit by a pitch, and reached base that way, and we won the game.

"Chico," I said to him in the clubhouse afterward, "when you first came up, you wouldn't have got hit by that pitch. You would have got out of the way."

"Willie," he said, "it's something I learned. And if they'd let me alone, I would have learned it two years sooner."

Now, when McCovey came up, a place had to be found for him. This was in '59. In those days, all McCovey could play was first base, so Cepeda was put in left field. He went willingly. All he wanted to do then, or ever, was help the team. But in his mind, inevitably, there was also that bigger-than-life reputation to live up to. He wasn't a real good outfielder and he knew it. So naturally, playing a position other than the one where he had done well and felt at home, he was affected by it. It preyed on his mind and hurt his concentration and his hitting.

Once again, the fans proved no help. Having constructed this extra-size hero, they were going to maintain him at all costs. So when McCovey made an error at first base, it was McCovey's fault. When Cepeda made an error in left field, this was McCovey's fault too, for driving him off first base.

Yet what were you going to do with those two bats? Leave one of them out of the lineup?

It got so that when Alvin Dark took over as manager in '61, he started out by playing Cepeda in right field—a tougher field than left—because he had a theory that the fans would think of this as a "new" position that Orlando understandably had to have time to learn, and thus they'd be patient and lay off him and McCovey both. As a theory this was great. I think it did quiet down the fans. Unfortunately it didn't quiet down the opposition, because obviously it would and did hurt our defense. So while the fans cheered, the Giants lost. As I remember, the experiment lasted two weeks. Finally, in sheer desperation, Dark put in a total switch, returned Cepeda to first, and put McCovey in left field. I guess this worked a little better, overall. But by then it was awful late in the game.

McCovey had been booed for no other reason than that his presence had forced Cepeda into an unfamiliar position, where he was bound to—and did—make mistakes that didn't square with the do-no-wrong image San Francisco had constructed for him. And the fans were out to protect that image—not Cepeda, just their own image of him.

And then, as time wore on, and the excuses grew fewer and fewer, the fans conveniently forgot it was themselves who'd labeled a fine young player overnight as an all-time great.

Conveniently forgot it.

And Orlando Cepeda came to the plate one day at Candlestick in 1964. He had no business even playing that day. He was on one leg; in pain; his knee swollen to nearly twice its normal size. But he'd had a bad leg that day in Chicago in '61 when he hit a home run with the bases loaded off Jim Brewer, the longest ball I have ever seen hit—it was still going up when it hit the dead-center bleacher tier just underneath the scoreboard at Wrigley Field, which is more than 500 feet from home plate. Maybe he could help us. That's why he went up there to hit now, this game in '64.

A couple of shots had gone wrong for him earlier. He'd turned wrong on the leg, and his limp by now was noticeable.

And before he even got to the plate, that Candlestick crowd was on its feet—booing the living socks off him.

This is what I mean by damage. It's happened in other towns, in other ways. San Francisco, over the years, has learned, just as I had to learn when I first came into the majors. In San Francisco, though, once the fans started to catch on to the game, they found they had something to unlearn for everything they were learning.

In a game in May of '65, we were ahead of the Houstons by a big score in the first game of a doubleheader, and manager Franks took me and McCovey and Hart out of the game, and now the Houstons started to get some runs, and an 18-year-old named Ken Henderson, now playing center field for us, caught a sinking liner and turned it into a double play at home plate. I've already recounted this play, in this book, from the professional baseball standpoint. That's not the point here. The point here is that the fans came to their feet for him, but there was an extra-nice sound to it. You get so your ear can tell you what the fans are saying. They were telling this youngster not just that he'd made an exciting play, but that he could make some not-so-good ones in the games to come and they'd understand.

Maybe Ken Henderson didn't hear this in the midst of that

standing ovation. But I heard it and—if Ken doesn't understand this now, he will sooner or later—I was as happy as he was. Not just for his play. Just as much because now, after this period of time, the San Franciscan has come to "know" his major-league baseball.

We came to the Coast in '58. It's traditional that a player performs better before the home crowds. That didn't become true of me till '62. I don't account for this change. The fans account for it.

You still have your oddballs. Every town has them and always will. But they're not grouped, and if they shout out of prejudice, at least it's not out of ignorance. Oh, even there, maybe one or two. But it's night and day from what it was.

One guy. He's there almost every game, because he drives a chartered bus, and he's always got some group or other to take to the ball park. He sits well up in the lower stand at Candlestick, a little to the right of home plate. And every time I come up, he lets me have it:

"'ey, Pop-Up Mays!"

Pop-Up Mays. To him, that's me, and nothing'll change it.

The press box sticks out right over where he sits, so they hear him there too.

"Buck," one of the writers said to me, "can you hear this 'Pop-Up Mays' character when you come to bat?"

"Yup," I said. "I can hear him."

I'm a human being. I can hear him.

I hear him in my sleep.

# 18

ONE THING THAT happened, in that transition period beginning with when Rig took over the club in '56 to when we moved to San Francisco and the first couple of years there, was that I began to click in the All-Star game. In the '65 All-Star game, I got my 21st hit—a record for All-Star performance, breaking a tie with Musial. I also hold the All-Star record for runs scored, most games played in the field, most put-outs, most chances. Also the record for the most triples and the most stolen bases, the last category both for single-game and overall totals.

I think my all-time favorite game was the 1959 All-Star game at Pittsburgh, when I got the winning triple, hit to center field where Harvey Kuenn, who later was to become a Giant, was playing then for the American League. Bob Stevens wrote one of the nicest lines ever said about me, describing that triple. "The only man who could have caught it," he wrote, "hit it."

What few fans remember is that in my "great" year of 1954, when I was MVP and we won the pennant and *Time* put me on the cover and everything else happened, I *didn't* make the All-Star team! Not as the starting center fielder, that is. I got in at the end, but it was Snider of the Dodgers who got the most votes to start—and deserved them.

This, though, may have been one of the things that plagued me when we first moved to San Francisco. The fans there were suspicious of me, a lot of them, on account of my "New York buildup," and the glamour and the nationwide TV and everything else, that come with the All-Star game, were I think a part of that. There's truth, too, to the charge that anybody who does well in just one game ought not to be "blown up." I readily confess the All-Star game had done that for me. It got so because I didn't start hitting homers right away when we started playing in S.F., the writers and fans pressured the Giants into taking movies of me to show me what I was doing wrong. This was fine, except I was hitting .375 at the time!! I like a good movie as much as the next guy, but I ain't about to take a .375 hitter and change his stance.

One of the main differences between me and DiMaggio was that I was a creature of TV; he was a creature of radio. Television was just getting big the year I broke in, which was the same year he retired. But TV, of course, only covers the big games, whereas radio covered them all, so it was logical for San Franciscans to compare me to DiMag on that basis and say, "Boy, they gave Mays ten times the build-up they gave Joe D.!"

As of right now, in case anybody's interested, more than 60 percent of my big-league games have been played in a San Francisco uniform, and the longer I play, the more impressive that statistic is going to become. My insurance agency has offices in three cities, but its home city is San Francisco. My home is San Francisco. I don't care where you're coming from, or what time of year it is, but you get off a plane in San Francisco, and you know you're home. You breathe that air, and it's stimulating and exciting and alive. I could live anywhere I want in the off-season, but I've chosen San Francisco. I love the place, maybe even more than it knows.

I've said that at the beginning it wasn't easy—no new town is ever easy. Getting a rock thrown through your living room window, or having the embarrassment of the mayor offering you his house to live in because somebody else turned you down when you were looking for a place—these things are no fun. Having them say you're nothing better than a piece of newspaper promotion—did any New York writer ever hit for me, let alone hit a home run for

me? did any New York writer ever pitch to me and let me hit one?
—this can be hard on you.

But like I say, things aren't the way now that they used to be.
They've changed. I've talked about the bad times in San Francisco
because, like I said before, the man said talk about everything in
this book.

And even Horace Stoneham finally drew his foot in the dirt and
said, "That line and no farther," where the early San Francisco pres-
sures were concerned. He was pressured into getting rid of Rigney—
let's concede that—but to the point of hiring a San Francisco man
to take his place? To that point, he wouldn't go. It was almost as if
Stoneham was having some secret laugh all his own. He named his
own houseman, Tom Sheehan, to the "interim" manager's job.

Sheehan knew his baseball, no doubt of it. I think he helped
Doubleday invent the game. But his future as a scout and front-
office man was secure, he didn't have any particular reason to want
to be a field manager, so there wasn't much discipline or drive, and
the '60 club sagged and wound up finishing fifth.

I don't think any team would have done any good that entire
first season at Candlestick, the year the park was opened. For the
'58 and '59 seasons, we'd played at Seals Stadium, and came close
to the pennant both years. In '59, in fact, it looked like we had it
won with two weeks to go. That San Francisco wind was there—
that San Francisco wind is everywhere—but we were going good,
and the chief fault with the ball park was that it was too small—a
minor-league park in every respect. There weren't enough seats
in the stands, nor enough concession booths or rest rooms or park-
ing to take care of the spectators in the seats they did have. And the
fans sat so close to you, the foul lines were so close to the seats, that
you'd hear every wise guy, every word of abuse.

Candlestick was bigger. Hell, Candlestick was too big. First day
I ever came to bat there, in hitting practice the day before the '60
season opened, it was windy and raw, and whoever was pitching
threw me a fast slider and I swung and looked and I was holding

just the thin handle of the bat in my hand. The ball had sawed my bat in two!

They made changes the following year, bringing the fences in and putting up a green backdrop behind center field so the hitters could see the ball better, which was important because the Giants play more day games than any other team except the Cubs, who have no lights in their park.

Also, they made a change in managers. Sheehan had lasted out the '60 season, which is what he was supposed to do, and now another former Giant—once again, Stoneham was ignoring any hints to pick a San Francisco man—was named to manage.

He'd never managed before, but he was manager material. Everybody knew that.

I got a letter from him, two days after he was named manager.

Dear Willie—

Just a note to say that knowing you will be playing for me is the greatest privilege and thrill any manager could ever hope to have.

It was signed:

ALVIN DARK.

# 19

THE BEST THING I could do to help Alvin Dark's debut as the new Giants manager was to show up. What I mean, there was an airlines strike and no planes were flying into Phoenix, so Dark was going to take over for the start of spring training with no players, and it would have looked bad. You don't want to take the edge off the way a man comes on managing his first big-league ball club, not if you can help it, especially not in a year like '61, because there weren't any Mets in New York at that time, so a lot of the old New York Giant writers had come to Phoenix to write about our club, and there was going to be a big spotlight on Dark right from the start.

So I managed to be there on time—it was three or four days, though, before the whole club was assembled—and we spent most of the time answering questions put by New York writers, seemed like. Actually, there was a good New York angle to the story. Five of us—me, Dark, and three of the coaches, Lockman, Jansen, and Westrum—not only were with that "miracle" Giant team of 1951 in New York, but actually were in the lineup at the time Bobby Thomson hit the homer.

While I don't think this prejudiced the San Francisco writers against Dark, they obviously weren't happy to see a bunch of New York writers, whom Dark knew well, monopolizing those first days of training. The San Francisco writers had a favorite of their own, too —Lefty O'Doul, who managed the Seals so many years in the Coast

League, and up till now Lefty had always come to Phoenix as a batting instructor during Giant training. When he showed up this time, though, Dark acted as though he didn't even know he was there. "I have no batting coach," Dark said. "If any of the players want to ask O'Doul for help, they can ask him on their own." About a week of that cold shoulder was all O'Doul felt like taking, and he left camp. And that was something the San Francisco writers *did* report.

Also, whereas most times managers make themselves pretty much available to the press, Dark instead stationed himself on the field once full workouts got under way, and pretty generally wouldn't talk to newspapermen while the sessions were going on. And finally, he wasn't one of those who'd drink or socialize with the newspaper boys in the evenings.

All told, you can see where this might have added up to a bad kind of first strike against the man, but actually the press didn't give him a bad time at all. After all, he'd inherited the supposedly beer-drinking, card-playing, after-hours bunch of 1960, whose team motto, somebody said, was "Shut up and deal!" and the very qualities in Dark that could make him seem straightlaced and distant and un-approachable were the qualities San Francisco cheered the most.

A nondrinker, early-to-bed man by lifetime habit, Dark was fitted to lead the Giants not only by discipline but by personal example. One of the truly fine amateur golfers around, he never touched his clubs that first spring in Phoenix except maybe for one off day, if I remember right. He wouldn't even take batting practice, or let Whitey Lockman do it, even though both could have started as players in our lineup. "We're not good enough to make this club," he stated.

There's no question that there was a new spirit on the club, and Dark was responsible for it. He worked us hard, but he worked us fairly, and while he had a lot of physical exercise on the program, everything had a reason. He didn't make a pitcher run in the out-

field, for example, just because he couldn't think of something else
for the pitcher to do.

What he did do with the pitchers was ask them to throw breaking
stuff the very first day. Jansen, the pitching coach, felt that the
standard pitching routine in a major-league camp was far lazier
and slower than it had any right to be, and Dark agreed with him.
(Over in Scottsdale, where the Red Sox were training, Sal Maglie
was the pitching coach, and when he heard what the Giants were
doing, he beetled those black brows of his and said, "The man's out
of his mind," but as part of Dark's plan of intensive shaping-up, the
speeding-up of the pitching workouts had its place too.)

Dark's target was to have his opening-day lineup actually take
the field for the exhibition game of April 1. He'd determined it would
be McCovey at first and Cepeda in the outfield, so Orlando never
touched a first baseman's mitt all spring. As for the wind at Candlestick—"In those hot summer dog days," Dark said, "San Francisco
has the only decent climate in the major leagues." Maybe he wasn't
kidding anybody, talking about the wind as if there was no wind.
But Alvin Dark was fashioning a new attitude, creating a new outlook. And it was having a fine and strong effect on the Giants.

I remember one exhibition game at Scottsdale, where the Red
Sox beat us in a dust storm when the umpire, an American League
man, called a close pitch ball four and forced over the winning run
in the last of the ninth. We'd been playing in that dust and heat for
four hours, seemed like, and everybody was tickled pink to get out
of there.

Not Alvin Dark, though. There might have been nobody left in
the stands to see it, but there he was at home plate, jawing head-to-
head with that plate umpire as though the World Series had de-
pended on that final call.

Well, maybe there was nobody left in the stands to notice it, but
I know of one man who noticed it. That was Bob Bolin, our pitcher.
He'd pitched well, and that last pitch maybe should have been

called a strike. It wouldn't be the first time an umpire helped finish a game nobody cared a hoot about.

But Bolin was a rookie then, fighting for a place on the Giants, and Alvin Dark was out there fighting for him, there in the heat and the dust with nobody around to see or care. The word got around real fast: *This is a stand-up guy. He'll fight for his men.* It got in the papers back home, too, and now Dark's stock really soared.

I think I am making the mistake here of painting Alvin as a dedicated but humorless man. Dedicated, yes. But humorless, no. He had a good sense of the comic, and he could laugh at himself. One morning, about eight A.M., it was raining in Phoenix, but Dark was on the phone, getting the Boston manager out of bed to try to schedule an extra "B" game for that day. The phone call was part of his dedication. But when he heard the startled, almost horrified, croak on the other end of the phone, he broke up, laughing at himself.

Cheerfully too—almost kiddingly, at times—he painted himself as a man who intended to "overmanage." In this, he was kidding on the square. In everything he did—from playing percentages down to outfield locations for certain hitters by certain fielders, to the intentional base on balls, to phony signs, to wholesale switching of his starting lineup as soon as the other pitcher was announced, to squeeze plays and pet "secret" plays, to "protection" sequences in his batting orders—all these things, Dark would use.

The best story reflecting this was one that happened a couple of seasons later. Dark was managing us in a game at Philadelphia, against his old friend and fellow "brain-master" Gene Mauch, and on that day Joe Cronin, the president of the American League, happened to be in the press box at Fenway Park in Boston, with the Western Union ticker at his elbow. Cronin had put in a phone call to his old friend Jerry Donovan, an official of the Giants, in San Francisco, and Donovan had his radio there, tuned in to our game in Philadelphia.

Now the ticker at Fenway Park reported that the Giants had just brought in their fifth pitcher, and the game was still in the first inning! Amazed, Cronin said to Donovan over the phone, "How bad are you guys losing?"

"One to nothing," Donovan said.

"You've given up one run in the first inning and you've used five pitchers?"

"What do you want from me?" Donovan said.

I can't say that I subscribe to overmanaging when it reaches a point like that. But don't fool yourself that it's all bad. Especially from Dark's standpoint in '61, when he was trying to snap a contending ball club back into shape.

"Look," he explained at one point, "I've come in from shortstop too many times and heard the manager come out and say to the pitcher, 'Don't give him anything good but don't walk him,' and the manager isn't back to the dugout before he hears the sound of the base hit. If you don't want to give him anything good, then walk him. At least, what happens after that is your responsibility. Responsibility for decisions like this *should* be the manager's. That's what I'm here for. If you're going to blame somebody, blame me."

Of course, in saying that, he was bargaining for more hell than maybe he expected. Once established, by his own pronouncement, that he intended to "overmanage," and that he intended to take the blame for anything that went wrong, Dark had to listen to an awful extra lot of blame. We had one game where one of our hitters missed a "take" sign and swung at a 3-and-0 pitch and popped it up in a critical situation. Now one of the San Francisco columnists, who didn't bother to find out the true situation, just made his own assumption and did a whole piece about how Dark's overmanaging had reached the point where he was telling hitters to swing at 3-and-0 pitches in ridiculous situations. And Alvin had no choice but to sit and take it. His own admitted overmanaging had got him to the point where he looked guilty regardless.

Another thing: Dark reasoned that he himself had never been the greatest ballplayer in history. Thus, he seemed to tell himself, anything he could do, the Giants he managed could do too. It was almost an overappreciation of our talents. There were a lot of things he could do that a lot of us couldn't do. Yet he expected them from us. One game, Dark asked Tommy Haller to squeeze Cepeda home from third, and Tommy just didn't believe the sign. He went back to the dugout, supposedly to get a new bat, but actually to ask Dark if he was kidding or not. Dark said flatly that he wasn't kidding. By this time everybody in the ball park knew the bunt was on, and of course they pitched out and nailed Orlando off third. You got the feeling at times that Alvin Dark thought he was managing 25 Alvin Darks.

Yet this too had its plus side, especially at the beginning. For as a result, he had ballplayers doing things they *could* do, but just hadn't bothered with up till then.

And let us face it, Dark also became a one-man advertising agency for Willie Mays. What the man did for me, I will never forget. I had had it hard in San Francisco, for reasons I've already outlined, and the lengths Dark went to in his first season as manager to enhance the figure of Willie Mays were lengths that few people suspect. I won't list all of them here—maybe no one quote, or move, that he made was outstanding on its own. Put them all together, though, and they were a pattern of one man going all out for another man.

Here are a couple of 1961 examples:

Dark said on the radio in San Francisco: "Without Willie Mays, the Giants are an ordinary ball club."

Dark heard that we had not won a game in San Francisco when I didn't appear in the lineup. For this reason, he started me the last game of the season (the second game of a doubleheader in Milwaukee—we'd already clinched third place in the first game) and played me for one inning. His private reason: "I don't want them to win without Willie in the lineup."

Those are just two examples, but you'll have to agree they're two pretty good ones. The man went on television, too, and called me the greatest ballplayer he'd ever seen—greater, he said, than Musial, Williams, or Mantle.

Not that he downgraded his other players. But he went out of his way for me, determined to do what he could to correct a San Francisco image of me which, he felt, was not my fault.

To say that all he was trying to do was win ball games, via securing fan appreciation for a player who enjoyed appreciation, is to say a fairly obvious thing. But it doesn't tell the whole story, and it doesn't lessen the way I felt toward him.

And this especially because I knew he was saying what he really felt. Not everything a baseball manager says is the straight dope. Actually it can't be.

In his first training season as manager, for example—this was in the spring of '61—Dark saw three of his players land in jail on "drunk-and-disorderly" charges late one night. Actually, the question of whether the players had done anything wrong was up for grabs. They'd been coming back to the Adams Hotel, and some joyriding juveniles had baited them, and there were some words exchanged, and our three were the ones the police put in the paddy wagon. Bob Begam, one of the top lawyers in Phoenix, climbed out of bed to go down to the jailhouse to represent our guys till they were released on $30 bail apiece (an amount that doesn't exactly indicate a capital crime), and to this day no one's at all sure how much at fault they were, if at all.

Now, though, Dark had this problem: if he felt the players were innocent, he had no business fining them. But if he didn't fine them, how would he make other fines stand up? Could you fine a man $25 for missing a sign but fine him nothing for getting himself mugged and fingerprinted?

So to protect his own system, Dark had to fine the players who'd been jailed. (It was $100 apiece, later rescinded.) But to protect his players, he had to tell the press they'd done nothing wrong and therefore had not been fined.

So he just plain lied to the reporters about it, and I don't know what else he could have done.

Still and all, here was the same problem in another form: Dark was doing things that had bad sides and good sides, both at one and the same time. The good sides were awful good. But the bad sides were going to have to catch up with him, sooner or later, and he'd suffer for them.

I myself favored at the time, and still do, all of those things he did, because I felt then, and feel now, that they balanced out on the plus side for the ball club. There was only one thing he did—at the time, it seemed most innocuous of all—that I thought he had no good reason for. And maybe this is what in the long run was the one thing that truly hurt him worst of all.

Like I say, it was innocuous. I thought the man might have played a little more golf. Stayed up a little later, if he felt like it. You run into all kinds of discipline under different managers. Little things, like swinging at a certain pitch when the manager's asked you to lay off that pitch—with Dark, the fine for that was a couple of golf balls. Bigger things, like a woman being in a ballplayer's hotel room on the road (a fine that, I might hastily add, I don't know ever was invoked against a Giant player). Or this much for violating a curfew or that much for failure to hustle.

My point is a very simple one: players are disciplined because they play. Managers and coaches don't play. For you as manager to voluntarily subject yourself to the same schedule of fines, across the board, as you have for your players, can just reach a point where it stops making sense. In some cases, it's great. But you can reach an absurd point, like where a coach is subjected to the curfew rule on the road and it's still his job to check on whether the players are violating the curfew. Now, how does he enforce this rule without violating it himself?

Understandably, Dark wanted to lead by example. But a baseball season can last up to six months or more, and there are rules and there are rules. Some of them, everyone should be subject to. But others need to be only for the players themselves, since they apply only to the question of physical fitness which isn't required of the manager or the coaches. Furthermore, someone like a manager has extra duties all his own. He has to make the appearances and the banquets, and so forth and so on, including some where everybody understands that, for training reasons, he can be there but the players can't.

So in the long run, the manager who handles it this way from the start has everyone's understanding. The manager who goes out of his way to put himself, in a blanket way, under the same training rules as his players, invites misunderstanding. To violate a rule that doesn't affect you means nothing, but to violate one that, while it may not affect you, you've nonetheless promised to observe, can lessen your whole structure of discipline and respect. And when you lose respect, you lose communication, and when you lose communication, the grumbling sets in, and there goes your hold on your ball club.

It isn't as simple or as clear-cut as that, of course, but it's a way of asking for trouble. On the other hand, if this is the only thing you could criticize Alvin Dark for when he first took over the Giants, he must have been a pretty fine manager. After all, it didn't take much for him to set an example by being in bed early. He went to bed early by habit.

And let me tell you, he *was* a pretty fine manager.

And the one thing he wanted, above everything else, was to win. This, maybe, accounted for his overmanaging. Everybody who's been around baseball for a while, seems like, gets some "pet play" in his head. And Alvin Dark, who dreamed, slept, and ate baseball, didn't lose a minute, once he got a job as manager, putting some of his "pets" to work.

The trouble with pet plays is, they have a way of going wrong. Or they work once and then they change the rules on you. One year in Cincinnati, Don Hoak got himself intentionally hit by a ground ball, to avoid what looked like a sure double play. He actually *fielded* the ball, as I remember, then tossed it to the shortstop. So the ball was dead for hitting the base runner; Hoak, the runner, was automatically out; and the hitter automatically got a single out of it. Well, they had to go and change that rule, so you can't get away with getting yourself intentionally hit anymore.

And Casey Stengel was supposed to have a famous "pet play" when he was managing the Boston club in the thirties. The idea was that with a man on third, the pitcher was supposed to throw directly at the batter's head and shout a warning at the same time. According to Casey's theory, everybody would "freeze" and the catcher could whip the ball down to third and catch the runner off. They tried it once and, according to Casey, "It worked too well. Everybody did freeze—the third baseman worst of all. So the ball went into left field."

Dark's real pet called for a truly specialized situation. You had to have men on first and third, and a left-handed pitcher working, and have a weak hitter at bat with two strikes on him, and be in a realistic situation as far as the score was concerned, like maybe a run or two ahead.

The purpose was to get that man home from third, on the theory that a weak hitter with two out and two strikes wasn't likely to do it for you.

Now, it had to be a left-handed pitcher because when he takes his stretch position he's facing first base. So that way, first he'd look at the runner leading off third, looking over his shoulder at him; then he'd look at first; then he'd deliver to the plate.

The minute he stopped looking at third, Dark had the runner there break for the plate. At the same time, the man at first was supposed to make a big bluff toward second. Ideally, the pitcher would throw over there to catch him in a run-down, which would give the other runner time to score before the out was made. But if the pitcher didn't fall for that, or if somebody yelled at him to throw the ball home, Dark reasoned that the chances were real good that in throwing home, in that state of alarm and from the stretch position, the pitcher would commit a balk and the run would come in that way.

We must have worked on this two solid hours in spring training, and then Cap started trying it in exhibition games. The amazing and actually funny thing about it was not how many times it didn't work, but how many times it came up. You'd think if you ran into that exact situation—a left-handed pitcher, the score right, the number of outs, the hitter, the count on the hitter, the base runners in the right places—if you ran into that one time a season, that'd be about it. Two times would be extending the law of averages.

But I think we actually got to try it something like five times inside of a month! It worked once, in an exhibition game, and not even Dark had expected it would work every time. It wasn't just that it didn't work the other times, but the ways it didn't work, that made him just throw up his hands and give up on it. Once the guy on first didn't break the way he should have. Once the guy on third didn't. Once everything worked and the pitcher balked but the umpire didn't call it. Once the pitcher didn't balk but the guy on third had such a good break he was going to beat the ball to the plate and actually steal home—only the hitter forgot and swung and missed for strike three and the third out.

As I say, pet plays have a way of not working. I can think of only one really new situation in baseball, and that was when I was just a kid. First basemen started holding the runners on the bag with two out. In the days before that, the custom was to play normal fielding depth with two out and let the runner take a big lead. (For this reason, the base-running of men like Maury Wills and Jackie Robinson might strike you as more impressive than that of some of the old-time base stealers, because about one-third of the time, it used to be that you had a "gift" lead off of first, whereas now they're holding you on all the time.*)

* I say "about" one-third of the time because actully there are more none-out situations than one- or two-out situations. There has to be at least one none-out situation every half-inning, but a double play eliminates the possibility of either a one-out or a two-out situation.

Ty Cobb said of me that I had restored the art of base-running to the game, and that is just about the finest compliment I can ever remember—except that I'm not positive it's the truth. There were great base stealers in the forties, like Wally Moses and George Case, but it wasn't till Jackie Robinson came along that the first basemen actually started playing the bag with two out. So if anybody "restored" the art, you'd have to think of Jackie ahead of anybody else. He actually rewrote the book on how baseball is played, because of that basic defensive shift that came in because of him, and I might say this is an interesting argument against those old-time critics who argue that baseball has become a slugger's game. For the only real change we've seen in something like two or more generations has been not on account of hitting but on account of *running!*

My point here is how little the game really has changed—I've just mentioned the only example I can think of. So pet plays don't really play a part, even though everybody has one in the back of his mind.

Herman Franks told me about a play Billy Meyer used to use. What's interesting about this one is that, if you use it just infrequently, in very carefully selected spots, it will work not only in the major leagues but in the minors, and in college, and in high school, and in Pony League—all the way back to the earliest they play where they can take a lead on the pitch—and it will work about the same against the best pros as against the youngest amateurs.

Bases loaded, 3-and-2, two out—everybody runs on the pitch. Right? Okay. Now—how about bases loaded, 3-and-2, *less* than two out?

Suppose everybody runs on that pitch too?

Meyer's theory was that it didn't matter who was pitching—the greenest kid or the most hardened professional. The sight of that man on third breaking for the plate on his delivery could cause him to balk—or, if he didn't balk, to throw *ball four!*

In other words, the chance of a strike was awful small, so the risk was awful small. And if it was a strike, the hitter might swing and connect. Maybe for a hit (you're ahead). Maybe for a ground ball (you're ahead). So the risk gets even smaller.

It figures down to a better-than-80-percent chance of scoring, given all the different possibilities, if the runners go on the pitch!

I don't know a thing to say against this play, used in the right situation, except somehow you don't see it. Like a magazine article Bobby Bragan did half a dozen years or more ago, showing how statistics prove you should let your best hitter lead off for you, just for the extra times at bat he'd get that way over a full season. Once again, a "pet" idea that makes all kinds of sense—except you never saw Bragan leading off with Henry Aaron, did you?

I've even got a pet of my own. Ready? Count no balls and two strikes, bases empty. Pitcher can really waste one now and throws so wide, catcher can't handle it. My pet play is that the batter should swing on this pitch, which will put him on first because the third strike got past the catcher. It's a funny idea, and I've never tried it, but I confess it's in the back of my head, just as a notion. Of course, the pitch might not be wide—it might be 'way inside, right at you. That becomes interesting, because getting hit by a pitch puts you on first same way as swinging and missing when the ball got by the catcher. I've got a mental image of swinging and getting hit at the same time.

But there is a great difference between "pet plays" and fundamental instruction, even though at times the results may seem the same. For instance, Alvin Dark spent a good deal of time at Phoenix, that first year, showing his *slower* runners how to steal bases. This is an interesting point, too, because sometimes it almost seems like you can tell from the way a man manages, what position he played during his active career. Not that it's a set-and-fast rule, but sometimes you get the feeling that the catchers who become managers are the ones who then put the "take" sign on the most when the count's 3-and-1. They're dealing from their own experience, and they remember the countless times they called for an "off" pitch, figuring the hitter would be looking for a strike and therefore would be chasing anything that came up to the plate.

Or take the managers who used to be outfielders. They played on their bats, not on their defensive ability, because nonhitters don't get to play the outfield. You've all heard the expression "strong down the middle." This means catcher, shortstop, second baseman, and, to a lesser extent, center fielder. But all it really means is that the catcher, second baseman, and shortstop can get into the starting lineup on the strength of their gloves. Everybody else has to hit his way on. Westrum hit less than .200 for us in '54, but he was our regular catcher, and he was just tremendous as a winning factor. But at the same time nobody was going to hit .189 and be our regular right fielder.

And so the outfielders who become managers, manage like "hitters." Seems like they're the last ones to take a hitter out of the batting order late in the game, so as to put in a defensive replacement to hold a small lead. They're thinking of still having that bat in there on the chance they might want more runs next time around.

And, when former pitchers become managers, they tend to think as pitchers and the former infielders tend to think like infielders. What position you used to play has, of course, nothing to do with your ability to lead a ball club, get the most out of your men, so forth and so on. But in the tactical department, you do spot a little throwback, a lot of times, that traces to where the manager used to play. Former pitchers and catchers, to cite just one more example, tend to use their own judgment on when to take out a pitcher or leave him in, more than former infielders or outfielders, who kind of lean more on their pitching coaches.

Anyway, here was Dark, a former shortstop, and I once saw him "force" the other team to use Jerry Lynch as a pinch hitter. Part of Dark's thinking was that that would get the other team's second baseman out of the lineup, since he was the one Lynch was going to hit for, and it would cause a less-gifted second baseman to take the field for them for the last three innings. The way this particular move worked out that day isn't important—if you win, you're a genius; if you lose, you're an idiot—but the point is that as an ex-infielder, he was thinking of that defensive situation at second base, whereas another manager who'd played something besides infield might not have been "thinking infield." Even there, I stress that this is just a *part* of the overall thinking. But it does seem like there are those little differences that a lot of times you can see at work if you think about them.

Dark as a shortstop, though, had a notion how our slower men could steal a base, and it was a good notion, and it might not have been brought up by a manager who hadn't played shortstop. On the face of it, it looked totally crazy. The idea was not only that a slower man could steal a base, but that he could do it *by delaying!* It took an Alvin Dark to think of this, but he'd played shortstop, and he knew that there's a point when the pitcher delivers the pitch that the infielder—the shortstop or second baseman—has to take his attention away from the man on first and get set for the result of the pitch instead. Now, that shortstop or second baseman not only always does this, but does it more basically when the runner on first isn't a threat to steal anyway. And you can't throw to second base—or, at least, you shouldn't—unless somebody's there to catch the ball when it comes.

So all Dark told our slower runners was, wait till the fielders snap their attention toward home plate, then take off. Your unexpected delayed steal will get you there when a faster man's expected steal wouldn't, simply because they're set to react to the fast man—maybe even pitch out—but they're not figuring on you. So they'll be slow to cover, and the catcher will have to hold up his throw, and you've got it stolen.

And this was not just what you'd call a "pet play." This was something that was soundly thought out—and it worked.

By the same token, when, somewhere into the 1961 season, Dark decided to take Cepeda back out of the outfield and work him at first base, he used a shortstop's thinking to work with Chico on a play that had always bothered him—the force throw to second from the first baseman. Cepeda had had a habit of throwing the ball into left field, a habit that stemmed, I think, mainly from a subconscious determination not to have the ball hit the runner going to second. Since that runner's headed where you're supposed to be throwing, if you subconsciously aim away from him, then you're aiming away from your target too. It isn't just a question of having a "scatter arm."

Anyway, what Dark did, as an ex-shortstop, was work not with Cepeda, but with our shortstop, José Pagan, who'd be taking that throw at second. He got José to hold up his glove as a target for Cepeda *out of line* with the runner's path. If Cepeda was back of first, Pagan would give him the outside target. If Cepeda had come in to field that ground ball, Pagan would be stretching his glove off the inside of the bag. In effect, what Dark had the sense to do, in correcting an "erratic" arm, was not to correct the arm but to correct the target instead. It was right, and it was clever. But maybe the reason Cap thought of it was he'd been a shortstop himself.

Now, there is still another category of "plays"—not just "pet plays," not just those that strike you that might not always occur to somebody else, but plays that almost everybody knows about, but that you put into use more than most others do.

One example is bringing a pitcher into the game just to issue an intentional base on balls, then taking him right out again. It looks crazy on the face of it—I mean, if you want to walk somebody on purpose, why not let the outgoing pitcher do it instead of having a guy working on his control in the bullpen, then coming in to throw four wide ones. But of course it makes sense, and Dark was one to use the play.

The joker is of course that a pinch batter doesn't have to actually get up to bat—he can be announced, then removed for someone else before he ever gets to swing—but a new pitcher does have to pitch to at least one hitter.

Bearing that in mind, let's see how Dark worked it in a typical situation, this one in an early '61 game against the Cubs.

We were playing at Chicago, and in the last of the ninth we were tied 1-1 and Billy Williams led off for them with a double. Everybody figured Ron Santo, the next hitter, would be bunting, but they went against the book and he popped up instead. Now, with one out Ernie Banks was at bat, and of course we were going to walk him on purpose.

But Dark brought in Billy O'Dell from the bullpen and had him issue the intentional walk instead of Bob Bolin, who had been pitching for us.

In this manner, O'Dell, a left-hander, had already pitched to his one mandatory man—Banks—and now Dark was free to bring in a right-hander if the Cubs, not wanting the left-handed-hitting George Altman to bat against the left-handed-pitching O'Dell, decided now to pinch-hit for Altman.

Which they did. They sent up George Freese, a good right-handed hitter, to swing for Altman. Immediately, Dark took out O'Dell and brought in Sam Jones, a right-handed pitcher.

So immediately the Cubs told Freese to sit down and sent up Bob Will, a left-handed hitter, to face Jones. Jones had to pitch to one hitter, of course, and Will was it, and the Cubs did have the percentage of the left-handed hitter going against the right-handed pitcher. But Dark didn't fear Will as a batter the way he feared Banks, Altman, or Freese, and sure enough, Jones got past him and pitched out of the inning, and we went on to win the game in extra innings.

This way we not only got through the ninth without having to pitch to Banks, Altman, or Freese—even though all three of those big hitters went up to hit—but two of them, Altman and Freese, were out of the game from then on, so we never had to worry about them again. And this all because a pitcher had come out of the bullpen, thrown four balls intentionally wide of the plate, then left the game!

Would you call that overmanaging? I'm not sure I would. All Dark did was have O'Dell be the one to walk Banks instead of Bolin. It was the Cubs who made all the first moves after that; all Dark did was suit to it.

When people get so they appreciate this play, their first reaction is to say why don't teams do this all the time? The answer to that, of course, is that just being a left-handed or a right-handed pitcher isn't enough to make it work. You have to be a *good* left-handed or right-handed pitcher to make the other side want to take an Altman or a Freese out of the lineup. And how many clubs have two top front-liners like O'Dell and Jones sitting in the bullpen, expendable so you can bring one in, have him walk a man, and give him the day off? If your schedule makes a couple of top men like O'Dell and Jones available this way on a day when the situation calls for it, okay. But it doesn't happen all the time. And some managers don't play the percentages as much as others.

The funniest percentage—by "funniest" I mean comical, the way it came out—was the way Gene Mauch managed against the Giants in '61. He walked me on purpose seven times through that season, three times to get to Cepeda. Those three times Cepeda got a single and two homers and eight runs batted in. A fourth time, the Phillies walked me to get to McCovey, who grounded out, but Cepeda, up after him, hit a two-run double. So Orlando's output against the Phils, following intentional walks to Mays, was, out of four times at bat, a single, a double, two homers and ten RBI's. After the season was over, Mauch was telling that story on himself. Somebody always asked him, "Do you ever intend to do that again?" And Mauch would reply: "I probably will."

This, in any event, was the Alvin Dark who started out managing the Giants of 1961.

I said then, "I never thought I'd say this about anyone—but I actually think more of Cap than I did of Leo!"

The other players were saying the same thing.

Mike McCormick, for instance: "That man's going to mean fifteen games for this ball club this year, all by himself."

Joey Amalfitano: "It gets so you can't win a ball game and you look at him and all of a sudden you think, hell, maybe we *can* win it."

Jim Marshall: "If you lay down on him, it's a crime."

Jim Davenport: "If you can't play for him, you can't play for anybody!"

# 20

WHEN I SAY APRIL and May are my best hitting months, then, like I say, you have to take that with a grain of salt. I've had my troubles those months too, but what I remember most of all was a "little" slump in April of '61. We'd gone on a road trip, starting in Los Angeles, where we won both games, then had come into Milwaukee, where, on a real cold Friday night, Warren Spahn pitched the second no-hitter of his career and beat us 1-0 on an unearned run. Sam Jones pitched for us, and all he gave up was five hits, all singles. As for Spahnie, he faced only the minimum number of men—27. He gave up two walks, but on the next hitter each time Spahn himself started the double play that wiped out the runner.

Day after that the Giants exploded. We got five home runs and 15 hits. In fact, everybody in the lineup hit safely except me.

So for that road trip so far, I was 0-for-my-last-7, and had only three singles in my last 15 times at bat. In fact, I was 10-for-my-last-40, and seven of those 10 were singles, and seven other times I'd struck out, so it's what I call a "little" slump.

On top of that, I went and got myself poisoned. Or so it felt like for a few minutes there. I was rooming with Stretch McCovey at the Schroeder Hotel in Milwaukee, and on this Saturday night, McCovey, who'd hit a pair of home runs that day, decided swinging a bat like that can make a growing young man hungry. So, rather than violate curfew, he fetched a double order of spareribs up to the room and we settled down for a midnight snack.

The ribs were tasty enough going down, but now, try as I could, I couldn't get to sleep, and there was a pain in my stomach and it kept getting fiercer and fiercer till finally I picked up the phone and got Doc Bowman, the trainer, and he tumbled out of his bed and came on up and fed me a spoonful of something and a couple of pills of something else. I wound up with about four hours' sleep, if that, and we had a day game the next day, and at the ball park I said to Alvin Dark, "Cap, I'm weak as a cat."

"Take some swings in hitting practice," he said. "See how you feel then."

Hitting practice felt all right—nothing sensational either way—and Dark said, "How about it?"

"I'll play," I said, and went back into the clubhouse, where one of the San Francisco writers was. He looked at me, and he said, "You look lousy."

"I feel lousy," I said.

"Don't brood about it," he said. He didn't know about the bad ribs the night before.

I started to laugh. "You writing I'm in a slump?"

"No," he said.

"I'll come out of it," I said. "I always do."

"You'll come out of it faster if you don't think about it," he said. (There it was: I was being "mental" again.)

"Listen," I said to him, "don't *you* ever get in a slump?"

"*Me?*" he said, and started to use some bad language.

I laughed again. "I read you," I said. "I know you get your slumps, same as the rest of us."

"Yeah?" he said. "Well, I don't have to go out and hit against Burdette."

"Don't go 'way mad," I said to him.

"Listen," he said, "all I wish is, I wish I knew what was so funny, that's what I wish."

"Just don't worry about anything," I said. "Your trouble is you worry too much."

"*I* worry?" he said. "*You're* the one who . . ." He threw up his hands ". . . Ah, forget it."

I was still laughing when he left the room.

Now, I remember that "little" slump, and those bad ribs, and that conversation with that writer, because that was the day I went out and hit four home runs in one game.

Maybe strange to tell, I have little or nothing to say about actually hitting those four home runs in one game. What I have to say about it, I've already said. I was coming up again in the ninth, when with two out, the hitter ahead of me grounded out to the second baseman, and the crowd booed their own man for retiring the hitter so I couldn't come to bat, and the truth is I *did* want to get another chance to swing—but I didn't want it that much.

Could I have become the first and only man in history to hit five home runs in one game? I suppose so. I would have liked to be Lloyd's of London and set the odds against me.

A guy showed me the chances on roulette one time. If you had $2 to spend, he said, and wanted to bet two numbers, then you had two numbers going on the spin of the wheel, and there are 38 numbers on the wheel, and you'd have a dollar on each of two numbers, and any number that comes up pays off at 35-1. So, he said, the mathematics are that you had two chances out of 38 to win $34, because the $35 you won on the number that came up would be reduced by the $1 you bet on the other number that didn't come up.

Now try it the other way, he said. Take the same $2, he said, but bet it twice on the same number, on *two* spins of the wheel instead of one. That way you had one chance out of 38 twice in a row. But you also had the chance that your number would come up *both times*. And you'd win $35 each time if it did.

Either way, of course, the odds don't favor you. But one way you have a shot at winning $70. The other way your best shot is $34.

Now, the house odds against you on one spin, if you're betting two numbers, are 36 out of 38, or about 94 percent. If you're betting one number at a time, but on two consecutive spins, the odds for the house are 37/38 × 37/38, or 1,369 out of 1,444, or about 95 percent. That is, 95 percent of the time you won't win on *either* spin of the wheel. Of course, you also have that fractional chance—1/38 × 1/38 —that you'll win on *both* spins. And it does happen. Numbers do repeat.

I said to this guy that my first feeling was that for a difference of maybe less than 1 percent in my overall winning chances, I'd rather bet the two numbers one at a time, instead of betting the same $2 on two different numbers on the same spin, where I know in advance one of my bets has to lose, and where I know my utmost potential is $34 against $70, or less than half.

"Your kind of thinking," he said to me, "is what keeps Nevada in business. They want you to bet twice instead of once, because they play 24 hours a day and you don't. They'd rather have 37 out of 38 chances against you twice than 36 out of 38 chances once. Sure you have a come-on. Why shouldn't you? You care very much what happens to you, but the house couldn't care less. They'll wait for the law of averages to bring them their edge. Who's doing the betting couldn't bother them less."

I thought about that some. I think instinctively, maybe I agreed with him all along. Not about roulette, because I don't play roulette. But that generally, the truth is I've never really wanted to go for that outside $70.

On the spur of the moment, I will gamble with anybody. A situation will come up in a ball game, and I'll go for it, even where maybe a lot of other guys wouldn't.

But as a general outlook—a "system," if you want to call it that— the answer is no. I'm a straight conservative. I can say honestly and truly that I have never consciously set out, or wanted, to lead the National League in anything.

In 1954, my first full season in the league, I was named Most

Valuable Player. For the next ten years, I never won the award
again. Over those ten years, I think it is likely I got more points in
the MVP balloting, overall, than any other player. And that is the
kind of thing that truly satisfies me.

It is hard to say this, because people look at a year like 1962,
when the Giants won the pennant, and I finished just behind Wills
in the MVP balloting, and it turned out whichever writers voted
in Houston, which was a new city that year, had cast their votes
for American League players as well as National Leaguers. And
that piece of sheer stupidity could, they tell me, have cost me the
award that year.

But couldn't that same stupidity have cost Wills the chance of
getting more votes than he actually did? Let me put it this way:
yes, I have goals. Over the years, I have wanted to hit .300 and
bat in 100 runs and score 100 runs and hit 40 homers a year. Some
years I've come in under those goals. Most years I've come in over
most of them. But there you have it. That's really the measure of
what I want.

I can repeat flatly that I do *not* set out to be the leader in any
single department. When I say this, I say it for a fact. I'm not
trying to be modest, and I'm not trying to show a lack of ambition.
Look at the goals I *do* have—written out just above here. Is there
anything modest or unambitious about them?

And right here, where I've started to talk about what I really don't
have much to say about—those four home runs in one game—I
suppose I can do some talking too about "my greatest day in baseball." I put that in quotation marks, because it's a standard inter-
viewer's question. I think there was even a book put out under
that title, with different players talking about the day they remember most. For myself, I've never been able to answer it. That is,
I can't name just any one day.

Bobby Thomson's homer would have to be one of my "greatest
days." And the time we came in to New York and they cheered
me in the rain. And my first major-league hit, the home run off

Spahn. And catching the ball off Walls for the pennant-clinching out in '62. Those four home runs in Milwaukee, certainly. The night in '63 when I homered in the 16th and Marichal beat Spahn 1-0. The catches off Clemente and Musial and Bouchee and Morgan and Amaro and Tommy Davis. The throws on Cox and Cunningham and Wills. Scoring from third on a short passed ball and from second on an infield out and from first on a single. Coming in to cover second base on a rundown play. Luring *good* outfielders into throwing behind me so I could move up.

And the look on the faces of the Milwaukee players the day they had bases loaded against us three times, twice with none out and the other time with one out, and haven't scored yet.

There's no question that most of the big memories come when you win. Somehow the same plays don't linger quite the same way, seems like, if you haven't got the game ball in the clubhouse with you. If you think I looked crazy climbing the wall in center field for the catch off Musial that time, you should have seen Dark climbing the one in the clubhouse after the game, when we'd lost by one run. Yet if most of the memories come when you win, maybe that's because when you do real good, you usually *do* win. And sometimes, it's not so much what you do as the moment you do it in.

I remember, for example, a game against the Braves at Candlestick, and, with two out in the ninth, Charley Lau was at bat for them and put up a little fly ball back of second base, toward right field. The way we were defending Lau, I was closer to the ball than our right fielder was, and Charley Hiller, at second base for us, was closest of anybody.

But Hiller had to track back for the ball, and the wind was doing something with it, so he and I just about came together, him with his glove up over his shoulder, going back, and me with my glove out in front of me, coming in.

In one final motion, I managed to snag the ball and avoid Hiller at the same time. Knowing how close together we were, I also realized how difficult it would be for anybody to see—actually see—

the catch, with the ball being blocked by bodies and gloves and everything else.

What made that moment, as I say, was that this was the last out of the game. I found myself grinning as I just kept going. It's only 100 feet or so, maybe less, from where I caught the ball to the side entrance to the clubhouses along the right-field line at Candlestick. And that's where I went, as fast as I could, with the ball still hidden in my glove.

I beat the rest of the guys into the clubhouse, since they were using the usual long tunnel from the dugout, and when they got there, they were laughing fit to split. I got to say, Hiller was laughing harder than anyone else. He started acting out how first him, then the umpire, started looking in his glove, then around on the ground, to try to find the ball. It was a funny moment—one you remember. And I'd also hit two home runs in that game, one with the bases loaded. But—"my greatest day"?—I just couldn't say that.

One night in Philadelphia, I scored from first on a single to left by Cepeda. They say you can't score from first on a single to left. I've done it twice. But they're right—the truth is, you *can't* do it—not all by yourself. The real base-running is done by the guy who hit the single.

In this case, their shortstop went out on the grass and cut the ball off as the outfielder threw it toward third. The shortstop knew I had third base safely. So he did the "smart" thing. He wheeled and looked at first, to see whether Chico had been "careless" in turning the base. Chico had been "careless." He was hopelessly trapped. So they threw over there real fast.

By which time, I was in the dugout. I'd just never stopped running. A throw from the shortstop to the plate would have nailed me by nine miles. But Cepeda had literally "smoke-screened" them into playing for him instead.

So he was trapped off first—or was he? The first baseman and second baseman had him in a rundown, and it was a standard defensive deployment, with the second baseman running Chico back toward first, then throwing to the first baseman, then ducking out of the play. So when Chico turned and started toward second again, the first baseman could throw to the shortstop covering the base there.

But the shortstop never showed up at second. He'd been close to third at the start of the play, and after seeing me score he'd gotten upset and was out of position anyway. So nobody covered second base, and now here was Cepeda racing for second with Pancho Herrera, the Philadelphia first baseman, chasing him with the ball. And Orlando dived safely into second base. Afterward, we told him he just should have kept running—that the Phillies generally and Herrera in particular were so mad by then, Herrera would have chased him all the way around the bases and across home plate!

I remember another night in Philadelphia—and this one needs some background to tell it right. The background really starts in Milwaukee, when we had a game there and Billy Loes was in pitching for us in relief. I hit two home runs in that game, but we lost 8-6, and it was my fault as much as anyone's. I just plain misjudged a fly ball. I don't do that very often, and when a guy doesn't make that kind of mistake, fans always think there must be some hidden factor at work when he *does* do it. But there was nothing hidden here. I blew it, that's all.

It was a bad time for Loes, who was kind of temperamental anyway. We were all fond of the guy and called him "Bugs," which I guess goes in a way to describe him. He once lost a ground ball in the sun.

Bugs wound up getting kicked out of the game. This is how one of the San Francisco papers described it:

. . . After umpire Vargo had called ball one on Loes' first pitch to Henry Aaron, Loes stormed toward the plate, shouting at the arbiter. Almost instantly, Vargo's right arm swept majestically around as he ordered Loes from the field.

"All right," Loes said to him, and tossed him the ball. "You pitch."

Then he tossed his glove too, and when the object accidentally brushed Vargo's arm there wasn't much more that could compound the situation.

"He threw me out of the game, so I gave him the ball," Loes said afterward.

"You gave him the glove, too," somebody pointed out.

"I'm an honest guy," Loes replied. "I don't want to fight a stacked deck."

This could have almost as many meanings as the listener could think of. The Giants had played badly back of Billy while he pitched last night. Willie Mays had literally misjudged a fly ball —a once-in-a-decade rarity for him—to give Joe Torre, the first batter Loes faced, a leadoff triple in the seventh. Harvey Kuenn, playing right field, had a chance to catch the ball, but Mays was under it. Willie suddenly said two words, the first of which was "Oh," and by then it was too late for anybody to catch it.

Loes now got the next two men out infield, holding Torre at third, but left fielder Orlando Cepeda was late in starting after Gino Cimoli's liner, and it reached the fence for a double.

Then starting off the last of the seventh, Willie McCovey at first base juggled Eddie Mathews' grounder and made a just-in-time hard throw into the stomach of Loes, covering first, for the out.

By now, all Bugs needed was a close call from Vargo. He got it on the next pitch.

The strange thing was that Loes wasn't fined or suspended for throwing the ball and glove to Vargo like he did. Actually, I think the reason was it all happened so fast. Bugs just handed Vargo the ball and glove and kept going. In effect, he was kicking himself out of the game. By the time Manager Dark got out to home plate to try to smooth things out, Loes had passed him and was in the clubhouse. (Vargo said to Dark, as Alvin arrived, "What do *you* want?" and Cap replied, "Darned if I know," and turned around and went back to the dugout.)

But now Dark was unhappy, because we'd lost, and Loes was unhappy, because *he'd* lost, and we got into Philadelphia, and the first game there, we got four runners to third base and four more to second and never scored a run and lost 1-0. Just as in the Milwaukee game where Loes gave the ball and glove to the umpire, again we left 12 men on base.

Now Dark honestly went a little bit out of his mind. Storming into the clubhouse, he picked up the nearest object—a stool—and threw it against a locker. Trouble was, his hand had got lodged under the lip of the stool, so when he threw the stool he threw half of the little finger of his right hand along with it and had to go to the hospital for stitches.

Things didn't improve any on the bus going to the ball park the next night, when some clown on the club asked Alvin to count to 100 by nines.

But by the time that night's game was over (we won, 12-5), things had begun to look up. By the time the following night's game was over, things had stopped looking altogether. We played the longest night game in major-league history—five hours, 11 minutes—and got a 7-7, 15-inning tie out of it. It was 4-4 going into the last of the 14th, and now Dark tried to stall out the curfew that says no inning can start after 12:50 A.M. His reasoning was that with everybody's lineup used up by now, we had a better chance playing the whole thing over. And he did everything he could think of, even including having our warm-up pitcher in the bullpen intentionally pitch wide ones so the ball would roll onto the playing field and make them call time. At 12:49 A.M., he signaled Hobie Landrith, our catcher, to give Jack Sanford, the pitcher, the sign to "slow down." Jack mistook this for the sign to "change up." So instead of not pitching at all, he threw a slow ball to Don Demeter —an 0-and-2 count, when you never throw a change-up, especially to Demeter. And Demeter swung and missed for the third out, so we went to the 15th inning!

Now, in the top of the 15th, we scored three times.

And, in the last of the 15th, so did they. The tying run came in —you won't believe this, but it's how it happened—when Landrith was returning a pitch to our pitcher (now Mike McCormick), and Mike didn't see it, and the ball went past him while the man came in from third!

So we had to replay the game next night, now as part of a twi-night doubleheader, and what we did, again, is told perhaps the quickest way by the story in the paper:

Willie Mays owns Philadelphia, Billy Loes owns a five-hitter, the Giants own a double triumph over the Phillies and second place in the National League. Also the caretaker at Connie Mack Stadium owns 142 empty beer cans.

The twi-night victory for the San Francisco club, ending the strangest 24 hours in baseball's modern times, saw them win the first game 8 to 7 in ten innings on Mays' third homer of the game and 299th lifetime.

In the second game Mays tripled home the first run, scored the second, doubled home the last, and gave Loes the confidence nobody thought he'd ever show again with a sensational double-play throw to the plate in the first inning. The Giants cruised, 4 to 1.

. . . When Mays walked in the sixth inning of the afterpiece, Philadelphia catcher Jim Coker could stand no more. He screamed. Umpire Tony Venzon threw him out and an eight-minute beer break followed as empty cans clattered out of the stands. None of the 14,997 fans, it appears, can aim. . . .

In that doubleheader, I had six hits for 18 total bases. I scored four runs, batted in seven, reached base seven times. The two times I was out were on extremely long fly balls to the outfield.

(Incidentally, I've had six hits in a doubleheader more than once, and seven at least once—but . . .)

"But," I say. I think two things: first, I think that if I ever have to select a "greatest day," that doubleheader in Philadelphia, one people don't think of right away when they talk about big moments I've had, would have to rank right up there. As much for the throw I made to the plate in the  second game as for any of the hits, because with that one I was making something up that I owed Billy Loes from the time before.

And the second thing is that all of the episodes I've brought up here—the doublehader in Philadelphia, the scoring from first base on the single, the "funny" play on the last out of that game against the Braves—all occurred within the stretch of less than two months, early in the 1961 season. And so, in that same stretch, did the four home runs in one game.

Suppose you were me. Would you pick your four homers in one game over that doubleheader in Philly? What *is* a "greatest day"?

Maybe, like I said a little while ago, your greatest day isn't a day, it's a night—it's not a game, it's an exhibition—it's not something in the game, but before it. It's not anything you do. It's what other people do. Like, as I said a little bit ago, when they stand in the rain, 50,000 of them, and scream and roar and shout and yell, and you stand there listening to it and the tears run down your cheeks. . . .

# 21

I CAN NEVER forget that moment—in late July of '61, when we came into New York to play the Yankees an exhibition game at the Stadium.

This is from the San Francisco *Examiner's* story:

The Giants had come home, and in a driving, steaming summer rainstorm, the big town turned out to say hello.

There was no pre-game practice. It was raining. The pre-game home-run contest (Cepeda and Mays for us, Mantle and Maris for them) was called off. It was raining.

Game time was held up half an hour past the scheduled 7:55 P.M. start.

"We'll never play tonight," Alvin Dark said.

"Look outside and you'll change your mind," he was told.

He went down the runway and up into the visiting dugout along the third-base line and looked.

"Wow," he said reverently.

There in the rain sat the people. Waiting.

(They could have all stayed home and watched it free on TV. But they were there.)

"Ladies and gentlemen," said the Yankee Stadium announcer, giving the lineup for the San Francisco Giants, "at second base, number fourteen, Joe Amalfitano."

236

The cheering started.

"Number seven, Harvey Kuenn, right field . . ."

It got louder.

"Number twenty-four, Wil——"

You never heard the rest of the Giant batting order announced here tonight.

An unbroken, throat-swelling peal of adulation sprang from the hearts of Giant-starved New Yorkers. It rolled and volleyed off the great tiering of this triple-decked palace and against the vague outline of the Bronx County court house, looming in the gray-black mist out beyond the huge scoreboard in right-center field.

They rocked and tottered and shouted and stamped and sang. It was joy and love and welcome, and you never heard a cascade of sound quite like it.

That was the moment. That was the one that will always have the best place in my heart. Not that there haven't been others. But no others like that one.

# 22

WE HAD A RUN at the pennant in '61, fell short, then in the winter we got Billy Pierce and Don Larsen from the White Sox in a trade for four minor leaguers, and if it'd been Leo, he would have been sniffing a pennant.

Dark was sniffing it too.

Didn't have to be Leo.

In mid-August the Dodgers came in for a three-game series at Candlestick. One of our "favorite" columnists—one who was always down on me, and not 100 percent fond of the Giants as a club either—wrote that Friday that we were a bunch of choke-ups, and this series would prove it. We swept the series.

Monday he wrote another column taking credit for snapping us out of our choked-up situation. He'd personally got us mad, he said.

'Course, if the Dodgers had swept the series, he would have done the other column, the one that says I told you so. So he was 100 percent protected either way.

We were a fighting, kicking, battling team—one of the winningest Giant clubs in all history—yet there were the Dodgers, always there to be caught.

In 1961, I'd had 40 homers, 123 runs batted in, 129 runs scored. In '62 I was to hit 49 homers, bat in 141 runs. (Batting average?— hardly any difference—.308 in '61, .304 in '62. My only .320-plus average since coming to San Francisco had been that first year,

'58, when I hit .347 and they were taking the movies of me to show me what I was doing wrong.)

In mid-September we left on our last road trip. We'd won 94, lost 51, trailed the Dodgers by half a game in the standings.

We opened in Cincinnati—a hot, muggy night.

It had been a hot, muggy night back in Birmingham that time I'd hit the inside-the-park homer as a teen-ager and went dizzy after I crossed home plate.

It was a hot, muggy night in New York in 1954, one time when I was in a spell of hitting six home runs in six consecutive games, and I got an inside-the-park home run against the Cubs. When I went out to the field for the next inning, I had to call time. Standing there in center field, I started getting dizzy again. I bent over and put my hands on my knees, and the feeling went away.

Now it was hot and muggy in Cincinnati, and I hadn't hit any home run. I was in the dugout. We were batting in the top half of the second inning.

The next thing I know, I was lying on the floor of the dugout.

My eyes were open, but I couldn't see anything.

Doc Bowman had smelling salts under my nose and I could hear him saying, "It's all right, Buck, it's all right. It's nothing."

I sat up. "What's wrong with me?"

"Nothing," Bowman said. "Isn't that right, Alvin?"

Alvin Dark said nothing.

Larry Jansen came over. "What do you say, Buck? Can you see all right."

"Sure," I said. "I can see."

"Then what is it?"

"I just feel like I don't want to have to move," I said. "I *can* move, but I'd rather not."

Doc Bowman snapped at a couple of the other players. *"Get that damn stretcher!"*

In the radio booth, they didn't know who it was at first. Then they saw it was me. I heard later Russ Hodges, who has been broadcasting Giant games longer than I've been a Giant, had tears in his eyes when he saw who it was. Cynics would say this was because it was a key player at a key point in the race. In a way, I wish that was all it was, because there really wasn't that much wrong with me. But I know Russ too well, and he knows me too well. He was crying because I was his friend, and at that moment he couldn't tell *what* was wrong.

They took me to a hospital in Cincinnati, and the doctors there tried all the tests they knew, and found nothing. But they also knew better than to say they found nothing. What if they—strange doctors in a strange town—had missed something? There wasn't one of them going to give me the okay to go out and play ball again, not so long as I was in Cincinnati, Ohio. They might recommend it to a doctor in Pittsburgh, which was our next stop, but not on their own, they weren't going to take that chance.

I knew then what it was and I know now what it was.

I was exhausted. Mentally, physically, emotionally, every other way.

When Dark first took over as manager in '61, he announced that he'd be resting me periodically.

I've already said everything I can say about "rest," and how hard it is on a manager, not just on me.

But the fact is, the first complete game I missed in 1962 was the day after I collapsed, when I was in the hospital in Cincinnati, in September.

I will always hope—there will never be a way for me to know for sure—that Cap didn't think I lay down on him.

All he would say was, "Mays will play again when he says he's ready."

There are people who liked me and didn't like Dark, and who said that this statement of his was proof that he was calling me a bailout—proof that he, as a Southerner, had been bred to think the Negro man wouldn't put out when it counted. "If he wanted

Willie Mays called out on close play at third base during pennant play-off with Los Angeles, October 2, 1962. *(Courtesy Wide World Photos)*

A pitcher trys the "brush back" pitch on Willie. *(Courtesy* Sport *Magazine)*

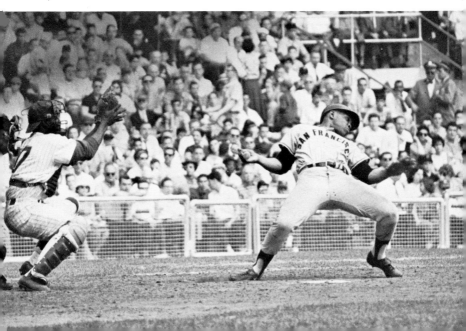

Last out of the game. To the surprise of everyone, including the second baseman, Charley Hiller, Mays catches the ball, hides it in his glove,

and carries it into the clubhouse where the players roar with laughter.
*(Courtesy Charles Doherty — San Francisco* Examiner)

Mays plays shortstop in 10th inning of ball game against the New York Mets! May 21, 1964. *(Courtesy Wide World Photos)*

Willie Mays poses with Giants coach, Herman Franks, and at right the baseball player's father, Willie Mays, Sr., August, 1964. *(Courtesy Wide World Photos)*

Willie Mays swings and connects for the 500th homer of his major-
league career, September 13, 1965. *(Courtesy Wide World Photos)*

Willie watching his team at bat . . . Frowns. . . . *(Courtesy* Life *Magazine)*

And then as his teammates get on base he permits himself a satisfied smile. *(Courtesy* Life *Magazine)*

Worries. . . . *(Courtesy* Life *Magazine)*

With two outs in the ninth inning, Willie Mays fouls off four 3-and-2 pitches, then hits the 501st home run of his career to win the game and keep the Giants in the 1965 pennant race. He doffs his cap. (*Courtesy* Life *Magazine*)

to protect you," they told me, "he would have said, 'Mays will play again when *I* say he's ready.'"

I think they overthink. Just like the people they pretend to hate the most, they see something when nothing's there and they fit it to whatever they want most to believe.

Sure the guy was heartsick. Who wouldn't be? He'd won seven in a row, had a shot at the pennant. Now, starting with that night I collapsed, he was to lose six in a row. We just plain fell out of the pennant race. I missed four full games. The next one I got into, I hit a home run to send it into extra innings, and we still lost.

They took a picture of me on the bench at Pittsburgh, one of the big wire services, and it appeared in papers all over the country. I was sitting there, huddled in a jacket, the unhappiest look in history on my face. *Aching to play,* one of the captions said.

The lovely touch about that was that it wasn't a picture of me. It was a picture of a bench warmer named Carl Boles, an extra outfielder we carried, who *was* aching to play. Boles looked a lot like me.

We came home from that trip—by now I was playing again—and with a week to go, we were four behind with seven to play.

I've talked about miracle pennants. The Giants of '51, who were 13½ out on August 11. The Giants of '54, who came from 35 games back the year before.

But never—NEVER—anything like 1962.

We didn't even win the damn thing. In that final week, we lost two games, one of them partially because I wandered off third base thinking three were out, and got tagged.

But those Dodgers, down in L.A., couldn't get a run to save their lives.

The Houston club came in for the final series. Joe Amalfitano, who'd played for us, now was with them. He said to me, "Can you score a run?"

"Yes," I said. "At least, I think we can."

"Then you've got the pennant," he said. "Those Dodgers are *never* going to score another run."

The Cardinals, who weren't going anywhere, were the last scheduled opponents the Dodgers had, and L.A. is a good "liberty town," so that final weekend some of the Cards had some pretty good hangovers. The line we heard was that the catchers were calling audibles because the pitchers couldn't see.

Yet they kept winning, the Cards, and on the final day of the season, with the score 1-1 in the eighth inning of our game with Houston, I hit Farrell for one of the longest home runs I've ever hit, and we won it 2-1.

In the clubhouse later, we learned the Dodgers had lost 1-0, so we tied them in the final day and there would be a play-off— the first play-off, of the four in National League history, that came about where the two teams didn't tie for the pennant till that last minute. Let me clarify that—the other three times, the two front-runners had come into that final day both tied for the lead. In 1962, we entered the final day a game behind. In other words, it wasn't totally in our hands. Even if we won, they still had to lose. If we lost, the race was over regardless.

Now it was a play-off—the Giants *vs.* the Dodgers—and we lost the toss this time, meaning the first game would be at Candlestick, then down to Chavez Ravine—but who cared?

That Giant team of '62 was to win 103 ball games, one of the two or three greatest Giant records of all time, but we hadn't won anything. The Dodgers had lost it. They'd lost it because Koufax got hurt. He pitched the first game of the play-off. I hit two homers off him, and everybody else hit too, and we won 8-0.

Then we went down there and built up a 5-0 lead in the second game and couldn't hold it, and the Dodgers came on to win it, so there would be a third game—October 3, 1962, 11 years to the day from the final game of that 1951 play-off.

But the two situations couldn't have been more different. In '51, we'd closed with that unbelievable rush against a team that was playing winning ball. In '62, we closed as well as we could, but the team we were closing on couldn't win for losing.

And it all came down to one game.

*I remember what I think nobody else remembers, from that one day: the way the clouds were against the sky. It was a good day, but it was October and it was getting late, and they were no longer white but ribbed with gray too, and you had the feeling that if you could reach high enough you could get the gray out of there.*

Me, I remember the clouds.

*The New York Times* had it on page one next day, with headlines equal to only one other story: Wally Schirra, the Astronaut, had successfully completed his orbital flight and been picked out of the Pacific.

But I remember the clouds.

I saw them, looking up automatically the way you always did when you came up out of the dugout at Chavez Ravine, carrying two or even three bats, to go out in the on-deck circle and await your turn to hit.

The date: October 3, 1962.

It started—that last half of the ninth—with the player I admired most. Only he was no longer a player. Now, Alvin Dark was manager.

That time, 11 years before, Leo Durocher had made a little speech. This time, with us behind 4-2 going into the top of the ninth, our last at bats, Manager Dark made a little speech, too, except you couldn't rightly call it a speech.

All he said was, "Matty, get your bat."

Durocher? He was there. As a Dodger coach, though, sitting over there in the other dugout, staring at us, snarling, using those words—but he remembered too. I know he remembered.

And Matty Alou went up to pinch-hit for our pitcher.

He hit the first pitch to right field for a single.

Kuenn forced him, but now McCovey got a pinch walk, and Felipe Alou walked too, to load the bases.

It was my turn, with bases loaded.

Eleven years ago, I'd prayed it wouldn't have to be me come up with bases loaded in that ninth inning of that last play-off game against the Dodgers.

Now, I prayed it *would* be me.

And it was.

That was the measure—the true measure, I believe—of how far I'd come as a major-league ballplayer.

I *wanted* to hit!

Wanted to, and did—slashed one up the middle, off the pitcher's leg for a run-scoring single that left the bases loaded, and now Cepeda got us the fly ball to right field that scored the tying run. A wild pitch, and big Alou and I both moved up, dictating an intentional walk to Ed Bailey to load the bases.

Now Davenport drew a walk, an inside pitch from Stan Williams 3-and-1, forcing in the go-ahead run, and a Dodger error gave us another run.

Once again, we'd scored four times in the ninth to go ahead, just as we had 11 years before. Now we still had to hold them off in their half, but no sweat. Billy Pierce came in and it was three up, three down.

The last out of the game was a half-liner to right-center that held up for me. I caught the ball and threw it into the stands.

In that crazy clubhouse afterward, I remember them offering me champagne and me just turning it down this time. Who needed it?

I remember Alvin Dark on television, shell-shocked, at his greatest moment of triumph complaining on nationwide TV that the Dodgers who thought he'd wet our infield at San Francisco ought to be prosecuted for keeping their own like it was a brickyard. . . .

And I remember Bob Stevens, looking at me like an owl and saying, "I didn't notice you using that basket catch on that last out."

I grinned at him. "You think I'm crazy?"

And I remember the flight home, and the pilot coming on the

intercom and telling us they weren't sure they could land at San Francisco, they might have to land at Oakland, because there were 30,000 fans down there and they'd broken police lines and were overrunning the runways.

They finally got us down and into a bus, but then the crowd broke the police lines again and threatened to turn the bus over.

"They want you, Mays!" the driver said.

From the back of the bus came a growl from somebody else: "Throw 'em Boles and let's get out of here!"

# 23

THE DIFFERENCE BETWEEN the World Series of '51 and '54, and now this one in '62, was, I'll swear, that the Giants couldn't have cared less. I don't mean we weren't trying to win it. I mean instead that any team that a week earlier was trying to figure out how to win second-place money, and instead now would get a World Series share if it *lost*, wasn't going to be particularly tense at the prospect of facing the Yankees.

We weren't, either. We carried it out to the full seven games, but what with the way we won the pennant, and travel, and rain, the thing got drawn out far more than that, and to many people it was an anticlimax by the time it ended.

Not that the Series itself ended on any note of anticlimax. That bottom half of the last inning, with the Giants trailing 1-0 and the fans singing "Bye Bye Baby!" in the stands at Candlestick, was one of the great heart-stoppers I've ever been in.

Matty Alou opened it for us with a pinch bunt single against Terry, the Yankee pitcher. Our next two hitters tried to bunt him along, but both failed. Now I came up and sliced a double to right. If it wasn't for the unseasonable rains at Candlestick, which had the ground so wet they actually had to bring helicopters down almost to ground level and have them fan the water away so we could play, the ball would have been through to the fence for the game-tying triple, but the way it was, Maris got to it in time to cut it off and hold Matty at third.

246

Then McCovey came up, and in one of the strangest moves—or nonmoves—I ever saw a manager make, Houk decided to let Terry pitch to him. McCovey had hit a homer off Terry in the second game of the Series, and a tremendous triple his last time up in this seventh game. The Yankees could have played the percentage and brought in a left-hander—they had at least one left-hander ready in the bullpen—or, at worst, they could have walked McCovey intentionally, with first base open.

But they did neither. In our dugout, we were so sure they were going to change pitchers that Kuenn actually was at the bat rack, picking out a bat to swing in place of McCovey.

But they let Terry pitch to McCovey. Willie Mac lashed a tremendous foul to right, then a scorching line shot to the right of second base. Richardson was in the way of it. It brought him to his knees, but he held on to it, and that was the Series.

Afterward, somebody said to Dark, "McCovey hit that ball so hard, if it *had* gone through for a single, could Mays have made it home from second?"

"By the time they got the ball home," Dark replied, "Mays would have been dressed."

I would have, too.

# 24

ONE PIECE OF FAN criticism that had bothered me over the years was, in truth, the oldest piece of fan criticism there is. Take a guy you don't like, get faced with the fact that he has a good record, and your answer can always be: "Yes, but what does he do in the clutch?"

It's not a 100-percent bad question, at least in the early stages of a player's career. Like me—I didn't want to hit in that ninth inning of that last '51 play-off game; but I sure did want to hit in the same spot in '62. I'd got to the point where I didn't mind pressure, then actually to the point where I *liked* it.

And here in 1962, it seemed to me, I'd stacked up some pretty good proof positive. Last time at bat in the regular season, score tied, I homered; last time at bat in the play-off, Giants behind, I singled; last time at bat in the World Series, Giants behind, I doubled.

I mean, what do you have to *do?*

But the strangest claims follow you, and the strangest people think you choke up.

All his playing lifetime, Ted Williams was beset by a Boston sports editor who claimed Ted couldn't hit in the clutch. The man used the 1948 American League play-off game, which the Red Sox lost; the last two games of the '49 pennant race, where the Red Sox lost both times to the Yankees although a win either day would have given Boston the pennant; and the 1946 World Series,

248

which the Red Sox also lost. Williams in those 10 games, the man always said, was a total bust.

How they got to that play-off or those last two games or that World Series, the man never said. He was using his own definition of "clutch." In that case, you can take those three games of my own, at the end of '62, that I was just talking about, and even though they had an opposite result, you could use the same reasoning and not count them when you talk about me. There've been plenty of times I didn't deliver when we needed a hit.

What astonished me, in the spring of 1963, was to hear Alvin Dark talking that way. Dark was maybe not the most diplomatic man in baseball history. He used to ream us out pretty good in clubhouse meetings, and when Marichal had his finger hurt while he was pitching in the '62 Series, Dark said later he didn't care if it rained till Christmas, Juan wouldn't pitch again against the Yankees. Actually, at the point he said that, it was true Marichal wouldn't be needed again, because the one, or (as it turned out) two remaining games of the Series, both at Candlestick, would have Sanford and Pierce ready as the Giant pitchers, and they were best at Candlestick against the Yankees. But you still wouldn't call what Dark said a real feat of diplomacy.

Anyway, in the spring of '63, Cepeda was a holdout, and Dark had a press conference in Phoenix and said he'd been keeping a "point system" on key production by hitters, and that Mays and Davenport had done the best, but Cepeda was far down the list on delivering the big blow at the right time. Of course, this could have been nothing more or less than Dark cooperating with the front office in an effort to get a holdout to come to terms, but once again you couldn't call it real diplomatic. Fact is, if I hadn't known it was Dark talking, I would have sworn it was some fan.

Like I say, you run into players who don't deliver when the chips are down. But either they begin to deliver or they don't last in the big time. You don't go as long as Cepeda did, batting .300 and knocking in 100 runs every season, and not help your ball club. I know what I say here isn't going to change any fan's mind who reads this, and I guess, despite all my nice words on the subject, we all have secret feelings about other people and how they perform "in the clutch."

Which doesn't change my feeling of surprise when I heard the manager talk that way for print.

# 25

IN 1961, MY SALARY as a Giant had been $85,000. In 1962 it was to be $90,000; and, beginning in 1963, $105,000 per year—the highest, I was told, ever paid a ballplayer in straight salary.

"You're getting more than the President," somebody told me.

"So did Ruth," I said. (They say one time they told the Babe he was getting more than President Hoover, and he said, "I'm hitting better, too.")

I don't know what was the main difference between Ruth and the President in those days, but in my case the main difference was one of us couldn't pay his taxes. Me.

Over the years when we were in New York, the Giants had advanced me money against future salary—well, maybe that's putting it wrong. They had lent me money, and the future salary was of course the implied security. I don't want to give the impression that Horace Stoneham was acting like a finance company. The truth is the opposite. No man I know reacts more generously or more loyally than Horace Stoneham.

But this was money they'd advanced me, and over the years it had come to more than $50,000 total, and it wasn't my money.

Why had I been borrowing from the Giants? Well, to begin with, it had never been a really big swatch of money at any one time. And the story that goes with it isn't a new story. It's familiar and dull and if I don't go into the details here, it's not to hide anything.

It's not worth hiding. Being not worth hiding, it's not worth discussing in detail either.

It's understanding I'm appealing for, not sympathy—and they tell me there's a difference—when I say that I was a poor boy from Birmingham, suddenly thrust into the glamour and the spotlight and the excitement of the big city. They say there's a broken heart for every light on Broadway. There's also a way to spend your money.

They say I was in bad hands, and made foolish investments, and so forth and so on. The truth is even duller than that. I wasn't in bad hands. Most of the time, if you compare those days with the way they are today, for all intents and purposes I wasn't in any hands. As for investment—if you mean by that companies or stocks or new ventures—forget it. I never did enough of that to matter. If, when you speak of foolish investments, you mean buying a new car bigger or sooner than you have to, or having 20 tailor-made suits instead of half a dozen you could buy off a rack, or going out on a whim and paying retail for the most expensive pool table you ever saw, or getting married and throwing thousands into drapes and carpets and even wallpaper—all right. That was me.

I say "was." It isn't me anymore.

I own as many suits as ever, and I don't drive around in a Fiat. But my expenses now are planned. I don't pick out the first shiny thing I see in the store window.

A lot of people get a little smarter as they grow older, and I like to suppose this can be said of me. The trouble is, sometimes things have a way of closing in on you anyway. This was true of me too, after the Giants moved to San Francisco.

As I've said, things weren't 1,000-percent for me there to begin with. They cheered me in the parade when the ball club came to town, but somebody threw a rock through my window. They showed me what a cosmopolitan city San Francisco was, but somebody else wouldn't sell me a house. (Like I said, George

Christopher, the mayor then, got so mad he asked me to move in with him.)

Between things like that, and the booing, and the fact that my friends all were still in New York, I went and bought a house back in New Rochelle—in Westchester just outside New York—for me and my wife in the off-season.

Now my marriage was going on the rocks, so the house in New Rochelle was becoming just one more of my famous "investments." On top of that, as the divorce was acted upon, there was the factor of alimony. And—finally—the Giants themselves now needed the money back that they'd loaned to me. I don't know the details behind that—it could well be that, having moved to the Coast, they had to close out their books back East, and right now.

Naturally, they proposed that instead of them writing me my check and me writing them their check, they just withhold the money from my salary that year. This was '62.

Which put me in the position of having to pay not only my going expenses but my new expenses, plus the taxes on a $90,000 salary—all this on an actual income that year of no more, possibly, than $35,000.

Potentially, I was in a position where my actual income wouldn't even pay my Federal and state taxes.

It's easy to interpret the foregoing that I'm making the Giants the heavies here, for closing in on me that way. That interpretation couldn't be farther from the truth. Aside from the obvious thing, which is that a happy man produces better, I know that Horace Stoneham, out of nothing more than straight personal affection, would have seen to it that I didn't wind up going to any debtor's prison.

But all that could have done would be get me farther into the tunnel, with no daylight at the other end.

I remember vividly one game in '62, when the Dodgers were in Candlestick and I was in court, making an appearance on account of the divorce settlement. I got to the ball park too late to start, and Dark held me out till the eighth, when we were losing and we needed a pinch hitter, and Alvin sent me up against Drysdale. I hooked one real good down the left-field line, but just foul. Then he got me. And after the game, Leo Durocher—coaching for the Dodgers, but still as always a Mays fan—crowed that if I'd just been put in the field when I got to the ball park, the Giants would have won (there'd been a long ball to center, while I was on the bench, that went for a key extra-base hit for them).

The next day we flew to Chicago, to start a series there, and that night I couldn't sleep. I had the shakes. I found myself, for no real reason that I knew, on the verge of tears. I called Dark on the phone. I said, "I don't know what's wrong with me."

"Come on up," he said, and I went up to his room, and he called Doc Bowman and Doc came and fed me a couple of sleeping pills that would have felled a horse. "Sleep in here with me," Alvin said, pointing to the other bed, and then, maybe for an hour, he and I talked till the pills put me to sleep.

Later on, Dark told a newspaperman friend, "Durocher says I could have won if I'd used Willie earlier. If I'd known then what I found out about how that court thing upset him, I wouldn't have used him at all."

But that was my state of finances—and my state of mind—there in '62.

Was there a cure for it? The answer was yes. The cure lay in the hands of a man named Jacob Shemano, who had just started up a new bank—the Golden Gate National Bank—in San Francisco. Shemano was its president. It was a one-office bank then, trying to get started. (I won't say "struggling" because, I learned, they weren't struggling. They were in good shape from the word go.)

In the few short years since then, they've grown to five branch offices and all kinds of high ranking, and they have done this with imagination. Imagination is something you don't always expect to find in a banker—in fact, some people get scared when they do find it. I guess image is a funny thing. If you see a blind man with a dog, you accept it. But if the dog isn't a police dog, you look twice. No rule that says some other kind of dog can't do the same job. But you're not conditioned to expect it.

I'd been introduced to Jake Shemano, and had decided to set my financial affairs before him. In late '62 we had a meeting. From a business standpoint, it was the most important single moment of my life.

"Jake," I said to him, "I've been advised to declare for bankruptcy." It was true—I had so been advised, and by a top man from New York. It seemed to him the only way out.

Shemano looked at me. "Well," he said at last, "it's good advice. It can be the way out for you. Except for one thing."

I said, "What's the one thing?"

"The one thing," he said, "is that if you do file for bankruptcy, I will say again that it can be the sound and logical move, in the shape you're in—*but* . . ." and that word *but* hopped around the room like the clang of steel in a rolling mill ". . . *but*, if you do, then I want nothing to do with it. You're a baseball player, not some slick corporation executive somewhere, living off stock options and pension plans and all the other stunts. Kids look up to you."

"I know that," I said.

"*Do* you know it?" he said. "You made $90,000 last year. You'll make better than $100,000 next year. What does it look like to a kid who finds out that Willie Mays, his idol, makes $100,000 and can't pay his taxes?"

"All right," I said. "I appreciate that. But what do I do? I'm down here in the pit. If I can't climb out of it, I'm not much of an idol to the kids that way either, am I?"

"No," he conceded. "You're not. But I can tell you one thing: there was a time when I was in worse shape than you. And they weren't even my own obligations. I'd underwritten some things for some other people, and they went sour. I was three times worse off then than you are now. But I came out of it."

"Then come out of it with me," I said.

"Not if you're talking bankruptcy," he said. "If you are, you can clear out right now."

"I'm not talking bankruptcy," I said. "I'm telling you what the man said. *He's* the one talking bankruptcy. And you just said yourself it's not bad advice."

"You're right, it's not," Jake said. "I just say there must be something better. And if you stay with me, we're going to find it."

"I'll stay with you," I said.

Yes, there was imagination there, and Shemano, along with his trusted lawyers and accountants and tax authorities were able to work out a way for me to pay off my debts, earn a top wage, and still not become a total prisoner of the revenue people. What's remarkable is not that they did just this, but that they did it without getting tricky, or "beating" the tax man, or squeezing through loopholes. Instead, for the first time in my life, I had a realistic financial program worked out for me—one that did two things wrapped into one, literally easing my problem of the present by helping my expectations for the future at the same time.

I was a specialist at one thing: center field.

Jake Shemano and his experts were specialists at something else.

They helped me. And, time and again, without charge.

I can't rate the importance of peace of mind to the way a ballplayer performs in action. But it's there. And they gave it to me. My gratitude to Jake and his organization could not be greater.

# 26

THE YEAR 1963 MARKED several things: one of the worst starts I ever got off to (though I was pulling up by then, I was still well under .300 at All-Star time; surprisingly, I wound up at .314 for the year); another collapse, this time Labor Day at home plate, as I was going up to hit; and my first real fight with Dark.

The fight really didn't amount to much—the reason I bring it up here is that it's really the *only* time I ever truly tangled with a manager. What happened was, we were in the eighth inning of a game at Chicago and we had something like a six-run lead, and somebody for them hit a long one to center that I didn't chase all out. It was off the wall for a hit, and suddenly now everything started wrong and they tied the game, then won it in extra innings.

After the game, Dark snapped at me and I snapped back. In a way, we were both right. I should have chased it, and he had no business getting on me for not chasing it. We didn't speak for two or three days after that; then things smoothed over.

Maybe it goes back to what I said about his first spring training, where he set too-strict rules for himself that obviously sooner or later he was going to violate, but in any event his hold on the players seemed to be less than it was before—maybe not his hold so much as his ability to talk to them and have them listen to what he was saying.

He held a lot of clubhouse meetings, and sometimes talked about things other than baseball, about how Jesus was the only man in history who was perfect, and about how he was for Barry Goldwater, and things like that, but what was surprising wasn't how many things he said but how many ballplayers didn't seem to be concentrating real hard on whatever it was he was saying.

There was a story in print that one time he took José Pagan to one side after a game and gave him a $50 bill and said, "Take the boys to supper," by which he meant the Latin players on the club. So José did. Couple of days later, in St. Louis, Dark said to Pagan, "José, I'm fining you for not hustling." Pagan said, "How much?" Dark said, "Fifty dollars." (I say this story was in print, and it was, but it also was told to me, by one of the players.)

Another time he benched Cepeda, then pinch-hit him, and Orlando bounced out to the pitcher and refused to run it out, he was so disgusted with himself. Dark screamed at him in the clubhouse afterward, and for a minute I didn't know what was going to happen next, the way Cepeda looked at him.

And then there was my collapse at home plate, in September. I went up to hit, bent over, and here came the dizzy business again. They walked me back to the dugout and sent me home and I stayed in bed for three days. Once again, we'd been in the thick of a pennant race. Once again, I'd had hardly any rest—I think I'd missed one full game all year up to that point.

This time, at least, the home fans could see it for themselves.

The year before, when I'd collapsed in Cincinnati, you should have seen the "rumors" the San Francisco papers printed. That I'd had a heart attack. That I was secretly an alcoholic. That I was epileptic. The number-one columnist in San Francisco, Herb Caen, told his readers the real reason I fell down might have been that one of my teammates hit me.

So, as a friend of mine later summed it up, I was an epileptic alcoholic, being hit by a friend while in the midst of a heart attack.

All this, mind you, in a town that genuinely liked me by now. Lord save me if it had happened in '58!

There's always the press, and they've always got to have a story every day. It's hard to blame them sometimes.

Take the start of the '64 season, when I was off to that truly fantastic hitting spree. The press was 1,000 percent on my side now.

"They're cheering you!" a friend said.

"Hit .486 they'll cheer you," I replied.

And then, in May, Alvin Dark called me into his office off the clubhouse at Candlestick.

"Willie," he said, "I'm making you captain of the Giants."

I stared at him.

"You deserve it," he said. "You should have had it long before this."

I found my voice. "They'll kill you," I said. "They'll tear you apart."

"You know what I think of them," he said.

"Yes," I said. "I know. I think that's caused you part of your grief."

"I'm not going to kiss up to them," he said.

"They know that," I said.

"Will you take the job?"

"Yes, Cap," I said. "I will. But you don't have to do it."

"Never mind what I have to do."

"You got the guts of a burglar," I said to him.

If it was true that Dark was losing communication with the players, then of course making me captain was a sound thing for him to do. Furthermore, to name the first Negro captain in baseball history took some thought as to timing, and the timing here was perfect. I was off to a tremendous start, the Giants were leading the league, yet it was soon enough in the season so naming a captain didn't look like just an empty gesture.

But I told him they'd land on him anyway.

And they did.

One of the bad things about the timing was that Jackie Robinson had just brought out a book, called *Baseball Has Done It,* in which various baseball men were quoted on the subject of Negroes in the game. Here is how Dark was quoted—I give this here in its entirety:

Since I was born in the South I know that everyone thinks that Southerners dislike Negroes or even being with them. This isn't true at all. The majority of the people in the South, especially the Christian people that I have associated with, have really and truly liked the colored people. As for socializing with them on different levels there is a line drawn in the South, and I think it's going to be a number of years before this is corrected, or it may never be corrected.

The way I feel, the colored boys who are baseball players are the ones I know best, and there isn't any of them that I don't like. When I first played with them on the Giant ball club—Willie Mays and Monte Irvin and a boy from Cuba by the name of Ray Noble, Hank Thompson, Ruben Gomez, the Puerto Rican—all these boys were, as far as I was concerned, wonderful boys and I never had any kind of trouble any way with them. In fact, I felt that because I was from the South—and we from the South actually take care of the colored people, I think, better than they're taken care of in the North—I felt when I was playing with them it was a responsibility for me. I liked the idea that I was pushed to take care of them and make them feel at home and to help them out any way possible that I could in playing baseball the way that you can win pennants.

This is the feeling I have always had; I have respected many colored fellows in the National League as far as playing baseball goes. The greatest competitor I have ever seen in my life is Jackie Robinson. He has to be one of the greatest competitors the game has ever seen. Things that happened on the baseball field showed me that he had to be one of the greatest competitors.

As far as my thoughts on integration are concerned, I'd rather stay away from it as much as possible. I think it's being handled a little wrong in that the people in the South, and I think I know them because I've lived with them, although I live in California now, I feel that too many people are trying to solve the Southerners' problems before they solve their own problems in the North. In Chicago, in New York and other cities where they're having racial problems—if these problems were solved by the Northerners or people from the West who come down South, if they would take care of their own problems first and let the Southerners work it out I know they would work it out because there are a lot of people in the South that feel that everyone's a human being, a son of God, if they are Christians, all born equally. I feel that right now it's being handled a bit too fast. It's true that in a number of cases things have to be done in order to get something accomplished, things that might be a little fast for a certain community at this particular time. But I know that the majority of the Christian people in the South want to help any person who has Negro blood in them in any way possible because they feel like we are all born equal, we are all the sons of God and in the end will all be brothers in one faith. Being a Christian, I feel that this will be solved one day in the South. But they're rushing it a little bit too quick right now.

The way I run a ball club is just like the way I played. As long as a man does his job I don't care who he is. I don't pick on any one in particular. If a fellow loafs, if a fellow misses a sign, if a fellow doesn't produce, it makes no difference to me what color he is. I want to win and that's why I want my players to put out. There has never been any trouble between colored boys and other players on this club during my connection with it. Colored boys have never given me any trouble as manager. I wouldn't care if I had nine colored players on the field at one time as long as they can win. I think that any ball club that wins is going to draw people, there's no doubt about it. But I will say this—we have had as many as seven in the lineup at one time and as far as I am concerned as long as the boys are out there to win, if there's nine of that kind on the club I'm going to play 'em if they're the best boys on the ball club. That is up to the organization as to how many I'm going to have of colored boys. They're going to sign up the best they can sign up. It doesn't make any difference who they are as long as they're going to win. That's all this game is. As far as I'm concerned the only fun in the game or in any sport is to win. Naturally, you've got to abide by the rules, but in professional sports it's win—you have to win.

I don't think that a ball club with colored players would change the people in Birmingham or anywhere in the South. The majority of people in the South like colored people. They consider them as human beings, but right now it's being rushed too fast. I think that if a ball club moved into Birmingham or any place in the South, just like in Houston, it would speed up integration in hotels. As far as opening the thoughts of older people down there I don't think it would help at all because the older people in the South have taken care of the Negroes. They feel they have a responsibility to take care of them. That's my opinion of how things are.*

This is how Alvin was quoted, and this is the book Charles McCabe, columnist for the San Francisco *Chronicle*, had in front of him when word came that I'd been named team captain.

McCabe was a  sports columnist who'd boasted in print that his

* Jackie Robinson, *Baseball Has Done It*, ed. Charles Dexter (Philadelphia: J. B. Lippincott Co., 1964).

prime virtue was he knew very little about sports. Nobody on the Giants, as far as I know, would talk to him. Except for his picture in the paper, few of us had ever seen him, because he didn't come around much.

Anyway, McCabe took the news that I'd been named captain, and took what he read from the Jackie Robinson book, and this is what he wrote in his column—again, in its entirety:

I had not intended to make any comment on Mr. Alvin Dark's comments on the Negro in baseball, believing that every man is entitled to one really huge goof a year in his public life.

Mr. Dark's views are those of an educated, committed, Christian Southerner. They are terrible.

The only reason I bring them up is that the manager of the San Francisco Giants, a largely Negro ballclub, recently named Willie Mays to be "captain" of the club. And "managerial material."

Willie Mays has as much reason to be captain of the Giants, even if in name only, as I have to be placed in charge of our space program.

His naming to the fictitious job was, apparently, a public relations gimmick to becalm the Negroes of this area, many of whom are rightly enraged by Mr. Dark's odd views on the race question, most of which could have been pronounced from a podium by Governor Wallace, of Alabama, to wild, wild applause.

Had Mr. Dark's views been made public in New York when the Giants were living there, and had the press there reacted as they predictably would, Mr. Dark would now be seeking employment in a field outside baseball. That he is not doing so is a tribute to the fact that the racial question is not met with such raw emotion in these parts.

If you didn't read the story in the Sporting Green of some

time back, I shall refresh you. Not with any real pleasure, mark you, because I'm sorry for an America where the educated class of the South thinks as Mr. Dark thinks.

The manager gave his views in a taped interview which was quoted in Jackie Robinson's book "Baseball Has Done It."

Mr. Dark allowed "there are a lot of people in the South who feel that everyone's a human being" but that right now the racial question is being "handled a bit too fast."

He said, "The majority of the people in the South, especially the Christian people I have associated with, have really and truly liked the colored people. As for socializing with them on different levels, there is a line drawn in the South, and I think it's going to be a number of years before this is corrected, or it may never be corrected."

As to the ultimate solution of the racial problem, which is in process of solution before the U.S. Senate now, Mr. Dark remains bleakly optimistic.

"Being a Christian," he said, "I feel that this will be solved one day in the South. But they're rushing it a little bit too quick right now."

He concluded on this note of pure ante-bellum Southern thinking:

"As for opening the thoughts of older people down there I don't think it would help at all because the older people in the South have taken care of the Negroes. They feel they have a responsibility to take care of them. That's my opinion of how things are."

This kind of chit-chat is garbage, and dangerous garbage, whether it comes from a politician or a baseball manager. The appalling thing about it is its obvious sincerity. Mr. Dark clearly believes, to the last comma and syllable, what he is saying.

His comments on the Negro problem are about as meaningful, and as called-for, as somebody idly remarking that some of his best friends are Jews.

His remarks quite rightly outraged large segments of the Negro and white community here. Ergo, Willie Mays is named captain.

The function and importance of the job of Giant captain can best be judged by the fact that the team has done without one for the past eight years. The last captain was Alvin Dark.

What Mr. Dark said about the Negro was bad enough, but not surprising. His views are shared by thousands of his fellows in the South, and they constitute the largest single social problem before us.

What the Giants' organization did to turn the heat off itself —naming an innocent as captain and "managerial material"— is another rougher, more sickening thing.*

So that was it. Dark had named me captain to "bail out" of an embarrassing position on the Negro question.

"I told you it was going to happen," I said to him.

"Do you believe it?" he said.

"No," I said.

"So long as you know better," he said.

(One comment I might make on the McCabe material is his talk about whether the Giants needed a captain. Whether they needed one or not in their present situation isn't important, because McCabe wouldn't have understood one way or the other in any event. But it's not true that because a club goes a number of years without a captain, that's proof a captain isn't needed. It's a question instead of who's managing, how he manages, and what his problems are. I guess that's so obvious I'm sorry I used up this paragraph talking about it.)

Anyway, the troubles went on. I got all but one vote for the

* "The Fearless Spectator," column headlined ALVIN DARK AND CAPT. WILLIE, San Francisco *Chronicle*, May 25, 1964.

starting center field position on the National League All-Star team, so personally I was surviving another San Francisco columnist who said 1964 would mark my downfall, because my eyes and legs had gone bad.

But we weren't pulling in front of the league the way it looked like we had a chance to do. Lord knows that's not the first time that's happened, but the backstage bickering was still going on, and we weren't a happy crew. One of the writers did a piece saying one of the players was for Goldwater. Then Dark went on TV and said *he* was for Goldwater too. What he was trying to do was say writers should stick to baseball, but the effect was that he was one who *didn't* stick to baseball. And, like I say, the players felt by now that Dark wasn't observing rules that he'd originally said he would observe. So communication was down, and making me captain didn't help much. The best fun I had was the first time I brought the lineups out to home plate. The umpires really gave it to me then.

"Let's check the ground rules, Twenty-four," one of them said to me. "Ball hits the scoreboard and sticks in one of the slots. What do we do?"

"Give the hitter a saliva test," I said.

Another one of them said, "Any of your pitchers spit on the ball, Captain?"

"No, sir," I said. "We have a rule. Ironclad. No pitcher ever spits on the ball."

"You're sure of that?"

"Yes, sir. He spits in his glove and puts the ball in there."

But the fun didn't last. Word reached us from upstairs that the old man—Horace Stoneham—had decided to replace Dark at the end of this season, win or lose.

Then, late in July, *Newsday,* a daily paper out on Long Island with a circulation of nearly half a million, ran a two-day interview with Dark.

Here are some of the things he was quoted as saying (the quotes

I use here are verbatim from the reprint in the San Francisco *Examiner*):

> We have trouble [atrocious mistakes] because we have so many Spanish-speaking and Negro players on the team. They are just not able to perform up to the white ball player when it comes to mental alertness.
>
> You can't make most Negro and Spanish players have the pride in their team that you can get from white players. And they just aren't as sharp mentally. They aren't able to adjust to situations because they don't have that mental alertness.
>
> One of the biggest things is that you can't make them subordinate themselves to the best interest of the team. You don't find pride in them that you get in the white player.
>
> [About Cepeda]: You don't know how hard we've tried to make a team player, a hustling ballplayer, out of Orlando. But nothing has worked for long . . . he doesn't sacrifice himself. . . . I'd have to say he's giving out only 40 percent.
>
> Stoneham won't trade Cepeda or Willie McCovey. They know it and they know they'll get paid well if their averages are good.

*Newsday* has a big circulation, and there are people who like to stir things around, so you can bet every Negro and Latin player on the Giants got these columns in his mail.

We were heading out on the road. We hit Pittsburgh. Next stop was New York.

During our stay in Pittsburgh, just about every Negro and Latin player on the club came to me—almost as if I was team captain!?!—to talk it over. My own thoughts, as I relayed them to these other players, could be broken down into three parts:

"Number one: If they ask you, all you know is Dark always

treated you fair. No matter what any of you think personally, no matter what reason you've got to think the way you do, all he ever did is try to get you to play harder and better.

"Number two: We've got a hell of a chance to win this pennant with Dark as manager.

"Number three: Don't ask me any questions. Some of you saw what happened, back in 1960, when they changed managers in midseason. It's like two dogs fighting over a bone. The bone never wins. Dark won't be back as manager next season. Let's leave it at that."

If Cap reads this, all I can say to him is, there was nothing happy, nothing vindictive, nothing triumphant, in that riot act I read in that room in Pittsburgh. If it interests him, the riot would have come if I hadn't said what I'd said. I take no gladness in it, no joy. It is a strange, sad thing for me to say, but Alvin Dark did more for me—and meant it—than any other man I've ever known.

We got to New York. I had a bad cold. There was a press conference that Dark held, and he said: "I thought I proved my feelings when I named Willie Mays captain. If I thought Negroes were inferior, would I have done that?"

I wasn't at that press conference. When I read about it next day, I was actively sick. Here that McCabe had accused him of using me to bail out—and he and I had laughed about it, both of us knowing better than to believe it.

And now here he was. Using me to bail out.

Not because McCabe knew what he was talking about. But because other things had come along, and you stick a man's back against a wall and he does the one thing he knows how to do, the thing that comes to his mind first.

That night, our last night in New York, he handed me the lineup card in the clubhouse before the game. He knew I had a bad cold. I looked at the card. My name wasn't on it.

I took a pencil and wrote my name on it.

I hit three home runs against the Mets in 1962. One of them was with two out and our side trailing by a run in the last of the ninth at Candlestick, in May. That got us tied, and Davenport homered to beat them in the 15th.

The other two came that night in New York, when I took the lineup card and put myself on it.

It's a world none of us made. It's nobody's fault, certainly not Dark's.

But he and I haven't talked to each other from that moment till this.

He was let go the last day of the 1964 season, and Herman Franks was announced as the new manager. In a strange way, the whole race business "saved" Dark's job. If it hadn't been for that, he was going to be canned two months before he was. This way, it would have looked "racial," so they stayed with him.

I wish the man nothing but the best.

# 27

I HAVE A DREAM every once in a while—some people might call it a nightmare, and a lot of times I guess it is—and different things can happen in this dream, but no matter what happens, it always happens in Philadelphia. Sometimes I wake up and it turns out I wasn't dreaming to begin with.

I broke into the majors in Shibe Park—I know they changed the name of the place to Connie Mack Stadium, but a lot of times you keep on using the name you got used to in the first place. Garry Schumacher every once in a while still calls the Dodgers "the Brooklyns." It's funny, you find baseball people will use the city names for some teams and the nicknames for others, like the Yankees are always called the Yankees, but the Houston club is always called Houston. The ball parks in New York—Yankee Stadium and Shea Stadium—one's called "Shea" and the other's called "the Stadium." In Chicago, they call Comiskey Park "Sox Park." In San Francisco, it's "Candlestick." There was a big fuss about the name of the place when it was being built, and they had a contest, and it was finally named Candlestick Park because it's next to a point of land called Candlestick Point, but a lot of people said that was no name for a baseball field and it had nothing to do with anything. It was really surprising, considering all the disturbance and ruckus, that it died down so fast and the name caught on as quick as it did. By contrast, half the people in Los Angeles call the ball park there "Dodger Stadium" and the other half call it

"Chavez Ravine." The ballplayers from other teams just call it "L.A." Same with St. Louis. The ball park there is just "St. Louis." Often you hear players use the right name—"Forbes Field"—when they talk about games at Pittsburgh, but I bet you could find dozens of players in the big leagues who not only don't call the Cincinnati park by its right name, but don't even know that Crosley Field is its name to begin with. In fact, for all the years we've been training in Phoenix, first at the old ball park on South Central and Mohave there and out past the stockyards at the new park on East Van Buren, I don't believe I know the names for either of them. One time some writer or fan said to me, in Phoenix one day, "See you tomorrow at Rendezvous," and I found myself wondering where that was. Turned out it was the name of the park where the Cubs were training at Mesa.

Anyway, that dream about Philadelphia—a lot *has* happened there, as far as I'm concerned. I broke in there, and had—back in '61, as I've already told—what was probably my greatest single playing night in the ball park there.

And on Thursday, July 8, 1965, in a night game there, I hit a home run off Ray Herbert—it was a long, high fly ball into the left-field seats—which was my 23rd home run of the season. But more important, it was the 476th of my National League career, which broke a tie with Stan Musial and put me second to Mel Ott for all-time National League homers.

"Were you trying for it?" somebody asked me later.

"I've been trying for it for a week," I confessed.

We were going good at that point—personally I was leading the league in homers and right at or around the league batting lead, at .338, in there somewhere—and the club was laying third in the race. We hadn't won as many as we had at that point the year before, but neither had anybody else. But we were hurting. To begin with, we were carrying two bonus kids, which put our roster of 25 men down to 23 right there, so far as big-league seasoning was concerned. And Orlando Cepeda's knee hadn't come around after he had it operated on in the winter, and he'd gone on the disabled list. And Jack Sanford's arm wasn't whole, and Marichal had missed a couple of starts, and one game we had two catchers out because of injuries and the other catcher had to play first base because McCovey was hurt so we had to rush a kid up from Tacoma and that was the way it was going.

You can credit an awful lot to Herman Franks, the manager, that we were running as good as we were in the pennant race. "I don't think you've got a thing to worry about, where those home runs are counted," he said to me, early in the season.

"I'm not worried," I said. "They'll come."

"That's not what I mean," he said. "As far as I'm concerned, you already have the record."

"You're crazy," I said.

"No," he said. "I mean for right-handed hitters. You've been the all-time league leader in homers by right-handers for a couple of years now. Ever since you passed Gil Hodges."

"That doesn't mean anything," I said.

"It does to me," he said. "Remember, us left-handed hitters have always had those shorter fences. It's quite a difference."

I began to laugh, and so did he. "Us" left-handed hitters, he said. Herman didn't get to play too much as a big-league catcher, and they aren't about to dedicate a new wing at Cooperstown to his lifetime batting average.

Maybe it's natural for a lot of people to expect other people to do what they used to do themselves, the way you hear a lot of times fathers expect from their sons. And on the other hand, maybe the man who wasn't a star himself isn't as surprised when some player doesn't do something right.

A lot of times, I feel like you can see this in different big-league managers. Like an Alvin Dark, for instance, would expect you to hit-and-run because he knew how himself. He wouldn't be boasting about it. Fact, he'd put it the other way—he'd say, "Shoot, if *I* could do it, *he* certainly can!" But he was still expecting it.

A Franks, on the other hand, was kind of a little looser. A Dark would say, "Here's what we're going to do." A Franks would say, "Here's what we're going to *try*."

I remember a talk we had in Los Angeles. We'd beat Drysdale 2-1. Drysdale had got a pair of singles, but each time Wills, the next hitter, forced him. Next night, we lost to Koufax 2-1. Koufax didn't reach base, and two times Wills, up behind him, now got on, then stole second, then came home on a pair of singles by Gilliam, and that was the ball game.

"Hey, Captain, you notice something?" Franks said to me.

"About what?"

"Drysdale gets on, we win. Koufax don't get on, we lose."

"I've been thinking of that," I said.

"Why didn't you say something?"

"Because it's crazy, that's why," I said. "Who ever heard of a defensive strategy of putting the *pitcher* on with nobody on base?"

"It'd have to be with two out," he said.

"And the score right for it," I said. "Close game."

"But the situation comes up," he said. "We had it night before last and we won. We had it last night and we lost."

"They'll know what you're doing," I said.

"It don't cost nothing to try," he said.

The idea of course was that you wanted to keep Wills from leading off the next inning. So with two out and bases empty, make sure the pitcher gets to first. Wills doesn't have the power to get him around with a hit, and meanwhile, by putting a pitcher on 90 feet ahead of him, not only do you keep him from leading off by bringing him up right now, but everything he does best—bunting, running, stealing—is either hurt or actually eliminated.

That night, sure enough, here came Claude Osteen, up to bat for them with two out and nobody on and them leading 3-0, which meant we were still in the game. Osteen had the lowest batting average on the whole Dodger club and hadn't drawn a walk all year. He got one now. Gaylord Perry didn't exactly throw four intentional wide ones, but none of those four balls was a close call for the umpire.

So Osteen went to first, and up came Wills, and bounced out, pitcher-first.

Next time we played them, at Candlestick, we beat Drysdale the first game, leading all the way, so the score didn't bring the situation up. But against Koufax the next afternoon, we tried it a couple of times.

Sandy was smart. He swung at bad pitches and was out. So Wills led off next inning each time. We didn't get Wills out all day long.

"If we walk the pitcher on purpose," Herman had said, "maybe they'll just have him walk down to second base on the first pitch to Wills. Then it's up to us—do we want to tag him out, in which case we get Wills up leadoff next inning, or do we want to let him go all the way around, and tag him finally off of third?"

"If he gets to third," I said, "Wills scores him with a single."

"I know it," Herman said. He grinned again, that conspirator's grin of his. "It's fun to try, though, isn't it? You have fun with baseball, don't you, Captain?"

"You know it," I said.

"So do I," he said.

One time an umpire called a low pitch and Herman sang out from the bench, "Hey, ump, you're mistaking something else for his kneecaps!" and they threw him out of the game.

I don't mean to say by this that Franks was the easygoing, couldn't-care-less type. He cared very much—to the point where he actually fined a coach after one game for making the signs too complicated—and he brooded when we'd lose a bad one.

But he knew that a bad game didn't necessarily mean a bad ballplayer. And he could fine a player for not hustling without believing the player didn't want to hustle, or didn't want to hustle for *him*. Ballplayers are human beings, and a lot of times you do wrong things without *meaning* to. There doesn't always have to be a reason.

Another thing, speaking of Franks and fines: he wasn't one of those who only fine when you're losing. The fines came when we were winning too, and Herman had the last word, except that there was a committee of four—me and an infielder and a pitcher and a catcher—that could appeal if they thought something wasn't just.

Like all managers, Franks would make some changes while we were losing. But he had another gift—he could make changes while we were winning. This is a lot harder to do, because nobody likes to draw to a pat hand. But a baseball season lasts 162 games, and I think it's smart to rest some players and give some work to others, a lot of times even when you've been winning.

All these things, I guess, were indicated in Horace Stoneham's thinking when, just before the 1965 All-Star game at Minneapolis, he decided to rehire Franks as manager for 1966.

"We gave Herman a raise and made it retroactive to the current season," Stoneham announced to the press. He added that it was evident the players were putting out for Franks—and I guess it *was* evident—and he said:

"I think we're in a very fine position to overtake the leaders, and this in spite of a succession of injuries that has made the job most difficult for Franks. The way he's handled these setbacks and the way he has handled the case of Willie Mays, who now needs rest, has impressed me very much."

*The case of Willie Mays—who now needs rest—*

# 28

ACTUALLY, MR. STONEHAM was referring not so much to the case of Willie Mays as to the case of Herman Franks. The Giants of 1965 (unlike the pennant winners of '51 or '54 or '62, unlike the powerful contenders of '59 or '63 or '64), had no business finishing as high as they did. Granted they were in first place by 4½ games the morning of September 17—they had no business that high either. Anyone who tells you the Giants folded after September 17, incidentally, has no business "experting" baseball. From then till we were eliminated on the next-to-last day of the season, we played .500 baseball, and that isn't exactly what you'd call a fold. Nothing like, for example, the way the Dodgers lost six straight in the final week of '62. The fact is that in '65 the Dodgers clinched the pennant by winning 14 out of 15, and it still took Koufax, pitching with short rest, to nail it down for them on the next-to-last day.

The story of the Giants in '65 is that they were a team without pitching, and pitching is the name of the game. When I say this, I don't mean to reflect on the skills of our pitching staff. It wasn't lack of personal skill as much as it was overwork and lack of a dependable starting rotation.

Faced with having to carry two bonus kids, Manager Franks made a sound decision. He knew that he had only one man—Marichal —as a regular starter; or at least, he found it out, when Sanford didn't come around and Hendley began to have difficulty. (Both those men were traded off before the season was much more than half over.)

Franks now had to give starting work to Bob Shaw and Bob Bolin, but the available pitching still wasn't strong. So he came to a decision—and it was not only sound, it was bold.

Herman decided he would go with just nine pitchers (most teams have 11). The two-man difference was the two bonus rookies we had to carry. If Herman could have reached out and got two top-drawer starting pitchers, maybe he would have carried 11 pitchers too. But where do you get them during a season?

So we went with nine pitchers, but they included two tremendous short-relief men in the bullpen—Masanori Murakami and Frank Linzy. We obtained Bill Henry as an extra left-handed reliever. The rest of the staff—Gaylord Perry, Ron Herbel, even Warren Spahn (we got him after the Mets let him go)—would swing between starts and long relief.

Then the extra two men would become extra bench strength, as a guard against injury or fatigue. (One of them, Lenny Gabrielson, who came in a trade from the Cubs, turned into a regular and did a fine job.)

Remember also that Franks went all season long without Orlando Cepeda, whose knee wouldn't let him play. You don't take a .300 batting average and 100 runs batted in out of the lineup and expect to do better the next year.

Yet Franks did do better, and you can't give him too much credit for it.

Herman has been called a manager who "gave the game back to the players." In a manner of speaking, I think there's something to that. He had a loose, easy way with us—for example, I don't think we had two clubhouse meetings all season long. Sometimes this is the sign of a soft heart. Early in the year, I remember, Herman said to me, "I'm not going out there again to take a pitcher out and have him talk me out of it. That's what's costing us."

I said, "You gonna get tough?"

"No," he said. "I'm gonna send Lavagetto out to get them."

So for a while, Cookie was the one who went out and got the pitcher, but that didn't last too long, because the authority was the manager's and he had to show it. Did I say awhile back that he fined a coach? Heck, he fined himself too. Fifty dollars' worth, I think, as the season wore on.

But we had a good spirit on the club. It was the first team since the Giants came West that didn't break fast from the wire, right out there on top. But we were never laying too far back, and come the first of August we started to make our move.

By now, Herman had moved me back to third in the order, ahead of McCovey. As I said earlier, there's things both for and against this, and Herman talked it over with a lot of people, me included. "I know the idea that I protect him, batting behind him," I said. "But he protects *me* too. And the way I'm hitting, I can use some." This was a half-funny reference to my July "slump," when I only hit two home runs all month and had that 0-for-24 spell in there.

Herman talked to me constantly about things, and encouraged the players to come to me too. Things like if our catcher went good in the first game of a doubleheader and wanted to work the second game, he'd come to me and I'd go to Herman and say, "If he wants to work, play his tail." Private and personal problems too. What was fantastic was the difference in being captain in 1965, compared to what it was like in '64. In '64, all I did was hand the lineups to the umpire before the game. In '65, the manager delegated me a great deal of authority, and consulted with me. The final decision was always his, but he'd seek me out for the way I thought about things, and the players knew it. There are a lot of things a player will say to another player that he doesn't want to say to the manager direct.

By late July, our lineup was fairly set. Haller catching, McCovey at first, Maxie Lanier at second, Dick Schofield at short, Jim Ray Hart at third, Jesus Alou in right, me in center, Gabrielson in left.

There were lots of switches. Matty Alou saw a lot of work, and Jim Davenport, and I'll never forget one night, at the start of September when the roster limit was off and we got some help from Tacoma, and this one kid went up to Herman in the clubhouse and said, "Mr. Franks, my name's Brown." "Okay, Brown," Herman said, "get your glove. You're starting in right field."

We did have injuries, and Herman wanted to try different combinations, especially for the percentage against that day's opposing pitcher, because when you're short on pitching like we were, every little edge counts.

Maybe what I'm saying is that it's hard to put your finger on just what it was Herman Franks *did* as a manager. All I know is, we didn't have the pitching Los Angeles had, or the hitting Milwaukee had, or the balance of power and pitching Cincinnati had, and on paper we didn't even have the team *we'd* had the year before. Something got us up as high as we finished, something besides baling wire and spit, and I have an idea that something had a great deal to do with a man named Franks.

Starting with August 3, anyway, we opened up. I was hitting again, and we had successive three-game series in Cincinnati and St. Louis, and those are two places it's nice to be when you're hitting. We swept all six games, then came back home and won two straight from the Pirates—eight in a row, our longest win streak since '62.

Then it was August 19, and I think I'd already had nine or 10 home runs in the month so far, and the Dodgers were in San Francisco for a four-game series, that Thursday, Friday, Saturday, and Sunday.

We trailed them in the standings by half a game.

I hit four home runs in that series, one in each game, and three of them put the Giants ahead (twice to stay), and the other got us tied. But I came up more than four times, and there were times I wish I could have even gotten a walk, because the best we could do was split the series. They won the first and third games, both in extra innings. We won the second and fourth.

It was in that second game that the umpire called Tommy Haller for tipping somebody's bat, and Tommy said later he thought maybe the hitter had contributed a little when the umpire wasn't looking, so later in the game Matty Alou kind of "backed into" John Roseboro, the Dodger catcher, with his bat, holding it a little farther back than you'd expect, and Roseboro didn't need a road map. "Better not anybody do that again," he said, or words to that effect.

Then came the Sunday game, Marichal for us, Koufax for them, and a capacity crowd on hand, and in the top of the second inning, first Maury Wills, then Ron Fairly went down for them. The Dodgers were ahead by a run because of Wills's bunting and base-running in the first inning, and the pitch that put him down wasn't one he could bunt—am I saying that diplomatically enough?—but the one to Fairly wasn't at all intentional or even, it seemed to me, even that close. He did the dive anyway, though, and when I came up, leading off our half of the second, I knew the first pitch was going to be a retaliation duster. I also knew it wasn't going to hit me— not because my reflexes are that good against Koufax's fast ball but because Koufax has never tried to hit anybody in his life.

So Sandy wound up for the first pitch to me and here it came. It was what we call a "courtesy pitch." It was to let us know they didn't appreciate their hitters having to bite the dust. Just for form's sake, you might say. It wasn't too fast, and it sailed about two feet over my head to the backstop. I just stood there and ducked a little, and then the count was ball one and the game went on.

When it came Marichal's turn to hit, leading off the bottom of the third, there was some question whether *he'd* be thrown at. Once again, though, Koufax wasn't about to throw at a man. Another pitcher might have, but not Sandy. On the other hand, Marichal had been the pitcher when Wills and Fairly went down, whereas

I'd been an innocent bystander in center field, so the gentlemanly "courtesy pitch" wasn't called for either. In other words, Koufax, being Koufax, had no choice except simply to pitch to Juan like he'd pitch to anyone else.

Roseboro had a choice, though—one no one was looking for. He took the second pitch and threw it back to Koufax, only he darn near threw it through Marichal's head. It was the first time I ever saw a duster come from behind the plate. I think it actually did tick Juan's batting helmet.

Now Marichal said something to Roseboro—later, the papers said that what he said was: "Why did you do that?"—and all of a sudden Roseboro was advancing on Juan and Juan was backing away, holding his bat pressed close to his body, moving out toward the pitcher's mound. Now Roseboro either pushed or punched him —I disremember which, and Juan swung with his arm and the arm had a hand and the hand held a bat, and that's all of the fight I ever saw.

I was up off the bench, and there were people all around, and I was headed for just one man—Roseboro. It said later in the papers that he and I were close friends and I hated to see my friend hit with a bat, but that wasn't what I was thinking. Roseboro and I *are* friends, but what I was thinking was that once they got separated, the thing that would bring them together again and start the fighting all over and maybe cause a full-scale riot would be—*Roseboro*. He's the one who'd had his head creased. So he was the first one who had to be held back.

Not that I doped it out that carefully in advance, but that was my motive. It wasn't till I got my arms around him that I saw the blood. For a minute I thought he'd got it in the eye, but I could tell he was all right, and some of the Dodgers came and got him and I think I went and got a towel and came back to help wipe the blood off. I'm not sure, because everybody was milling around and half a dozen other "almost" fights were fixing to start, and later on I saw a picture of me all alone among the Dodgers, over by their dug-out, so I guess that's where I wound up.

Sandy Koufax, of course, was as upset as everybody else by what happened, and by the time peace was restored he'd lost something of his pitching rhythm. He got two out, but then he walked Davenport and McCovey, and now he had me at bat, and believe me, he wasn't fixing on throwing anything close. Not only Koufax—*no* pitcher was going to risk a close pitch the rest of the game. But in this case particularly, with the riot just concluded and Mays ("the peace-maker") at bat, Koufax didn't even trust himself to try for the inside corner.

He was deprived of one of the spots he likes most to pitch me, and I knew it, and he knew it, and I knew he knew I knew he knew, and he didn't want to risk the outside fast ball that might be a wild pitch with two on, and trying to get the outside corner with his curve was pitching in to my strength.

In other words, he had no way to pitch to me.

The intentional base on balls was no answer, because Hart was up after me, and the jam pitch inside was the one Koufax specialized in when pitching to him and he couldn't throw it to him either—not this soon after the riot.

So Sandy squared his shoulders and challenged me, and threw a fast ball across the plate, but he knew I knew, and the hope was that I'd get under it too much. It wasn't much of a hope, and I don't take much pride in the advantage I had over him. I swung and the ball cleared the fence in center field and another fence beyond that one, and we were ahead 4-2 and that's how the game ended.

They set Marichal down for nine days, which meant he'd get to pitch a week from Wednesday in Philadelphia, then the following Sunday in Chicago. Although it wasn't announced officially till later, we knew that the league office didn't want him to be in Los Angeles at all for the series of Labor Day and the day after. This not just because of our little riot, but because of the really serious one they'd just got through having in the Watts area of L.A.

What they didn't think of was that if it had rained in Chicago on Sunday when it was Marichal's turn to pitch, after his suspension, then if he couldn't appear in L.A. Monday or Tuesday it would be the equivalent of an added suspension. We hoped they'd make the nine-day suspension actually nine days from the time of the riot, which would have permitted Juan to pitch in Philadelphia a week from Tuesday and give him a cushion in case of rain in Chicago, letting him pitch there either Saturday or Sunday. It wouldn't have given Juan any extra starts for the year, and because they were admittedly thinking about keeping him out of L.A., it would have been a much safer way to arrange it. I think they actually considered it, but the Dodgers left San Francisco and opened up in New York for their next series, so they got to the New York press and television people and fed the hue and cry against Marichal and so anything that looked like the league was easing his penalty—even if in fact it wasn't so—was out of the question, and they had to stick by their first ruling.

As it turned out, it rained in Philadelphia on Wednesday September 1, which was the night Juan was first eligible to pitch again. So he pitched Thursday, and on two days' rest he went back against the Cubs Sunday, and that way he didn't go to L.A. but it didn't cost him a start. I just don't think the league fully realized what a chance it was taking—and this in a pennant race where going into September four teams were something like a game and a half apart at the top of the pile.

It's said that Latin Americans have hot tempers. I don't know about that. They have hot weather, and hot weather seems to go hand in hand with fights and riots a lot of time. I never heard of a riot in Lapland, but maybe it's because I don't read the papers that close. I remember tackling Orlando Cepeda one time in Pittsburgh when he went after Danny Murtaugh with a bat, and the only fight I ever had on the ball field in the big leagues was with Elio Chacon, who was playing second base for the Mets in 1962, when I was leading off second and they threw back there a couple of times, and all of a sudden instead of just trying to tag me, Chacon was beating on me with his fists. I don't remember much of the details. They said afterward I picked him up and dropped him into short center field. I don't think it was that way exactly, but I know I didn't do any swinging, and it was all over in a couple of minutes. I didn't do anything to cause the fight. Even Chacon admitted that. He said instead that the year before, I'd spiked him in a slide at second base, which was true. But it hadn't been intentional, and it took him a year to infer it was.

Anyway, with the Marichal thing, temper or no temper, it was Roseboro who'd made the first move that touched it off, coming at Juan the way he did. And speaking of hot heads among Latin Americans, the quietest Giant of all was Matty Alou. You wouldn't know he was there, half the time, except for one night in Pittsburgh, just after the Marichal-Roseboro episode. Matty made the front pages that night.

Herman sent him in to pitch!

Ordinarily, there's a rule that a man has to be listed as a pitcher before he's allowed to pitch in the majors. This is to keep them from making a farce out of games where a team is far behind.

But with our nine-man staff reduced to eight with Marichal's suspension (and a couple of sore arms among them), President Giles of the National League told Herman to go ahead and pitch anybody he wanted. On top of all that, we had to play five games in four days at Pittsburgh, not because the schedule planned it that way but because we played one tie—we were ahead by two runs with one out in their half of the tenth when the rains came and their tarpaulin somehow didn't work (it never does when the home team's behind). So that was washed out, and here we went again, and we were to lose four straight to the Pirates and one game was so bad that finally Herman brought in Matty, and he pitched two shutout innings, striking out Willie Stargell twice while he was at it, and it was the damnedest sight you ever saw. Later in the season, when we were losing one to Cincinnati 17-2, the crowd was yelling for Matty to pitch some more. By that time, of course, Marichal was back so Matty's pitching was illegal—but not any more illegal than it looked those two innings he worked in Pittsburgh. He gave them all the motion, all the business, and a nickel curve that the Pirates hadn't seen in so long they couldn't hit it anyway.

Stargell was victimized by me, too, in that Pirate series. I made the longest throw of my life—one bounce from 406 feet away—and got him at the plate. It was one of those extra-base jobs that you pick up and just wheel and throw back toward the infield, figuring somebody there will know what to do with it—your job is to get the ball back in the direction of civilization. And somehow none of our fellows felt like touching it, and it went on through to Tommy Haller, and here came Stargell cruising in and the ball was waiting for him. I'll say it was sure quite a throw; on the other hand, it isn't quite accurate to describe it by saying, "Mays took dead aim from four hundred and six feet away and got his man."

From Pittsburgh, we went into New York, where I hit two home runs. The first one, my 16th of the month, tied Lou Gehrig's lifetime total of 493 homers and Ralph Kiner's National League record for a one-month output. The second one, of course, passed both those marks. Kiner, who broadcasts for the Mets, sat there and watched it happen. Afterward, we had one of the most refreshing interviews I can remember. I said: "Are you sore?" He said: "Sure I'm sore."

We split in Philadelphia, then got two out of three in Chicago, and then we went into L.A. for the last two Dodger-Giant games of the year.

The first game was on Labor Day—nationally telecast and played before a capacity crowd. One ironic touch was that neither Koufax nor Marichal had a normal rotation that would permit either of them to see action in this series—Marichal with a suspension, Koufax without one. So instead of Koufax, we saw Drysdale, and inside of two innings he had a 4-0 lead.

I will always treasure the memory of the roaring welcome that Giant-hating crowd gave me when I came to bat for the first time. It was a salute maybe to the hot pace I'd been going at, but much more, obviously, to my reputation as the "peacemaker" in the Roseboro incident.

At this time, it was even being written that this had played up my credentials as a future manager. Much of what was being said was summarized in a piece written by Milton Gross, of the New York *Post*, which I saw reprinted in the *Chronicle*, in San Francisco, as follows:

Undoubtedly it does Herman Franks a great injustice to ask who will be the next Giant manager. Could it be Willie Mays? Don't snicker. He's been the assistant manager all year.

"Man," Willie screamed in protest, "don't call me that. Herman's a good man. He's been doing a good job. He don't misuse a man. He don't abuse him."

True, true, but Mays is such a great one, he's not only been the Giants' team leader this season, he's been a coach, a whip-cracker, a shoulder for the young and an example for the old.

"I don't want to think of things like managing," said Willie. "I got enough to think about playing, but I'll tell you this. In my mind there ain't any job I can't do on a baseball field."

. . . The point is Willie does not completely reject the possibility of becoming the first Negro manager. He'd rather not discuss it seriously, but he's serious when he says he knows in his own heart he could do it.

Item: Second-baseman Hal Lanier is considered the "captain" of the Giants' infield. It is his duty to talk to the pitcher, give him a breather, a moment to think. It was Willie who appointed Lanier to this task, and it is Willie to whom Lanier looks for instructions in the field during the course of the game.

"Nobody in the whole organization taught me more about this game than Mays," Lanier confessed. "I watch him out in the outfield, and when he waves me to go in and talk to the pitcher, I go. The pitcher knows I'm coming into him on Willie's order, and that's good enough for him."

This is so great a departure from what Mays used to be that it is almost startling to listen to Willie say it. In the past he would never offer advice to another player unless the player came and asked. It is more than a measure of maturity for the 34-year-old. Why the change?

"This year," said Mays, "they talked to me. This year they told me to do it. This year I'm encouraged to say what's on my mind."

"They" are president Horace Stoneham, vice-president Chub Feeney and even Herman Franks.*

Now I will speak for myself. I do want to stay in baseball. My insurance business, and such investments as I have made in recent years, do not affect my concentration on the game now, and there is no reason why they should in the future. I'm as candid as I can be when I say that I know younger players listen to me, just as I listened when I was young, and I think my experience has qualified me to teach and—yes—to lead.

I'm equally candid when I say there are drawbacks to my becoming a manager. It may astound you if I say that the question of race is not what I consider the most important of these drawbacks. With the authority Herman gave me as captain in 1965, I feel that, if anything, any "white resistance" to a Negro manager would have shown itself already, and more easily, by resistance to a Negro captain, and it just hasn't happened. The squawks, if any, would come from the outside.

But, as I've already indicated in this story, I wonder seriously about whether a man who was a star as a player can become the

* Milton Gross, New York *Post*, as reprinted in the San Francisco *Chronicle* on Monday, September 13, 1965.

best kind of manager. Does he expect his players to do what he did? Or, even if he doesn't, do his players think he does?

Alvin Dark once said a very revealing thing. He said that much of the Giants' poor base-running could be charged to players who tried to run the bases like Mays. It may be true. You want your men to do what is their best, not what was your best. The stupidest thing in the world is a man with his own gifts trying to act like somebody else. You can be taught, and you can be inspired. But you've still got to be you.

You've still got to be you, and I've still got to be me, and as far as I'm concerned, I've still got some playing left to do.

How much? I don't know for sure. Barring injury, I think I may have three or four seasons left—and I mean what amounts to *full* seasons. When all's said and done about how I did all that resting in 1965, I still appeared at the plate well over 600 times (counting walks), which was second on our club only to Jim Ray Hart; I was one below Matty Alou for the club lead in stolen bases; I had a career high of 52 home runs and what I believe was a career low of 70 strikeouts. I remember just before the 1964 season started how one columnist in San Francisco, who's no longer writing regularly, wrote that my legs and eyes were both going bad. So in '64 and '65 I hit 99 home runs and both years had fewer than 75 strikeouts, and if that means my eyes were going bad, I'll take that disease. Also in those two seasons I scored 239 runs and for the Giants, who don't play the running game, led the club in stolen bases one season and was one away from the club lead the other. If that means my legs are going bad, I'll take *that* disease.

Don't get me wrong. Nobody lately took me for Peter Pan. But I'm not headed for the barn, either. Even with more rest, I was able in '64 and '65 to put two more productive seasons back-to-back than at any similar two-season period in my entire career— and I'm not averaging out per games played or times at bat, either. I mean straight totals. For instance, take that two-year total of 99 home runs in '64 and '65. My best two-year output before that was in '54 and '55, when I was 10 years younger. Those two years I had 92 homers in 1,145 at bats. In '64 and '65 I had 99 homers in 1,136 at bats. So you can't even charge my better "old-age" performance to the 162-game schedule that's true now but wasn't back then. Any way you look at it, the production was up, period, and I just ain't spavined. Period.

As I look back on what I've said just now, it has a bad sound to me, and maybe it will to some readers too. A kind of chesty, boastful sound, like why does Willie Mays have to recite his averages? On the other hand, I can't think of a truer way to emphasize the main fact about any talk about me as a manager—which is that such talk is premature.

Sure, I get tired easier than when I was 20 or 25. As a result, I'll look bad at the plate sometimes. But when I was 20 or 25 I looked bad at the plate too—for a different reason, mainly inexperience, but the result was the same. Am I one step slower getting to a fly ball? Maybe. But maybe, too, I'm two steps closer to it before it's even hit, for knowing now where to play.

And so for now I want to go on thinking about playing ball, not about not playing ball.

The columnist—not a San Francisco columnist, a New York columnist—who said I was going to ask for $150,000 in 1966, may have (unintentionally, maybe) supported that idea: that I think there's a good deal of baseball left in me. His story appeared at the tail end of the '65 pennant race. It said the Giants had given me $105,000 in order to boost me over Mickey Mantle's $100,000 with the Yankees. That's not true. I made $90,000 in '62 and was advanced to $105,000 in '63. It was after my $105,000 for '63 had been announced that Mantle's $100,000 was announced. I pointed this out to that writer and he said, "I heard different." That's like saying Goldwater is President, and when you say Johnson won the election, the writer says, "I heard different." Sometimes I dunno.

The truth is still the truth, isn't it? The part about Horace Stoneham trying to ace out the Yankees by boosting my pay over Mickey's is just plain not so.

And it's not so that I'd intended to ask for $150,000 in '66 the way that writer said I had. The truth is I never gave one thought to my '66 salary before the '65 season was over, which is when he wrote the piece. I think what happened is that somebody told Jake Shemano, my friend at the bank, that I was worth $150,000. Whereupon Jake said: "I agree." And they based that newspaper story on that.

It is maybe far too late, at this place in my story, for me to say what I guess has occurred to you already—that this book is different from most "memory" books by athletes, because it isn't being done by somebody whose career is over. I can't tell you about my last salary negotiation, because my last salary negotiation hasn't happened yet. I can't look back and "rate" players or managers or talents. The pitcher I write about today may be throwing at my head tomorrow. And I'm joking when I say that, but you know what I mean. It's not just that I have to "stay in business," as they say. That part of it isn't what means the most. What means the most is that the business itself changes, from day to day and week to week and month to month. This book is being written at one time, but it can and will be read, I suppose, at a hundred different times. The business of stroking your beard and looking back at a career already completed—I just can't do it.

I remember when I first saw Bill White and said, "This is going to be a good one." It wasn't a hard thing to say. I think I can say the same thing today about Maxie Lanier, the Giants' second baseman. His real name is Hal, but his father was Max Lanier, the pitcher, so everybody calls him Maxie. You've heard of some of the things he can do, and he gets better with each passing day. There was a time, for instance, when he wanted any fly ball he could get to. Now he knows: if you catch a fly ball backing away, you're not going to throw out the man at home coming in from third after the catch. So now he lets the outfielder, the one with the body momentum coming in toward the plate, be the one to make the play. It doesn't result in any more outs at home plate. The result instead is that far fewer runners on third ever try to break for home.

Most of all about Maxie, though, I think for his age he is one of the smartest and best base-runners I've ever seen. And I mean base-*runner*—not base-*stealer*. A guy who can steal is a creature of the scoreboard. Put his team two runs behind, he ain't going nowhere. But the *runner*—he can take his shot anytime, any score, any inning. He can protect other runners, lure throws, con the opposition into throwing behind him, "sense" the momentary bobble or the slow-reacting pickup. The best base-stealer in the game is a prisoner not only of the scoreboard but of his own teammates. If they play long-ball, there's no sense in his stealing. Put a Maury Wills on that old window-breaking Yankee team of the thirties, and Maury doesn't steal any 100 bases. Not that he can't. He just doesn't.

But to speak of a Wills, or a Maxie Lanier, or a Bill White— none of this means I can sit here and reel off my "all-time team," position by position. The reason is simple. I haven't seen it yet.

So much for that. Now, if I remember right, we left off in the third inning at Los Angeles in front of that big Labor Day crowd, with the score 4-0 against us and Drysdale going for them.

We won the thing 7-6, in 12 innings. Jim Hart tied it with a two-run homer in the eighth, then Tom Haller (who threw Wills out stealing twice in that game) retied it in the ninth, then Davenport looped the game-winning single into left-center in the 12th.

Next day Hart homered again, we won 3-1, and for the first time in all of 1965, we were in first place in the National League.

We whooped it up pretty good in the clubhouse after that Labor Day win, although when a reporter asked me if I thought we'd win the pennant, I said simply, "There's a long way to go." At the same time, in his little office off the clubhouse, I heard later that Franks was saying the same thing to another reporter.

Coming down to Sunday the 12th, we'd won eight in a row and had 22 left to play and Herman said to me, "How many?"

"Fourteen," I said.

"That's what I want," he nodded. "Fourteen."

We both figured that if the Giants could win 14 of their remaining 22 games—which would have given us 95 wins on the year—it would be enough to take it.

Actually, the Giants won exactly 14 of their remaining 22, got their 95—and the Dodgers got 97.

So we didn't fold. In fact, we were to make it a 14-game winning streak, then lose one, then win three more in a row.

Following the Labor Day set at L.A., we had a 6-0 home stand, a 7-3 road trip, a 5-5 home stand. All told, the Giants won 22 of their last 30 games. So it wasn't us folding. It was like '51, when they played good but we played better. This time the positions were reversed. Somebody else just got hotter than we were.

My 500th home run came off of Don Nottebart at Houston, the night of September 13—a line drive into the center-field seats. It got us tied at 1-1 and there was a standing ovation from the fans there when the "500" went up on the message board.

Waiting for me in the dugout when I got back was Warren Spahn.

"Damn it," he said, "I saw the first one and now I've seen the five hundredth."

I grinned at him. "Same pitch, too."

"The hell it was," he said. "I threw you a curve that day back in fifty-one."

"It wasn't a curve," I said. "It was a fast ball. And it wasn't a day. It was a night."

"Day."

"Night."

"Curve ball."

"Fast ball."

Finally we compromised. We made it a twilight game and a fast curve. Actually, I *know* it was a night game. But he may be right about the curve part. Pitchers remember pitches longer than hitters.

The Houston people tried to get me the ball that night, but some woman in the center-field stands had caught it and said she wanted to keep it. I said, "Heck, let her keep it if she wants it."

The one that I hit for number 512, though—the good Lord willin' and the creeks don't rise—I'd like it if the lady who catches that one will let me have it. That will be, of course, the new all-time National League record for home runs. Like I say, the good Lord willin' and the creeks don't rise. . . .

Marichal went the distance for us the night I hit my 500th, to pick up his 22nd win of the year. If you had told any of us then that Juan wouldn't win another game the rest of the season, we would have said you were nuts. Juan not only was pitching well, but he had the desire. The next night—the 14th—we entered the ninth down by three runs. But with two out Jesus Alou singled a run in, and then, after something like four foul balls, I hit a homer off Claude Raymond to get us tied, and everybody in our dugout was up, yelling and carrying on, except one man—Marichal. He was just kind of walking around, peeking under cushions and behind the water cooler.

"What's the matter with him?" Herman Franks wanted to know.

"He's looking for his glove," somebody said. "He wants to go in and pitch."

"He pitched nine last night!" Herman croaked. "Is this whole team nuts?"

"Sic 'em!" somebody else said happily. "Go get 'em! Kill! Kill!"

Those were kind of war cries we used on the team bus going out to the ball park when we were on the road. Nobody was too serious about it. One time the bus broke down in front of a bookstore, and while the Giants were marking time, waiting for them to fix the bus or get cabs or something, some of the players wandered into the store. That included Bob Shaw, who was supposed to pitch that night.

"What book does he want to buy?" somebody asked.

"*How to Pitch,*" somebody else said.

"This team," Warren Spahn said to me at one point during that final September, "is the loosest I ever saw. I mean, for a club that might win a pennant."

"Maybe," I said, "it's because everybody picked us to finish sixth to begin with."

In a sense, that may have been part of it. In the final analysis, we were to lose a 4½-game league lead with 16 games to go— a four-game lead with 12 to go. When you have a four-game lead with 12 to go, you start selling World Series tickets. And that sure looks like you blew it.

But what was the recent pattern in the National League? Didn't the 1964 Phils blow a 6½-game lead with 12 to go? Didn't the '62 Dodgers lose their last six to blow a four-game lead with seven to go? And those were clubs that were among the preseason favorites. That final September was the hottest single month, won-and-lost, the Giants had in the eight seasons since they'd moved to San Francisco. We wound up winning 95 games, and you have to go back to 1908 to find a Giant team that won that many but still couldn't win the pennant.

More than half my home runs—28 of them—came in the last two months of the '65 season, from August 2 on. I make this point to suggest once again that not only didn't the Giants fold under pressure, but neither did their center fielder. Yet maybe I've made that point once too often, because the marvelous thing was our own San Francisco fans. They were disappointed, the way the race came out, and you can't blame them. But they weren't landing on the players at the end there, or accusing people of choking. They'd come a long way since those days of '58 when big-league ball was new to the Pacific Coast. We'd all come a long way.

Garry Schumacher showed me how long I'd come, once the season was over. He'd asked Seymour Siwoff, the demon baseball statistician, to get up a list of my home runs over the years, and he showed it to me. It's quite a list. It shows the day, the opponent, the opposing pitcher, whether we were home or away, how many were on base, even the inning. It begins on page 307 at the back of this book.

Going over the list, you make a mistake if you only look for who the pitchers were. Sure, a Spahn and a Law and a Drysdale are going to be there—because they've been around as long as they have. You don't hit 15 home runs off a guy you only face once. Like I said before, I have had, over the years, few if any "favorite" pitchers, and even then, home runs by themselves would be pretty much a matter of accident. Here's just one example of what I mean: the first four years we played on the Coast, the Dodgers were in the Coliseum at L.A., and visiting teams didn't want to pitch left-handers there. Visiting teams also would always play the Giants either just before or just after the Dodgers. So for four years we saw more left-handed pitching—and less right-handed—than any normal balance could give you. (Because of that peculiarity, in '61 Joey Jay of the Reds had won 18 games before he pitched against us the first time.)

I do notice from the list that 248 of my 505 homers through '65 were hit away from home. Even weighting it a little farther, for the fact that over the years you do come up to bat more often on the road (because your team always hits in the ninth even if it's ahead), that figure should prove that my two home parks—the Polo Grounds and Candlestick (also Seals Stadium for the '58 and '59 season) weren't particularly built for my power, which is essentially to left-center. In the Polo Grounds the power alley was well over 400 feet, and in Candlestick it's where the wind comes from. There's always the fan who thinks the Polo Grounds was made for me, or Candlestick is a "crackerbox," but now the figures are available, and this is one thing they do show. I think it is not unfair for me to say that among the leaders in home runs, I've been favored by my home surroundings—"tailoring," you might call it—less than any other man.

Favorite parks? Oh, yes. Starting with my first full year in
1954—and I start there because I have no way of checking how
many times I saw different ball parks in my partial seasons of
'51 and '52—we played four full seasons (44 games) at Ebbets Field
in Brooklyn. In those 44 games I hit 26 home runs there!!

Again starting in '54, not only to be able to count the games
played there but to add Milwaukee to the list since they'd moved
by then from Boston, we can also see from the list my home run
output in each of the six "away" parks that stayed the same through
1965. They are Milwaukee, Philadelphia, Chicago, Cincinnati, St.
Louis, and Pittsburgh.

If you asked me to pick my favorite from that list, I'd say
what everybody always said—St. Louis. In 124 games there, '54
through '65 I hit 33 home runs. In the same number of games (at
least the same number of Giant appearances—tie games here or
there, or my not playing on occasion, could change it a little), I
got 29 homers in Milwaukee, 24 each in Cincinnati and Pittsburgh,
only 15 in Philadelphia (though I always liked to hit there—there
are other kinds of base hits besides home runs, like I always try
to remind myself when I'm swinging from the heels and missing).

I think for average, one of my poorest parks has been Wrigley
Field in Chicago. That's just a guess. But it's built so the extra-
base hits there are mostly down the foul lines, and I don't do much
hitting down the lines.

But for home runs—as they say on North Beach, *mama mia!*
The list showed that I'd hit 42 homers in Chicago between the
start of '54 and the end of '65!

The list of homers, of course, ends with the one I hit the last
day of the 1965 season at Candlestick, my 52nd of the year—a new
personal record for one season, and an individual Giant record too.
Despite winning the day before, we'd been mathematically eliminated by the Dodgers. Cincinnati, who was playing us that final
weekend, was still in the race for third place, so Franks agreed to

start his regulars. He didn't intend, however, to let them go the whole game.

"The league won't like that," somebody said to him.

"Listen," he said, "I rested 'em when I was going for a pennant, didn't I? Do you want me to kill them now because somebody else is going for third place?"

We won the game anyway, so nobody said anything.

Herman had an idea that after I came to bat for the second time, he'd send me out to the field next inning, then send out somebody to take my place and bring me in, so that on the way to the dugout the fans could give me a farewell yell. He'd already done it with McCovey, who'd had a great season—no Giant appeared in more games than he did, and he'd hammered 39 homers and batted in 92 runs.

But they gave me an ovation after I hit the home run, and I just kind of grinned when I got to the bench and went into the clubhouse to get dressed. I didn't want to milk the fans for applause, and Herman agreed. Even though we'd finished far better than anyone expected, he felt bad because we'd blown a 4½-game lead, and I did too. And besides, you couldn't ask those fans of San Francisco for anything more—loyalty, support, cheers—than they'd given their 1965 Giants. The same for the San Francisco press—a fine, seasoned group by now—right up there with the top writers in the country, for my money.

So I went in and took a shower, and for some reason I was thinking of baseball's "longest day"—the time in '64 we played a doubleheader with the Mets and the second game went 23 innings and I got more tired and more tired and kept taking a lighter bat up to the plate till finally it looked like a Little League bat and Sudol, the umpire, said, "That bat's illegal." And I said, "Then kick me out." And he said, "If I'd known we were all going to be here this long I wouldn't have kicked Dark out!"

And I thought too of our next-to-last series of '65, against the

Cardinals at Candlestick, and how when it was over—we'd gone into the last of the ninth behind 8-0 and scored six runs and had two men on and the winning run at the plate when it ended—two of the umpires, working their last Candlestick series of the year, detoured over to me and just stuck out their hands, silently.

I finished my shower and went upstairs to the radio booth, where Russ Hodges was working—he and Lon Simmons have seen just about all our games in San Francisco—and he grinned at me and said, "Want to do an inning?"

"Ain't no way," I said. Great baseball announcers, like Hodges and Simmons, make it sound so easy you think anybody can do it. Anybody *can't* do it.

I missed the thought of being in the World Series. Not because of the excitement—once you're in the Series, the worst you can do is pick up that loser's check: your big job's already done. Many players have told me their most exciting moment is the first scheduled game of a new season—the moment you begin playing for keeps. And I agree. No, I missed the Series because San Francisco deserved it. By now, I've played nearly 1,300 of my 2,000 games in a San Francisco uniform. New York is a lot of things—wonderful things—but one of the things it has to be, is past history.

I joked with Chub Feeney, who was in the radio booth that last day of the '65 season, about how even with 1-for-2 on my final day my average stayed at .317 for the year and how he was trying to keep down my salary drive for next year. It is something to have friends like him, and Russ, and Horace Stoneham, and Jake Shemano.

"I'm a lucky guy," I said to Feeney.

"You don't look so lucky here," he said, and showed me the new *Life* magazine that had a copy of me getting the wind knocked out of me in a tag play at the plate in Milwaukee, that final road trip.

I read the *Life* spread. It said in its headline—"To his team he gives the best—and he gives baseball its finest hours."

Of my work in the final stages of the '65 pennant race, the *Life* thing said:

"Earlier this month the National League had appeared to be headed into the first six-team dead-heat finish in history. Suddenly —but not inexplicably, for Mays is the reason—five of the six teams were outpaced, outclassed and outplayed by the most brilliant virtuoso performance ever seen in baseball. Whatever the outcome of the pennant race—the Los Angeles Dodgers and the Cincinnati Reds were battling all the way—the incomparable and dazzling Willie had given baseball its finest hour in years."

Elsewhere in the same story, it referred to my "pixie grin" and, in a caption to a picture, added: "Willie bruises a lot because of his habit of crashing into outfield walls."

Maybe I'm entitled to one pixie-like remark—after reading something as wonderful as that.

Which is:

If I had a habit of crashing into outfield walls, I wouldn't be around by now to have been able to do this book.

Or to win the Most Valuable Player award for 1965—the first man in history, they told me, to win it twice as much as 11 years apart. One way of looking at it is, that's a lot of walls I didn't crash into over a span of 11 years.

Or—as proud a moment as I can remember—to be called to Washington and have Sargent Shriver and Vice President Humphrey sit down with me and enlist me in the Job Corps, asking me to tour the encampments and talk to the guys there—just *talk* to them.

"They'll listen to you," the Vice President of the United States said to me. "You give them hope. Will you do it?"

I nodded, a little dumbly. I said I would do it. I am doing it.

And what do I want for me?

What I want for me is maybe what I want for Michael. I don't want him to play baseball. The cheers, yes: anybody wants cheers. The money, yes: money is the measure of accomplishment, and to earn much is to do much, unless you're the boss's son, but baseball is one place where even being the boss's son isn't going to help you that much. I don't want them to measure Michael against me the way they measured me against my own father, because it isn't a question of who loses; instead, it's a situation where if anybody loses, it's wrong. For why should somebody have to be a loser, in a setup like that?

But he is going to have the chance, I hope, to see the clouds against the sky two times, two different times, the way I did: the first time when he wasn't yet a man, and the second time when he was.

And to know that, whatever he does, like his old man he maybe never quite grabbed the sky. But they'll say in the book that he reached for it.

*Willie Mays's Statistics*

## Mays as a Record-Holder

(The following notes compiled by
coauthor Charles Einstein)

THE "BOOK" ON Willie Mays's records cannot be presented here, simply because he continues as an active player. At the close of the 1965 season, he needed eight more home runs for the National League lifetime record of 513 (Mel Ott hit 512). By the end of 1965, Mays owned three fielding records (for outfielders) in All-Star games (most games, most put-outs, most chances) and five batting records (most runs, most hits, most triples, most stolen bases, most stolen bases in one game). As a major-league player, Mays owns some interesting "curio" records. David Grote of the National League points out, for example, that Mays is the only major leaguer to have hit 50 home runs and steal more than 20 bases in one season, or to get more than 30 of each in one season, or more than 200 of each lifetime. In 1965, Mays extended the following National League records that he already held: Most consecutive seasons 300 or more total bases (from 11 to 12); highest slugging average, lifetime (.589 to .593); most times two or more home runs in one game (50 to 54). In 1965 also he set the following National League records: Most home runs in one month (17); most seasons, 40 or more home runs (6); most seasons, 150 or more games (12); most seasons, 100 or more runs (12); most consecutive seasons, 100 or more runs (12).

The 12 seasons reflected in several of these records represent all 12 *full* seasons that Mays had been in the majors through 1965.

As he himself points out in this book, his time with the Giants before that—the last 121 games of 1951, the first 34 games of 1952—
total one season when put together. Thus in a real sense he is correct
in terming 1954 his first full year. Applying the same yardstick to
eight other acknowledged all-time outfielding greats, one can then
draw up the following table, showing the batting records of each
in his first *full* season. (By "full," we arbitrarily designate a minimum requirement of 130 games, a figure which, when compared to
others such as Ruth, Mantle, and Aaron, does not necessarily favor
Mays, since several others had appeared prominently in earlier
seasons. So the following table, while not definitive, is a fair one,
and holds some fascinating insights all its own.

| Name | Bats | Year | Team | Standing | G | AB | H | HR | TB | B.A. | SL.A. |
|---|---|---|---|---|---|---|---|---|---|---|---|
| Ty Cobb | L | 1907 | Detroit AL ............ | 1 | 150 | 605 | 212 | 5 | 286 | .350 | .473 |
| Tris Speaker | L | 1909 | Boston AL ............ | 3 | 143 | 544 | 168 | 7 | 241 | .309 | .443 |
| Babe Ruth | L | 1919 | Boston AL ............ | 6 | 130 | 432 | 139 | 29 | 284 | .322 | .657 |
| Joe DiMaggio | R | 1936 | New York AL ......... | 1 | 138 | 637 | 206 | 29 | 367 | .323 | .576 |
| Ted Williams | L | 1939 | Boston AL ............ | 2 | 149 | 565 | 185 | 31 | 344 | .327 | .609 |
| Stan Musial | L | 1942 | St. Louis NL ......... | 1 | 140 | 467 | 147 | 10 | 229 | .315 | .490 |
| Mickey Mantle | R-L | 1952 | New York AL ......... | 1 | 142 | 549 | 171 | 23 | 271 | .311 | .494 |
| Willie Mays | R | 1954 | New York NL ......... | 1 | 151 | 565 | 195 | 41 | 377 | .345 | .667 |
| Henry Aaron | R | 1955 | Milwaukee NL ...... | 2 | 153 | 602 | 189 | 27 | 325 | .314 | .539 |

305

# Willie Mays's Lifetime Figures

## Born, Westfield, Alabama, May 6, 1931

Bats Right.  Throws Right.  Height, 5 feet, 11 inches.  Weight, 180 pounds

| Year | Club | League | Position | G | AB | R | H | 2B | 3B | HR | RBI | SB | Avg. |
|---|---|---|---|---|---|---|---|---|---|---|---|---|---|
| 1950 | Trenton | Interstate | OF | 81 | 306 | 50 | 108 | 20 | 8 | 4 | 55 | 7 | .353 |
| 1951 | Minneapolis | A.A. | OF | 35 | 149 | 38 | 71 | 18 | 3 | 8 | 30 | 5 | .477 |
| 1951 | New York | N.L. | OF | 121 | 464 | 59 | 127 | 22 | 5 | 20 | 68 | 7 | .274 |
| 1952 | New York | N.L. | OF | 34 | 127 | 17 | 30 | 2 | 4 | 4 | 23 | 4 | .236 |
| 1952-53 | | | | | | | (In U.S. Army) | | | | | | |
| 1954* | New York | N.L. | OF | 151 | 565 | 119 | 195 | 33 | 13 | 41 | 110 | 8 | .345 |
| 1955 | New York | N.L. | OF | 152 | 580 | 123 | 185 | 18 | 13 | 51 | 127 | 24 | .319 |
| 1956 | New York | N.L. | OF | 152 | 578 | 101 | 171 | 27 | 8 | 36 | 84 | 40 | .296 |
| 1957 | New York | N.L. | OF | 152 | 585 | 112 | 195 | 26 | 20 | 35 | 97 | 38 | .333 |
| 1958 | San Francisco | N.L. | OF | 152 | 600 | 121 | 208 | 33 | 11 | 29 | 96 | 31 | .347 |
| 1959 | San Francisco | N.L. | OF | 151 | 575 | 125 | 180 | 43 | 5 | 34 | 104 | 27 | .313 |
| 1960 | San Francisco | N.L. | OF | 153 | 595 | 107 | 190 | 29 | 12 | 29 | 103 | 25 | .319 |
| 1961 | San Francisco | N.L. | OF | 154 | 572 | 129 | 176 | 32 | 3 | 40 | 123 | 18 | .308 |
| 1962 | San Francisco | N.L. | OF | 162 | 621 | 130 | 189 | 36 | 5 | 49 | 141 | 18 | .304 |
| 1963 | San Francisco | N.L. | OF | 157 | 596 | 115 | 187 | 32 | 7 | 38 | 103 | 8 | .314 |
| 1964 | San Francisco | N.L. | OF-1B-3B-SS | 157 | 578 | 121 | 171 | 21 | 9 | 47 | 111 | 19 | .296 |
| 1965* | San Francisco | N.L. | OF | 157 | 558 | 118 | 177 | 21 | 3 | 52 | 112 | 9 | .317 |
| Major League Totals | | | 14 Yrs. | 2,005 | 7,594 | 1,497 | 2,381 | 375 | 118 | 505 | 1,402 | 276 | .314 |

* Received most-valuable player award.

# WILLIE MAYS'S HOME RUNS—LIFETIME *

| No. | Date | Inning | Men on Base | At | Opponent | Pitcher |
|-----|------|--------|-------------|-----|----------|---------|
| 1 | May 28 | 1 | 0 | H | Bos. | Spahn |
| 2 | June 6 | 2 | 1 | H | Cin. | Ramsdell |
| 3 | June 17(1) | 8 | 0 | A | Pitt. | Pollet |
| 4 | June 18 | 7 | 1 | A | St.L. | Presko |
| 5 | June 22 | 10 | 2 | A | Chi. | Leonard |
| 6 | June 23 | 6 | 2 | A | Chi. | Lown |
| 7 | June 27 | 4 | 1 | H | Bkn. | Newcombe |
| 8 | July 3 | 13 | 0 | H | Phil. | Thompson |
| 9 | July 4(1) | 8 | 0 | A | Bkn. | King |
| 10 | July 7 | 10 | 0 | H | Bos. | Estock |
| 11 | July 15(2) | 4 | 0 | H | Pitt. | Werle |
| 12 | July 17 | 8 | 1 | H | Chi. | McLish |
| 13 | July 18 | 6 | 0 | H | Chi. | Hiller |
| 14 | July 20 | 8 | 2 | H | Cin. | Byerly |
| 15 | July 22(1) | 7 | 0 | H | Cin. | Raffensberger |
| 16 | July 22(1) | 9 | 1 | H | Cin. | Raffensberger |
| 17 | July 28 | 6 | 0 | A | Cin. | Raffensberger |
| 18 | Aug. 30 | 2 | 1 | H | Pitt. | Friend |
| 19 | Aug. 30 | 5 | 0 | H | Pitt. | Law |
| 20 | Sept. 15 | 4 | 0 | H | Chi. | Minner |

| No. | Date | Inning | Men on Base | At | Opponent | Pitcher |
|-----|------|--------|-------------|-----|----------|---------|
| 21 | Apr. 19 | 8 | 0 | A | Bkn. | Branca |
| 22 | May 13 | 4 | 0 | H | Cin. | Wehmeier |
| 23 | May 14 | 2 | 1 | H | Cin. | Raffensberger |
| 24 | May 27 | 4 | 0 | A | Bkn. | Wade |

* Compiled exclusively by the Elias Sports Bureau, publisher of *Little Red Book of Baseball*.

## 1954 (41)

| No. | Date | Inning | Men on Base | At | Opponent | Pitcher |
|-----|------|--------|-------------|-----|----------|---------|
| 25 | Apr. 13 | 6 | 0 | H | Bkn. | Erskine |
| 26 | Apr. 18 | 3 | 1 | A | Bkn. | Erskine |
| 27 | Apr. 30 | 14 | 0 | A | Chi. | Hacker |
| 28 | May 6 | 6 | 1 | A | Cin. | Perkowski |
| 29 | May 8 | 2 | 0 | A | Pitt. | Law |
| 30 | May 11 | 7 | 0 | H | Cin. | Baczewski |
| 31 | May 13 | 2 | 0 | H | Chi. | Church |
| 32 | May 16(2) | 5 | 1 | H | Mil. | Johnson |
| 33 | May 24 | 7 | 0 | A | Phil. | Dickson |
| 34 | May 24 | 8 | 1 | A | Phil. | Dickson |
| 35 | May 28 | 2 | 1 | H | Bkn. | Labine |
| 36 | May 29 | 5 | 0 | H | Bkn. | Erskine |
| 37 | May 30 | 2 | 1 | H | Bkn. | Podres |
| 38 | May 31(1) | 2 | 1 | A | Pitt. | Yochim |
| 39 | June 3 | 7 | 2 | A | St.L. | Presko |
| 40 | June 3 | 9 | 1 | A | St.L. | Brazle |
| 41 | June 12 | 7 | 0 | A | Chi. | Hacker |
| 42 | June 19 | 2 | 0 | H | St.L. | Poholsky |
| 43 | June 21 | 2 | 0 | H | St.L. | Staley |
| 44 | June 21 | 5 | 0 | H | St.L. | Lint |
| 45 | June 22 | 2 | 0 | H | Mil. | Conley |
| 46 | June 23 | 2 | 0 | H | Mil. | Wilson |
| 47 | June 24 | 2 | 1 | H | Mil. | Spahn |
| 48 | June 25 | 2 | 1 | H | Chi. | Rush |
| 49 | July 3 | 8 | 0 | A | Pitt. | Littlefield |
| 50 | July 5(2) | 2 | 0 | H | Phil. | Dickson |
| 51 | July 6 | 4 | 0 | A | Bkn. | Roe |
| 52 | July 7 | 5 | 1 | A | Bkn. | Newcombe |
| 53 | July 8 | 1 | 1 | A | Bkn. | Erskine |
| 54 | July 8 | 7 | 2 | A | Bkn. | Meyer |
| 55 | July 11(1) | 4 | 0 | H | Pitt. | Friend |
| 56 | July 16 | 4 | 0 | A | St.L. | Raschi |
| 57 | July 18(2) | 5 | 0 | A | Cin. | Valentine |
| 58 | July 24 | 8 | 1 | A | Mil. | Spahn |
| 59 | July 27 | 9 | 0 | H | St.L. | Haddix |
| 60 | July 28 | 6 | 0 | H | St.L. | Poholsky |
| 61 | Aug. 15 | 9 | 0 | A | Bkn. | Loes |
| 62 | Aug. 26(1) | 8 | 1 | A | Chi. | Pollet |
| 63 | Aug. 29(1) | 2 | 0 | A | St.L. | Haddix |

| No. | Date | Inning | Men on Base | At | Opponent | Pitcher |
|-----|------|--------|-------------|-----|----------|---------|
| 64 | Sept. 16(2) | 8 | 0 | H | Mil. | Crone |
| 65 | Sept. 18 | 6 | 2 | H | Phil. | Ridzik |

### 1955 (51)

| No. | Date | Inning | Men on Base | At | Opponent | Pitcher |
|-----|------|--------|-------------|-----|----------|---------|
| 66 | Apr. 24 | 4 | 1 | A | Bkn. | Newcombe |
| 67 | Apr. 24 | 6 | 0 | A | Bkn. | Labine |
| 68 | Apr. 27 | 2 | 0 | H | Mil. | Conley |
| 69 | May 8(2) | 5 | 1 | H | Pitt. | Law |
| 70 | May 10 | 6 | 1 | A | Cin. | Klippstein |
| 71 | May 10 | 8 | 0 | A | Cin. | Minarcin |
| 72 | May 13 | 10 | 0 | A | St.L. | Haddix |
| 73 | May 17 | 4 | 0 | A | Mil. | Conley |
| 74 | May 25(2) | 7 | 0 | A | Phil. | Dickson |
| 75 | May 27 | 8 | 1 | H | Bkn. | Erskine |
| 76 | May 29 | 8 | 1 | H | Bkn. | Podres |
| 77 | May 30(1) | 8 | 1 | H | Phil. | Simmons |
| 78 | June 1 | 9 | 1 | H | Cin. | Nuxhall |
| 79 | June 2 | 7 | 0 | H | Cin. | Podbielan |
| 80 | June 4 | 4 | 0 | H | Chi. | Pollet |
| 81 | June 4 | 12 | 0 | H | Chi. | Hacker |
| 82 | June 14 | 2 | 0 | A | Chi. | Jones |
| 83 | June 29 | 3 | 3 | A | Bkn. | Labine |
| 84 | June 29 | 5 | 0 | A | Bkn. | Labine |
| 85 | June 30 | 10 | 1 | A | Bkn. | Roebuck |
| 86 | July 2 | 5 | 1 | A | Phil. | Simmons |
| 87 | July 4(1) | 6 | 0 | A | Pitt. | Friend |
| 88 | July 4(2) | 11 | 1 | A | Pitt. | Donoso |
| 89 | July 5 | 2 | 1 | A | Pitt. | Littlefield |
| 90 | July 5 | 8 | 0 | A | Pitt. | Pepper |
| 91 | July 7 | 6 | 0 | H | Phil. | Meyer |
| 92 | July 7 | 8 | 0 | H | Phil. | Negray |
| 93 | July 19(2) | 1 | 0 | H | St.L. | Jackson |
| 94 | July 21 | 1 | 0 | H | St.L. | Arroyo |
| 95 | July 24(2) | 8 | 1 | H | Cin. | Staley |
| 96 | July 27(2) | 1 | 1 | A | Chi. | Hacker |
| 97 | July 27(2) | 6 | 0 | A | Chi. | Hacker |
| 98 | July 31 | 1 | 0 | A | Mil. | Spahn |
| 99 | Aug. 1 | 7 | 1 | A | St.L. | Lawrence |
| 100 | Aug. 7(1) | 7 | 2 | A | Cin. | Nuxhall |
| 101 | Aug. 9 | 1 | 1 | A | Bkn. | Podres |

| No. | Date | Inning | Men on Base | At | Opponent | Pitcher |
|-----|------|--------|-------------|-----|----------|---------|
| 102 | Aug. 16 | 5 | 1 | H | Bkn. | Podres |
| 103 | Aug. 19 | 3 | 0 | A | Pitt. | Law |
| 104 | Aug. 30(2) | 3 | 0 | H | Cin. | Gross |
| 105 | Aug. 30(2) | 5 | 0 | H | Cin. | Staley |
| 106 | Sept. 5(1) | 7 | 2 | H | Pitt. | Law |
| 107 | Sept. 5(2) | 8 | 0 | H | Pitt. | Donoso |
| 108 | Sept. 11 | 6 | 1 | A | Chi. | Hacker |
| 109 | Sept. 14 | 4 | 0 | A | Mil. | Spahn |
| 110 | Sept. 14 | 9 | 0 | A | Mil. | Spahn |
| 111 | Sept. 16 | 6 | 0 | A | Bkn. | Loes |
| 112 | Sept. 17 | 5 | 0 | A | Bkn. | Meyer |
| 113 | Sept. 18 | 6 | 0 | A | Bkn. | Erskine |
| 114 | Sept. 20(1) | 1 | 1 | H | Pitt. | Law |
| 115 | Sept. 20(2) | 5 | 1 | H | Pitt. | Law |
| 116 | Sept. 25(1) | 1 | 1 | H | Phil. | Roberts |

## 1956 (36)

| No. | Date | Inning | Men on Base | At | Opponent | Pitcher |
|-----|------|--------|-------------|-----|----------|---------|
| 117 | Apr. 22(2) | 9 | 2 | A | Phil. | Miller |
| 118 | Apr. 29(2) | 3 | 0 | H | Phil. | LiPetri |
| 119 | May 4 | 7 | 0 | A | Mil. | Burdette |
| 120 | May 15 | 3 | 0 | H | Chi. | Hacker |
| 121 | June 8 | 5 | 0 | A | Mil. | Jolly |
| 122 | June 13 | 1 | 1 | A | Chi. | Rush |
| 123 | June 13 | 4 | 0 | A | Chi. | Rush |
| 124 | June 14 | 2 | 0 | A | Mil. | Spahn |
| 125 | June 17(1) | 7 | 0 | H | Cin. | LaPalme |
| 126 | June 24(1) | 1 | 1 | H | Mil. | Burdette |
| 127 | July 2 | 3 | 0 | A | Bkn. | Lehman |
| 128 | July 8(1) | 1 | 1 | H | Pitt. | Law |
| 129 | July 8(1) | 4 | 0 | H | Pitt. | Law |
| 130 | July 12 | 4 | 0 | A | St.L. | Poholsky |
| 131 | July 15(2) | 8 | 1 | A | Cin. | Gross |
| 132 | July 29 | 4 | 0 | H | St.L. | Poholsky |
| 133 | Aug. 3(1) | 8 | 1 | H | Chi. | Kaiser |
| 134 | Aug. 9 | 3 | 0 | H | Phil. | Rogovin |
| 135 | Aug. 12(2) | 7 | 0 | A | Pitt. | Face |
| 136 | Aug. 14 | 8 | 1 | A | Bkn. | Labine |
| 137 | Aug. 15 | 4 | 0 | A | Bkn. | Newcombe |

| No. | Date | Inning | Men on Base | At | Opponent | Pitcher |
|-----|------|--------|-------------|-----|----------|---------|
| 138 | Aug. 16 | 5 | 2 | A | Bkn. | Erskine |
| 139 | Aug. 17 | 4 | 0 | H | Pitt. | Munger |
| 140 | Aug. 19(1) | 3 | 1 | H | Pitt. | Face |
| 141 | Aug. 31 | 3 | 0 | H | Bkn. | Newcombe |
| 142 | Sept. 1 | 4 | 0 | H | Bkn. | Drysdale |
| 143 | Sept. 2(2) | 1 | 0 | H | Bkn. | Koufax |
| 144 | Sept. 7(1) | 1 | 1 | A | Bkn. | Erskine |
| 145 | Sept. 7(1) | 7 | 0 | A | Bkn. | Roebuck |
| 146 | Sept. 9 | 1 | 0 | A | Bkn. | Drysdale |
| 147 | Sept. 14 | 1 | 1 | H | St.L. | Poholsky |
| 148 | Sept. 14 | 8 | 0 | H | St.L. | Jackson |
| 149 | Sept. 15 | 1 | 0 | H | St.L. | McDaniel |
| 150 | Sept. 17(1) | 7 | 0 | H | Mil. | Phillips |
| 151 | Sept. 22 | 6 | 0 | H | Phil. | Roberts |
| 152 | Sept. 25 | 6 | 2 | H | Pitt. | Arroyo |

### 1957 (35)

| No. | Date | Inning | Men on Base | At | Opponent | Pitcher |
|-----|------|--------|-------------|-----|----------|---------|
| 153 | Apr. 20 | 7 | 2 | H | Phil. | Miller |
| 154 | Apr. 21(2) | 6 | 0 | H | Phil. | Sanford |
| 155 | Apr. 22 | 3 | 2 | H | Pitt. | Arroyo |
| 156 | May 18 | 4 | 1 | A | Cin. | Nuxhall |
| 157 | May 21 | 8 | 0 | A | Chi. | Drott |
| 158 | May 25 | 3 | 0 | A | Bkn. | Podres |
| 159 | May 30(2) | 1 | 1 | H | Phil. | Cardwell |
| 160 | June 2(1) | 6 | 0 | A | Pitt. | Kline |
| 161 | June 4 | 1 | 0 | A | Mil. | Crone |
| 162 | June 5 | 1 | 1 | H | Mil. | Pizarro |
| 163 | June 12 | 6 | 2 | H | Chi. | Rush |
| 164 | June 14 | 8 | 1 | H | Cin. | Nuxhall |
| 165 | June 27 | 1 | 1 | A | Cin. | Gross |
| 166 | July 12 | 9 | 0 | H | St.L. | Jones |
| 167 | July 14 | 12 | 1 | H | Chi. | Brosnan |
| 168 | July 15 | 3 | 1 | H | Chi. | Elston |
| 169 | July 21(2) | 1 | 1 | H | Mil. | Burdette |
| 170 | July 28(2) | 9 | 0 | A | Mil. | Conley |
| 171 | July 29 | 7 | 0 | A | Mil. | Pizarro |
| 172 | Aug. 2 | 8 | 0 | A | Cin. | Klippstein |
| 173 | Aug. 3 | 1 | 0 | A | Cin. | Fowler |
| 174 | Aug. 3 | 8 | 1 | A | Cin. | Fowler |

| No. | Date | Inning | Men on Base | At | Opponent | Pitcher |
|-----|------|--------|-------------|-----|----------|---------|
| 175 | Aug. 4(1) | 8 | 0 | A | Cin. | Nuxhall |
| 176 | Aug. 4(1) | 12 | 0 | A | Cin. | Klippstein |
| 177 | Aug. 5 | 3 | 1 | A | Bkn. | Drysdale |
| 178 | Aug. 8 | 5 | 0 | A | Bkn. | Craig |
| 179 | Aug. 21 | 1 | 0 | H | St.L. | McDaniel |
| 180 | Aug. 22 | 1 | 1 | H | Chi. | Drott |
| 181 | Sept. 1 | 4 | 0 | A | Bkn. | Podres |
| 182 | Sept. 2(2) | 3 | 1 | H | Pitt. | O'Brien |
| 183 | Sept. 3 | 6 | 1 | H | Pitt. | King |
| 184 | Sept. 7 | 9 | 0 | H | Bkn. | Craig |
| 185 | Sept. 14 | 4 | 0 | A | St.L. | Mizell |
| 186 | Sept. 15(2) | 1 | 0 | A | Chi. | Mayer |
| 187 | Sept. 18 | 6 | 0 | A | Mil. | Burdette |

## 1958 (29)

| No. | Date | Inning | Men on Base | At | Opponent | Pitcher |
|-----|------|--------|-------------|-----|----------|---------|
| 188 | Apr. 26 | 6 | 0 | H | Chi. | Hobbie |
| 189 | May 9 | 2 | 2 | H | L.A. | McDevitt |
| 190 | May 9 | 6 | 0 | H | L.A. | Negray |
| 191 | May 10 | 1 | 0 | H | L.A. | Podres |
| 192 | May 12 | 2 | 0 | A | L.A. | Drysdale |
| 193 | May 12 | 5 | 3 | A | L.A. | Roebuck |
| 194 | May 13 | 1 | 1 | A | L.A. | Newcombe |
| 195 | May 13 | 2 | 1 | A | L.A. | Newcombe |
| 196 | May 15 | 1 | 0 | A | St.L. | McDaniel |
| 197 | May 16 | 6 | 2 | A | Chi. | Phillips |
| 198 | May 17 | 8 | 0 | A | Chi. | Freeman |
| 199 | May 21 | 10 | 0 | A | Cin. | Jeffcoat |
| 200 | May 23 | 9 | 1 | A | Mil. | Spahn |
| 201 | June 6 | 1 | 0 | H | Cin. | Haddix |
| 202 | July 1 | 1 | 0 | A | Chi. | Drabowsky |
| 203 | July 2 | 7 | 0 | A | Chi. | Drott |
| 204 | Aug. 4 | 3 | 0 | A | Chi. | Drott |
| 205 | Aug. 13 | 8 | 2 | H | St.L. | Wight |
| 206 | Aug. 14 | 8 | 0 | H | St.L. | Muffett |
| 207 | Aug. 16 | 5 | 1 | H | Chi. | Drott |
| 208 | Aug. 17 | 4 | 2 | H | Chi. | Briggs |
| 209 | Aug. 23 | 3 | 1 | H | Cin. | Purkey |
| 210 | Aug. 26 | 6 | 1 | H | Mil. | Burdette |
| 211 | Aug. 30(2) | 8 | 1 | H | L.A. | Labine |

| No. | Date | Inning | Men on Base | At | Opponent | Pitcher |
|---|---|---|---|---|---|---|
| 212 | Aug. 31 | 2 | 1 | H | L.A. | Birrer |
| 213 | Sept. 1(1) | 3 | 0 | H | L.A. | Labine |
| 214 | Sept. 1(2) | 6 | 1 | H | L.A. | Kipp |
| 215 | Sept. 4 | 8 | 1 | A | L.A. | McDevitt |
| 216 | Sept. 28 | 4 | 0 | H | St.L. | Jones |

### 1959 (34)

| No. | Date | Inning | Men on Base | At | Opponent | Pitcher |
|---|---|---|---|---|---|---|
| 217 | Apr. 20 | 1 | 0 | A | L.A. | Drysdale |
| 218 | May 3 | 1 | 1 | A | Mil. | Burdette |
| 219 | May 8 | 8 | 0 | H | L.A. | Klippstein |
| 220 | May 13 | 1 | 2 | H | Phil. | Gomez |
| 221 | May 14 | 4 | 2 | H | Phil. | Semproch |
| 222 | May 17 | 5 | 1 | H | Cin. | Purkey |
| 223 | May 18 | 4 | 0 | H | Mil. | Spahn |
| 224 | May 24 | 9 | 0 | A | L.A. | Fowler |
| 225 | May 27 | 8 | 0 | H | St.L. | Blaylock |
| 226 | June 11 | 8 | 2 | A | Pitt. | Face |
| 227 | June 26 | 3 | 0 | H | Phil. | Owens |
| 228 | June 29 | 13 | 0 | A | L.A. | Williams |
| 229 | June 30 | 3 | 1 | A | L.A. | Drysdale |
| 230 | July 5(2) | 1 | 1 | A | St.L. | Blaylock |
| 231 | July 10 | 11 | 0 | A | Cin. | Pena |
| 232 | July 18 | 8 | 1 | A | Pitt. | Haddix |
| 233 | July 26 | 4 | 1 | H | Chi. | Anderson |
| 234 | Aug. 6 | 7 | 0 | H | Mil. | Pizarro |
| 235 | Aug. 13 | 1 | 1 | A | Chi. | Ceccarelli |
| 236 | Aug. 15 | 3 | 0 | A | Chi. | Drabowsky |
| 237 | Aug. 16 | 1 | 1 | A | Chi. | Anderson |
| 238 | Aug. 27(2) | 1 | 0 | A | Phil. | Cardwell |
| 239 | Aug. 28 | 2 | 2 | A | L.A. | Drysdale |
| 240 | Aug. 30 | 3 | 1 | A | L.A. | Sherry |
| 241 | Sept. 3 | 6 | 1 | H | Chi. | Henry |
| 242 | Sept. 5 | 1 | 0 | H | St.L. | Mizell |
| 243 | Sept. 9 | 3 | 0 | H | Pitt. | Haddix |
| 244 | Sept. 10 | 1 | 0 | H | Pitt. | Law |
| 245 | Sept. 10 | 5 | 0 | H | Pitt. | Law |
| 246 | Sept. 14 | 6 | 0 | H | Cin. | Brosnan |
| 247 | Sept. 17 | 4 | 2 | H | Mil. | Rush |

| No. | Date | Inning | Men on Base | At | Opponent | Pitcher |
|-----|------|--------|-------------|----|----------|---------|
| 248 | Sept. 23 | 7 | 0 | A | Chi. | Anderson |
| 249 | Sept. 23 | 9 | 0 | A | Chi. | Henry |
| 250 | Sept. 26 | 1 | 0 | A | St.L. | Mizell |

### 1960 (29)

| No. | Date | Inning | Men on Base | At | Opponent | Pitcher |
|-----|------|--------|-------------|----|----------|---------|
| 251 | Apr. 24 | 1 | 0 | A | Chi. | Anderson |
| 252 | May 6 | 6 | 0 | H | Pitt. | Law |
| 253 | May 17 | 2 | 1 | A | Cin. | O'Toole |
| 254 | May 26 | 9 | 2 | A | Phil. | Gomez |
| 255 | May 28 | 5 | 1 | A | St.L. | Sadecki |
| 256 | May 28 | 7 | 1 | A | St.L. | Simmons |
| 257 | May 30(2) | 3 | 1 | H | Chi. | Drott |
| 258 | June 10 | 5 | 1 | H | Mil. | Spahn |
| 259 | June 15 | 8 | 0 | H | Pitt. | Haddix |
| 260 | June 17 | 4 | 1 | H | Phil. | Short |
| 261 | June 19 | 7 | 0 | H | Phil. | Roberts |
| 262 | June 21 | 5 | 2 | A | Mil. | Brunet |
| 263 | June 24 | 6 | 0 | A | Cin. | Hook |
| 264 | June 24 | 8 | 0 | A | Cin. | Grim |
| 265 | June 30(1) | 4 | 1 | A | Pitt. | Friend |
| 266 | June 30(2) | 1 | 0 | A | Pitt. | Mizell |
| 267 | July 3 | 5 | 0 | A | Phil. | Robinson |
| 268 | July 4(1) | 6 | 0 | A | Chi. | Ellsworth |
| 269 | July 22 | 1 | 0 | H | Pitt. | Mizell |
| 270 | July 23 | 5 | 1 | H | Pitt. | Haddix |
| 271 | July 24 | 1 | 1 | H | Pitt. | Cheney |
| 272 | Aug. 13 | 6 | 0 | A | Mil. | Buhl |
| 273 | Aug. 15 | 1 | 1 | A | St.L. | Broglio |
| 274 | Aug. 15 | 9 | 0 | A | St.L. | McDaniel |
| 275 | Aug. 21(1) | 8 | 0 | A | Chi. | Elston |
| 276 | Aug. 22 | 6 | 0 | A | L.A. | Sherry |
| 277 | Aug. 25 | 2 | 3 | H | Cin. | Osteen |
| 278 | Aug. 27 | 6 | 0 | H | Mil. | Burdette |
| 279 | Oct. 2 | 3 | 2 | H | St.L. | Nelson |

### 1961 (40)

| No. | Date | Inning | Men on Base | At | Opponent | Pitcher |
|-----|------|--------|-------------|----|----------|---------|
| 280 | Apr. 14 | 8 | 0 | H | Phil. | Mahaffey |
| 281 | Apr. 18 | 7 | 0 | H | Cin. | Purkey |

| No. | Date | Inning | Men on Base | At | Opponent | Pitcher |
|---|---|---|---|---|---|---|
| 282 | Apr. 30 | 1 | 0 | A | Mil. | Burdette |
| 283 | Apr. 30 | 3 | 1 | A | Mil. | Burdette |
| 284 | Apr. 30 | 6 | 2 | A | Mil. | Morehead |
| 285 | Apr. 30 | 8 | 1 | A | Mil. | McMahon |
| 286 | May 13 | 3 | 3 | H | Mil. | Buhl |
| 287 | May 13 | 5 | 1 | H | Mil. | Buhl |
| 288 | May 27 | 4 | 1 | A | Chi. | Drott |
| 289 | May 30(1) | 9 | 0 | H | Cin. | Henry |
| 290 | June 8 | 2 | 0 | H | Phil. | Buzhardt |
| 291 | June 13 | 7 | 1 | H | L.A. | Williams |
| 292 | June 14 | 2 | 0 | H | Mil. | Spahn |
| 293 | June 21 | 6 | 0 | A | Mil. | Burdette |
| 294 | June 22 | 7 | 0 | A | Mil. | Buhl |
| 295 | June 22 | 9 | 1 | A | Mil. | Buhl |
| 296 | June 25(2) | 9 | 0 | A | St.L. | Sadecki |
| 297 | June 29(1) | 1 | 1 | A | Phil. | Green |
| 298 | June 29(1) | 3 | 1 | A | Phil. | Green |
| 299 | June 29(1) | 10 | 0 | A | Phil. | Sullivan |
| 300 | July 4(2) | 2 | 0 | A | Chi. | Curtis |
| 301 | July 8 | 3 | 2 | H | St.L. | Jackson |
| 302 | July 9(1) | 3 | 1 | H | St.L. | Simmons |
| 303 | July 13 | 8 | 0 | H | Pitt. | Friend |
| 304 | July 16 | 2 | 0 | H | Phil. | Owens |
| 305 | July 16 | 7 | 0 | H | Phil. | Sullivan |
| 306 | July 17 | 1 | 0 | H | Phil. | Green |
| 307 | July 20 | 8 | 1 | A | St.L. | McDaniel |
| 308 | July 30 | 5 | 0 | A | Phil. | Owens |
| 309 | Aug. 12 | 3 | 2 | H | Cin. | Purkey |
| 310 | Aug. 20 | 3 | 1 | H | L.A. | Koufax |
| 311 | Aug. 22(1) | 1 | 1 | A | Cin. | Purkey |
| 312 | Aug. 22(2) | 6 | 1 | A | Cin. | Johnson |
| 313 | Aug. 23 | 9 | 1 | A | Cin. | Henry |
| 314 | Sept. 8 | 1 | 1 | H | L.A. | Podres |
| 315 | Sept. 9 | 7 | 1 | H | L.A. | Drysdale |
| 316 | Sept. 10 | 3 | 0 | H | L.A. | Williams |
| 317 | Sept. 14 | 6 | 1 | H | Phil. | Buzhardt |
| 318 | Sept. 19 | 3 | 3 | H | Mil. | Spahn |
| 319 | Oct. 1(1) | 7 | 1 | A | Mil. | Burdette |

## 1962 (49)

| No. | Date | Inning | Men on Base | At | Opponent | Pitcher |
|---|---|---|---|---|---|---|
| 320 | Apr. 10 | 1 | 0 | H | Mil. | Spahn |
| 321 | Apr. 11 | 1 | 1 | H | Mil. | Willey |
| 322 | Apr. 13 | 5 | 0 | H | Cin. | O'Toole |
| 323 | Apr. 16 | 6 | 2 | H | L.A. | Hunter |
| 324 | Apr. 28 | 2 | 3 | H | Chi. | Lary |
| 325 | Apr. 29(1) | 4 | 1 | H | Chi. | Balsamo |
| 326 | Apr. 30 | 1 | 0 | H | Pitt. | Mizell |
| 327 | May 2 | 6 | 0 | H | Pitt. | Francis |
| 328 | May 5 | 3 | 1 | A | Chi. | Koonce |
| 329 | May 6 | 1 | 1 | A | Chi. | Buhl |
| 330 | May 19 | 7 | 0 | H | Hou. | Giusti |
| 331 | May 24 | 6 | 0 | H | Phil. | McLish |
| 332 | May 24 | 7 | 1 | H | Phil. | McLish |
| 333 | May 25 | 3 | 2 | H | Phil. | Hamilton |
| 334 | May 26 | 8 | 0 | H | N.Y. | Hook |
| 335 | May 26 | 10 | 1 | H | N.Y. | Hook |
| 336 | June 1 | 5 | 0 | A | N.Y. | Craig |
| 337 | June 2(1) | 2 | 1 | A | N.Y. | Moorhead |
| 338 | June 3 | 6 | 0 | A | N.Y. | Miller |
| 339 | June 8 | 3 | 1 | A | St.L. | Gibson |
| 340 | June 9 | 1 | 1 | A | St.L. | Sadecki |
| 341 | July 2 | 7 | 1 | H | N.Y. | Anderson |
| 342 | July 4(2) | 1 | 2 | H | N.Y. | Hunter |
| 343 | July 4(2) | 4 | 1 | H | N.Y. | Hunter |
| 344 | July 7 | 1 | 0 | H | Pitt. | Podres |
| 345 | July 19 | 4 | 0 | A | L.A. | Lemaster |
| 346 | July 20 | 1 | 1 | A | Mil. | Law |
| 347 | July 22 | 3 | 0 | A | Mil. | Haddix |
| 348 | July 23 | 7 | 0 | A | Chi. | Kemmerer |
| 349 | July 24 | 1 | 0 | A | Phil. | Farrell |
| 350 | July 24 | 4 | 0 | A | L.A. | Farrell |
| 351 | July 29 | 7 | 0 | A | Chi. | Drysdale |
| 352 | Aug. 6 | 1 | 1 | H | Hou. | Green |
| 353 | Aug. 6 | 2 | 1 | H | Hou. | Smith |
| 354 | Aug. 10 | 1 | 0 | H | Hou. | Podres |
| 355 | Aug. 14 | 7 | 2 | A | L.A. | Gerard |
| 356 | Aug. 15 | 3 | 1 | A | Pitt. | Buhl |
| 357 | Aug. 17 | 4 | 0 | A | Mil. | Shaw |
| 358 | Aug. 28 | 4 | 0 | H | Phil. | Shaw |

| No. | Date | Inning | Men on Base | At | Opponent | Pitcher |
|---|---|---|---|---|---|---|
| 359 | Aug. 30 | 1 | 0 | H | Mil. | Spahn |
| 360 | Sept. 2 | 7 | 0 | H | Cin. | Wills |
| 361 | Sept. 3 | 3 | 2 | H | L.A. | Williams |
| 362 | Sept. 10 | 1 | 1 | H | Pitt. | Haddix |
| 363 | Sept. 16 | 8 | 2 | A | Pitt. | Face |
| 364 | Sept. 19 | 3 | 2 | A | St.L. | Jackson |
| 365 | Sept. 22 | 8 | 0 | A | Hou. | Brunet |
| 366 | Sept. 30 | 8 | 0 | H | Hou. | Farrell |
| 367 | Oct. 1 | 1 | 1 | H | L.A. | Koufax |
| 368 | Oct. 1 | 6 | 0 | H | L.A. | Sherry |

### 1963 (38)

| No. | Date | Inning | Men on Base | At | Opponent | Pitcher |
|---|---|---|---|---|---|---|
| 369 | Apr. 9 | 3 | 0 | A | Hou. | Farrell |
| 370 | Apr. 13 | 8 | 0 | A | Chi. | Toth |
| 371 | Apr. 19 | 4 | 0 | H | Chi. | Jackson |
| 372 | Apr. 21(2) | 2 | 0 | H | Chi. | Koonce |
| 373 | May 5(1) | 1 | 2 | A | N.Y. | Cisco |
| 374 | May 16 | 3 | 1 | H | N.Y. | Hook |
| 375 | May 17 | 1 | 0 | H | N.Y. | Cisco |
| 376 | June 2 | 1 | 1 | A | St.L. | Broglio |
| 377 | June 2 | 8 | 0 | A | St.L. | Humphreys |
| 378 | June 2 | 9 | 0 | A | St.L. | Shantz |
| 379 | June 5(1) | 1 | 1 | A | Chi. | Ellsworth |
| 380 | June 13 | 10 | 0 | H | Chi. | Ellsworth |
| 381 | June 28 | 8 | 1 | H | Cin. | Worthington |
| 382 | June 30 | 7 | 2 | H | Cin. | Worthington |
| 383 | July 2 | 16 | 0 | H | Mil. | Spahn |
| 384 | July 3 | 2 | 0 | H | Mil. | Lemaster |
| 385 | July 13 | 7 | 1 | A | Phil. | Duren |
| 386 | July 16(1) | 4 | 0 | A | Pitt. | Cardwell |
| 387 | July 20 | 2 | 0 | A | Cin. | Nuxhall |
| 388 | July 23 | 2 | 1 | H | N.Y. | Craig |
| 389 | July 23 | 6 | 0 | H | N.Y. | MacKenzie |
| 390 | July 25 | 5 | 2 | H | N.Y. | Hook |
| 391 | July 28 | 6 | 1 | H | Pitt. | Schwall |
| 392 | July 29 | 5 | 2 | H | Pitt. | Law |
| 393 | Aug. 2 | 7 | 0 | A | Chi. | Elston |
| 394 | Aug. 3 | 3 | 0 | A | Chi. | Buhl |

| No. | Date | Inning | Men on Base | At | Opponent | Pitcher |
|-----|------|--------|-------------|-----|----------|---------|
| 395 | Aug. 4 | 10 | 0 | A | Chi. | McDaniel |
| 396 | Aug. 5 | 9 | 0 | A | Hou. | Woodeschick |
| 397 | Aug. 14 | 6 | 1 | A | Cin. | Tsitouris |
| 398 | Aug. 17 | 8 | 0 | A | St.L. | Broglio |
| 399 | Aug. 25 | 2 | 0 | H | Cin. | Nuxhall |
| 400 | Aug. 27 | 3 | 0 | H | St.L. | Simmons |
| 401 | Sept. 6 | 8 | 0 | H | L.A. | Koufax |
| 402 | Sept. 7 | 1 | 1 | H | L.A. | Drysdale |
| 403 | Sept. 15 | 1 | 2 | A | Pitt. | Schwall |
| 404 | Sept. 18 | 2 | 0 | A | Mil. | Sadowski |
| 405 | Sept. 22 | 1 | 0 | H | N.Y. | Hook |
| 406 | Sept. 24 | 7 | 0 | H | Phil. | Bennett |

## 1964 (47)

| No. | Date | Inning | Men on Base | At | Opponent | Pitcher |
|-----|------|--------|-------------|-----|----------|---------|
| 407 | Apr. 14 | 3 | 1 | H | Mil. | Spahn |
| 408 | Apr. 14 | 8 | 0 | H | Mil. | Spahn |
| 409 | Apr. 15 | 3 | 2 | H | Mil. | Sadowski |
| 410 | Apr. 17 | 6 | 2 | H | St.L. | Craig |
| 411 | Apr. 18 | 5 | 0 | H | St.L. | Broglio |
| 412 | Apr. 19 | 8 | 0 | H | Cin. | Nichols |
| 413 | Apr. 24 | 4 | 0 | A | Cin. | Ellis |
| 414 | May 1 | 4 | 0 | A | L.A. | Drysdale |
| 415 | May 3 | 8 | 0 | A | L.A. | Perranoski |
| 416 | May 4 | 1 | 1 | H | Hou. | Johnson |
| 417 | May 8 | 6 | 0 | H | L.A. | Ortega |
| 418 | May 12 | 3 | 0 | A | Hou. | Brown |
| 419 | May 12 | 5 | 1 | A | Hou. | Brown |
| 420 | May 16 | 9 | 0 | H | N.Y. | Bearnarth |
| 421 | May 21 | 1 | 1 | H | Phil. | Wise |
| 422 | May 21 | 5 | 0 | H | Phil. | Klippstein |
| 423 | May 22 | 6 | 0 | H | Pitt. | Face |
| 424 | May 28 | 8 | 1 | A | St.L. | Simmons |
| 425 | June 17 | 1 | 0 | H | Cin. | Nuxhall |
| 426 | June 18 | 7 | 0 | A | St.L. | Sadecki |
| 427 | June 20 | 4 | 0 | A | St.L. | Hobbie |
| 428 | June 21 | 9 | 0 | A | St.L. | Craig |
| 429 | July 1 | 1 | 0 | H | Pitt. | Veale |
| 430 | July 8(2) | 2 | 2 | A | Chi. | Broglio |
| 431 | July 9 | 1 | 0 | A | Chi. | Jackson |

| No. | Date | Inning | Men on Base | At | Opponent | Pitcher |
|---|---|---|---|---|---|---|
| 432 | July 10 | 1 | 1 | A | Chi. | Ellsworth |
| 433 | July 10 | 4 | 0 | A | Chi. | Burdette |
| 434 | July 15 | 5 | 1 | A | Mil. | Lemaster |
| 435 | July 19(1) | 4 | 0 | H | Hou. | Farrell |
| 436 | Aug. 5 | 4 | 0 | A | N.Y. | Fisher |
| 437 | Aug. 5 | 8 | 0 | A | N.Y. | Wakefield |
| 438 | Aug. 9 | 1 | 1 | A | Cin. | Tsitouris |
| 439 | Aug. 11 | 3 | 1 | A | St.L. | Simmons |
| 440 | Aug. 12 | 7 | 2 | A | St.L. | Craig |
| 441 | Aug. 14 | 6 | 0 | H | Mil. | Sadowski |
| 442 | Aug. 16(1) | 3 | 0 | H | Mil. | Lary |
| 443 | Aug. 16(1) | 8 | 0 | H | Mil. | Lary |
| 444 | Aug. 20 | 2 | 1 | H | Cin. | Nuxhall |
| 445 | Aug. 28 | 6 | 1 | A | Mil. | Blasingame |
| 446 | Sept. 7(1) | 1 | 0 | A | Pitt. | Gibbon |
| 447 | Sept. 7(2) | 4 | 2 | A | Pitt. | Bork |
| 448 | Sept. 18 | 1 | 1 | H | Pitt. | Veale |
| 449 | Sept. 18 | 5 | 0 | H | Pitt. | Veale |
| 450 | Sept. 19 | 8 | 1 | H | Pitt. | Francis |
| 451 | Oct. 3 | 3 | 0 | H | Chi. | Buhl |
| 452 | Oct. 3 | 9 | 1 | H | Chi. | McDaniel |
| 453 | Oct. 4 | 4 | 0 | H | Chi. | Jackson |

## 1965 (52)

| No. | Date | Inning | Men on Base | At | Opponent | Pitcher |
|---|---|---|---|---|---|---|
| 454 | Apr. 13 | 8 | 1 | A | Pitt. | Friend |
| 455 | Apr. 14 | 3 | 1 | A | Phil. | Bunning |
| 456 | Apr. 20 | 2 | 0 | H | Pitt. | Friend |
| 457 | Apr. 25(2) | 9 | 0 | H | N.Y. | Spahn |
| 458 | Apr. 28 | 1 | 0 | H | Phil. | Culp |
| 459 | May 3 | 9 | 0 | A | St.L. | Simmons |
| 460 | May 4 | 1 | 1 | A | St.L. | Sadecki |
| 461 | May 5 | 8 | 0 | A | St.L. | Schultz |
| 462 | May 7 | 2 | 0 | H | L.A. | Osteen |
| 463 | May 7 | 4 | 0 | H | L.A. | Osteen |
| 464 | May 13 | 3 | 0 | H | Chi. | Broglio |
| 465 | May 15 | 1 | 0 | H | Hou. | Dierker |
| 466 | May 16(1) | 2 | 0 | H | Hou. | MacKenzie |
| 467 | May 18 | 1 | 2 | A | Chi. | McDaniel |
| 468 | May 20 | 7 | 0 | A | Chi. | Jackson |

| No. | Date | Inning | Men on Base | At | Opponent | Pitcher |
|-----|------|--------|-------------|-----|----------|---------|
| 469 | May 22(1) | 1 | 1 | A | Hou. | Bruce |
| 470 | May 22(2) | 1 | 1 | A | Hou. | Farrell |
| 471 | June 9 | 1 | 1 | A | N.Y. | Fisher |
| 472 | June 11 | 3 | 2 | A | Pitt. | Cardwell |
| 473 | June 12 | 1 | 1 | A | Pitt. | Friend |
| 474 | June 18 | 4 | 1 | H | N.Y. | Cisco |
| 475 | June 23 | 2 | 0 | H | Pitt. | Veale |
| 476 | July 8(2) | 7 | 0 | A | Phil. | Herbert |
| 477 | July 30 | 5 | 0 | A | Mil. | Sadowski |
| 478 | Aug. 2 | 6 | 0 | A | Mil. | Johnson |
| 479 | Aug. 5 | 1 | 2 | A | Cin. | Tsitouris |
| 480 | Aug. 5 | 2 | 0 | A | Cin. | Locke |
| 481 | Aug. 7 | 5 | 1 | A | St.L. | Stallard |
| 482 | Aug. 7 | 7 | 1 | A | St.L. | Briles |
| 483 | Aug. 8 | 6 | 0 | A | St.L. | Purkey |
| 484 | Aug. 12(1) | 6 | 0 | H | Pitt. | Friend |
| 485 | Aug. 12(2) | 6 | 0 | H | Pitt. | Law |
| 486 | Aug. 16 | 4 | 0 | H | N.Y. | Parsons |
| 487 | Aug. 18 | 1 | 0 | H | N.Y. | Miller |
| 488 | Aug. 19 | 1 | 1 | H | L.A. | Drysdale |
| 489 | Aug. 20 | 3 | 1 | H | L.A. | Reed |
| 490 | Aug. 21 | 8 | 0 | H | L.A. | Miller |
| 491 | Aug. 22 | 3 | 2 | H | L.A. | Koufax |
| 492 | Aug. 26(2) | 9 | 0 | A | Pitt. | McBean |
| 493 | Aug. 27 | 8 | 1 | A | N.Y. | Parsons |
| 494 | Aug. 29 | 3 | 2 | A | N.Y. | Fisher |
| 495 | Sept. 4 | 6 | 1 | A | Chi. | Broglio |
| 496 | Sept. 5 | 4 | 1 | A | Chi. | Ellsworth |
| 497 | Sept. 8 | 2 | 2 | H | Hou. | Nottebart |
| 498 | Sept. 8 | 8 | 1 | H | Hou. | Taylor |
| 499 | Sept. 12(2) | 8 | 1 | H | Chi. | Abernathy |
| 500 | Sept. 13 | 4 | 0 | A | Hou. | Nottebart |
| 501 | Sept. 14 | 9 | 1 | A | Hou. | Raymond |
| 502 | Sept. 19 | 1 | 0 | A | Mil. | Cloninger |
| 503 | Sept. 25 | 4 | 1 | H | Mil. | Sadowski |
| 504 | Sept. 28 | 8 | 0 | H | St.L. | Jaster |
| 505 | Oct. 3 | 4 | 0 | H | Cin. | McCool |